BEST-SELL

CHAPTERS

Middle Level

Chapters from 10 Books for Young Adults

with Lessons for Teaching the Basic Elements of Literature

Raymond Harris

JAMESTOWN PUBLISHERS

a division of NTC/CONTEMPORARY PUBLISHING GROUP
Lincolnwood, Illinois USA

Cover Design: Steve Straus
Cover Illustration: Lori Lohstoeter
Interior Design: Patricia Volpe
Interior Illustrations: Units 1, 10: Lyn Fletcher; Unit 2: Marcy Ramsey;
Units 3, 5: Heidi Chang; Units 4, 8: Timothy C. Jones; Unit 6: Maurice P. Dogué;
Units 7, 9: Phillip W. Smith

ISBN: 0-89061-656-6 (hardbound)
ISBN: 0-89061-652-3 (softbound)

Published by Jamestown Publishers,
a division of NTC/Contemporary Publishing Group, Inc.
4255 West Touhy Avenue,
Lincolnwood (Chicago), Illinois 60646-1975, U.S.A.
© 1998 NTC/Contemporary Publishing Group, Inc.

890 QB 0987654321

Acknowledgments

Acknowledgment is gratefully made to the following publishers and authors for permission to reprint excerpts from these works:

Summer of My German Soldier. From *Summer of My German Soldier* by Bette Greene. Copyright ©1973 by Bette Greene. This material is not to be reproduced without permission from the publisher. Used by permission of Dial Books for Young Readers, a division of Penguin Books USA Inc.

I Know Why the Caged Bird Sings. From *I Know Why the Caged Bird Sings* by Maya Angelou. Copyright ©1969 by Maya Angelou. Reprinted by permission of Random House, Inc.

Julie of the Wolves. From *Julie of the Wolves* by Jean Craighead George. Copyright ©1972 by Jean Craighead George. Selection reprinted by permission of HarperCollins Publishers.

To Kill a Mockingbird. From *To Kill a Mockingbird* by Harper Lee. Copyright ©1960 by Harper Lee. Copyright renewed ©1988 by Harper Lee. Reprinted by permission of HarperCollins Publishers, Inc.

The Westing Game. From *The Westing Game* by Ellen Raskin. Copyright ©1978 by Ellen Raskin. Used by permission of Dutton Children's Books, a division of Penguin Books USA Inc.

Of Mice and Men. From *Of Mice and Men* by John Steinbeck. Copyright ©1937, renewed ©1965 by John Steinbeck. Used by permission of Viking Penguin, a division of Penguin Books USA Inc.

A Separate Peace. From *A Separate Peace* by John Knowles. Copyright ©1959 by John Knowles. Reprinted by permission of Curtis Brown, Ltd.

Anne Frank: The Diary of a Young Girl. From *Anne Frank: The Diary of a Young Girl* by Anne Frank. Copyright ©1952 by Otto H. Frank. Used by permission of Doubleday, a division of Bantam Doubleday Dell Publishing Group, Inc.

The Hobbit. From *The Hobbit* by J.R.R. Tolkien. Copyright ©1966 by J.R.R. Tolkien. Reprinted by permission of Houghton Mifflin Co. All rights reserved. Canadian rights by permission of Unwin Hyman, an imprint of HarperCollins Publishers Limited.

The True Confessions of Charlotte Doyle. From *The True Confessions of Charlotte Doyle* by Avi. Copyright ©1990 by Avi. Decorations copyright ©1990 by Ruth E. Murray. Published with permission of the publisher, Orchard Books, New York.

The author thanks Louise Loewenstein, Educational Consultant, for her contributions and suggestions in choosing the stories for this second edition. Gratitude and thanks are also due the teachers and librarians who contributed suggestions and generously shared their knowledge of what young readers like, especially Roger Genest, Barbara Menard, Ben Nicholson, Lucinda Ray, Pam Shoemaker, and Peg Vohr.

Finally, Christine Powers Harris has been the sustaining force of the entire effort. Her insights and talents are reflected in all the lessons and especially in the unit on fantasy.

Contents

To the Teacher

Introduction

The new *Best-Selling Chapters*, Second Edition, has been revised to give your students more writing experience and more practice in critically discussing literature.

The popular format of *Best-Selling Chapters* has not changed, but you will find new features in this Second Edition—an expanded writing section within each unit and a writing process reference section. Every lesson helps students improve their writing skills by giving them insights into how an author uses theme, develops a character, creates a setting, or uses language. Seeing the novel through the author's eyes gives students a new awareness of just how a writer writes. In other words, students learn to read *and* to write from the writer's point of view.

The chapters from novels selected for *Best-Selling Chapters* have proven themselves favorites among young adults. The interactive lessons with each selection provide students with just enough challenge to demonstrate the obvious pleasures of familiarity with basic elements of literature. These interactive lessons not only allow students to prove to themselves that they can read with insight and understanding, but also teach students how they can apply an author's technique to their own writing.

The selections are all contemporary. Three were chosen from among the best of contemporary young adult novels: *The Westing Game, Julie of the Wolves,* and *Summer of My German Soldier.* Four other chapters are from classics that were not written for any special age group, but which have been taken to heart by middle and junior high readers as enduring favorites: *I Know Why the Caged Bird Sings, Of Mice and Men, A Separate Peace,* and *To Kill a Mockingbird.*

The last three selections introduce students to different genres. *The Hobbit* is a delightful book for teaching fantasy. *Anne Frank: The Diary of a Young Girl* is an important document for our times and is so popular among teens and preteens that it is a good choice for introducing students to autobiography and biography. Avi's award-winning novel *The True Confessions of Charlotte Doyle* deals with Charlotte's struggle to overcome her traditional views of social and economic class distinction and is one of the best ways of introducing the genre of historical fiction.

The Contents of a Unit

The book has ten units. Each unit contains the following:

1. **An illustration and discussion questions.** Each unit begins
   with a two-page illustration that depicts a key scene from the
   reading selection. This illustration enables visually oriented readers
   to place themselves easily in the story situation. The page that
   follows contains questions based on the illustration.

   You will notice that the illustration serves as an introduction to
   the lesson as well as to the selection. The accompanying questions
   also direct the students' thinking to essential ideas they will encounter in the lesson. In discussing the questions, students will be
   previewing both the story and the lesson. This activity heightens
   students' anticipation of participating in the story (because they
   are anxious to know if their interpretations of the illustration are
   correct) and sharpens their perception of the literary concept that
   will be discussed in the lesson.

2. **Introduction to the selection.** Each unit contains a brief, four-
   part introduction. The first part, About the Novel, sets the scene
   and explains a bit about the characters and the story situation.
   Experiences that are alluded to in the story but may be beyond
   the knowledge of most young readers are explained. For example, the
   names of parts of a sailing ship are explained in the introduction to
   The True Confessions of Charlotte Doyle. This part of the introduction also provides information about the author and suggests other
   novels by the author that the students may want to read.

   The second part of the introduction, About the Lesson, simply
   and concisely defines the literary concept to be studied in the lesson.

   The third part of the introduction consists of four questions
   intended to call the students' attention to particular passages in the
   chapter that are used to illustrate the four major points discussed
   in the lesson. The students should keep these questions in mind and
   look for the answers to them as they read the story.

   The fourth part of the introduction offers a variety of writing
   suggestions directly related to what will be discussed in the lesson.
   For example, if the lesson discusses character, students are asked to
   list ideas and suggestions for creating their own characters. Students will use their ideas for writing activities within each of the
   four lesson sections. Most of the writing exercises will take some
   time, so you may want to set aside a class period for students to

work on a writing project. You may want to discuss with your students the reference section Using the Writing Process at the end of the book. Remind students to refer to that section, beginning on page 439, and to the checklist when they begin a writing assignment.

3. **The reading selection.** With a few exceptions, the reading selections are unabridged, unadapted originals taken from the novels. The chapter from *The Hobbit* has been judiciously shortened since it was too long, when accompanied by a lesson, for students to handle comfortably. Representative selections were taken from *Anne Frank: The Diary of a Young Girl*. Students of average reading ability in grades 6–8 will be able to complete their reading of a selection in a sitting or two.

4. **The literary lesson.** Each lesson begins with a general explanation of a major literary concept. Then four major elements of the concept are discussed individually, and each is illustrated with an appropriate passage from the selection. After the literary element is explained in relation to this passage, the students are presented with a second passage from the story that illustrates the same element. This passage is followed by two questions that allow the students to critically discuss what they have just learned.

   Each of the four major elements discussed in the lesson is followed by Writing on Your Own, which helps students analyze a literary technique and apply that technique to their writing. For instance, within the four lesson sections that deal with setting, the students are asked to create a setting of their own. But first they build from basic elements of setting: the first exercise asks them to write about setting and the feelings it creates; the second, putting your reader into the story; the third, setting and how it reinforces ideas or themes; and finally, setting and the action.

   Seven of the ten lessons deal with elements of literature: character, setting, theme, language, conflict, symbolism, and tone and mood. Three lessons serve as an introduction to genre: autobiography and biography, fantasy, and the historical novel.

5. **Reviewing and Interpreting the Chapter.** Sixteen comprehension and interpretation questions following each lesson provide a quick check of four major reading skills: remembering facts, following the order of events, understanding word choices, understanding important ideas; and four interpreting skills: understanding levels of meaning, understanding character, understanding

setting, understanding feelings. Each question is labeled according to the skill it tests. A Comprehension Skills Profile is provided at the back of the book so that you can keep track of the kinds of questions each student misses most often. There is also a Comprehension Scores Graph that can help you keep track of overall progress in reading comprehension.

6. **Discussion Guides.** Through nine discussion questions in each unit, students are asked to consider three aspects of the chapter: the literary concept emphasized in the lesson, general ideas and implications of the chapter, and the author's technique or special relationship to the story situation. These questions encourage students to critically think about their reading and give them practice in critically discussing literature.

7. **Writing Exercise.** The writing exercises have always been one of the most popular elements in both *Best-Selling Chapters* and *Best Short Stories.* You will find that the expanded exercises within the lessons and the final writing exercise in each unit are directly related to what has been presented in the lesson and will encourage students to apply ideas and literary concepts to their own work. This exercise asks students to pull together all the elements they have discussed and written about in Writing on Your Own to create their own stories.

How to Use This Book

Best-Selling Chapters, Second Edition, has four major objectives:

◆ To help readers understand basic structure and the elements of literature

◆ To sharpen reading comprehension skills

◆ To encourage critical reading

◆ To give readers an opportunity to make a conscious effort to introduce elements of literary style into their own writing

Here are suggestions for ways to use the various parts of each unit:

1. **Discuss the illustration.** Ask the students to look carefully at the illustration. On the page following the illustration there are a key question and supporting questions. Read the key question aloud.

You can have the students respond spontaneously or ask them to hold their opinions until they have discussed the supporting questions.

Have either an open class discussion or small group discussions of the supporting questions. Then return to the key question and ask the students to respond to it in light of the answers they have arrived at in their discussions. Emphasize the importance of supporting or clarifying their opinions and conclusions by pointing out supporting details in the illustration.

These questions help students focus on both the selection they will read and the lesson that follows. Read the story and lesson first yourself so that you can direct the discussion of the illustration to assure that it is a good preview of the selection and lesson.

2. **Have students read the introduction to the novel.** You may wish to add information to the introduction from your own experience with the novel or the author. Point out that the author has written other works that they may want to read. Some of these works are mentioned in the introduction.

Call attention to the four questions that conclude each introduction. The students should keep those questions in mind as they read the selection. Point out how each of the questions is related to the definition of the literary concept given in About the Lesson. Discuss what the students should look for in the reading selection in order to be able to answer the questions. The questions guide the students, as they read, toward an awareness of the literary concept discussed in the lesson.

The introduction is followed by a writing exercise in which students list story ideas related to the literary concept discussed. You may want to provide time for the students to discuss their ideas before they make their lists.

3. **Have students read the selection.** Tell the students that you want them to enjoy the selection for its own sake, but point out that you also want them to read the selection *critically.*

To keep the students' attention focused on the literary concept discussed in the lesson, you may want to have them keep a copy of the questions from the introduction beside them as they read, or write the questions on the chalkboard. Also, remind the students that they will have to answer comprehension questions in Reviewing and Interpreting the Chapter—another reason for reading critically.

4. **Explain the literary lesson.** Each lesson is divided into five

parts. It begins with a general introduction to the literary concept that will be covered. After the students have read the introduction, discuss it with them to make sure they have a general understanding of the concept. Then have the students read and study the other four sections of the lesson, one at a time. Each explains a different element of the major literary concept on which the lesson is focused. The students should also complete the exercise at the end of each section. After they finish each section, pause for a discussion of the lesson so that the students can find out whether their answers or opinions to the questions are right or wrong, and why. Because many of the questions ask the students to draw their own conclusions or give their own opinions, it is important to explain that the Answer Key gives *suggested* answers.

5. **Have students discuss Writing on Your Own.** Each of the four lesson sections is followed by a writing exercise that focuses on the separate literary element discussed in that section. Provide time for students to discuss their ideas with classmates before they begin Writing on Your Own. These prewriting exercises help students prepare for the final writing exercise in the unit.

6. **Have students answer the questions in Reviewing and Interpreting the Chapter.** In classes in which reading comprehension is the primary concern, you may want to have the students answer these questions immediately after reading the selection. They should answer without looking back at the chapter. The comprehension and interpreting questions focus on eight important reading skills:

Remembering Facts	Understanding Levels of Meaning
Following the Order of Events	Understanding Character
Understanding Word Choices	Understanding Setting
Understanding Important Ideas	Understanding Feelings

7. **Have students correct their answers.** Students can check their answers to the Reviewing and Interpreting the Chapter questions by using the Answer Key that starts on page 451. Students should be encouraged to correct wrong answers and to consider why one answer is wrong and another right. Have students count the number of *each kind* of question they get wrong and record these numbers in the spaces provided at the end of the comprehension questions.

8. **Have students record their progress.** Students should plot the

number of *correct* answers they got for each story on the Comprehension Scores Graph on page 462. Instructions for how to use the graph are given on the page with the graph. When students plot their scores, a visual record of their progress quickly emerges.

Students should mark the number of *wrong* answers they got in each comprehension skill area (there are two questions related to each of the eight skills) on the Comprehension Skills Profile on page 463. This shows at a glance which skills a student needs to work on. Students usually enjoy keeping track of their progress, especially when they are allowed to manage this task themselves. Seeing visual proof of improvement in scores invariably provides the incentive to strive for even more improvement. You should also monitor the students' progress so that you can recognize any problems and deal with them early.

9. **Spend time on discussion.** There are three kinds of discussion questions for each selection—nine questions in all. The first three focus on the literary concept studied in the lesson. These questions give students a chance to demonstrate their new skills and allow you to expand upon the lesson if you wish. Questions four through six are more general and allow students to use their imaginations and apply themes in the selection to their own experiences. Finally, the last three questions deal with the author's experience and technique, and focus attention on the subjective aspects of literature.

10. **Have students do the Writing Exercise.** The writing exercise at the end of each unit allows students to improve their writing through imitation. Each writing exercise asks students to apply what they have learned about the literary element discussed in the lesson. If the students have not done the four Writing on Your Own exercises within the lesson, you may want them to go back and do them now. To make use of the truism that we learn to write by reading, encourage students to imitate the authors of the novels, if they wish. But an individual, freewheeling style may also be encouraged, especially among the better writers in a class.

11. **Using the Writing Process.** This reference section, beginning on page 439, is an extended lesson on what a writing process is and how to use it. The lesson helps students with the writing assignments they will encounter in the book. It explains the three major parts of the writing process: prewriting, writing, and

revising. The reference is followed by a checklist of the major points. Students should refer to this checklist each time they begin a writing exercise.

Before students begin the first writing exercise in the book, you will probably want to review Using the Writing Process with them. Read each section with the students and discuss and illustrate the main points. Make sure they understand that the three steps in the writing process are not strictly sequential. Point out that good writers move back and forth from one to another, focusing more on prewriting at the beginning and revising toward the end of the project. You may want to spend several class periods discussing and experimenting with the various stages.

To the Student

This textbook can help you become a better reader. Its goal is not to make you memorize facts or details. Instead, its goal is to help you enjoy and understand your reading. It teaches you how to become more involved in what you read. Once you do that, books will have more meaning for you.

The reading selections in this book have been chosen because they have proved to be favorites among young adults. There is a selection from each of ten different novels that you will probably enjoy. Each selection has an introduction that provides hints about what the rest of the book is like so that you will see how exciting and interesting it is. Be sure to read the introductions and the suggestions for writing your own stories. They are important for understanding the reading selection.

Each reading selection is followed by a lesson. In the lesson you will learn about how a story is written. Writing a story takes certain skills—the author's "tricks of the trade," so to speak. The lessons point out some of these skills and how they work in the stories. You will read descriptions of theme, character, and setting. You will begin to see how authors use language and how they tell you their ideas. Exercises that go with the lessons allow you to practice and "show off" what you have learned. Each lesson section is followed by a short writing activity that helps you apply newly learned techniques to your own writing. Reviewing and Interpreting questions, Discussion Guides, and a final Writing Exercise, which follow each lesson, let you check to see how well you understand the lesson as a whole.

Lessons and skills that you learn here will serve you well even beyond your school career. In the future you will read with a sharper eye. You will be alert to details and ideas that you may have missed before.

You can also use some of what you learn here in you life outside school. Skills that you learn in order to read well can also be used in talking or thinking about people. Understanding more about characters in novels can help you understand more about the people you know. Grasping ideas is another skill you learn in reading that you need to use in your daily life. You will also learn about detecting changes in tone and understanding the source of conflict.

Whatever effort you put into using this text will reward you with increased abilities. You will read with better judgment and more enjoyment. And you will learn to be more alert to what goes on in your life and the world around you.

Unit 1   Character

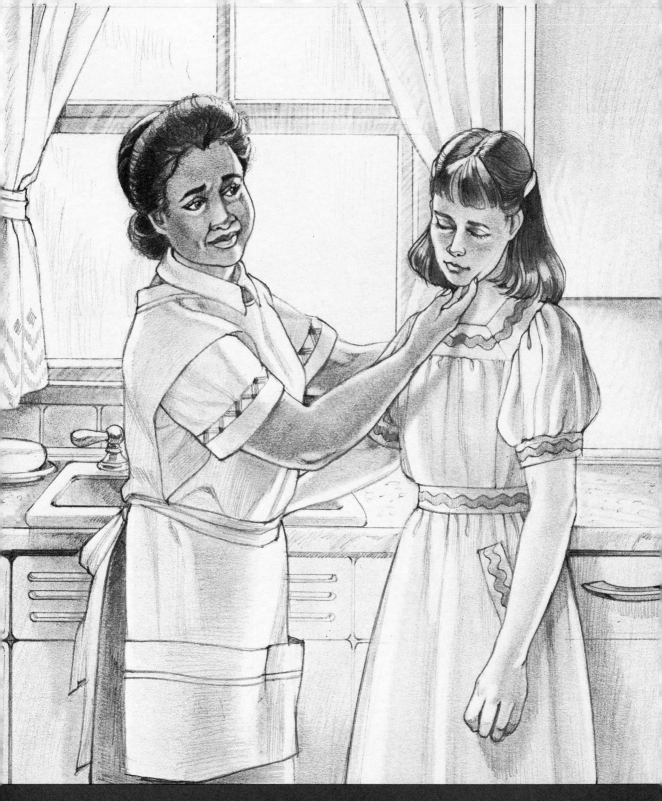

Summer of My German Soldier
BY BETTE GREENE

About the Illustration

What can you tell about each of these people? Describe
each one separately. Point out details in the drawing to
support your response.

Here are some questions to help you think about the
chapter:

◆ How would you describe the expression on the
woman's face? Why do you think she is touching the
girl?

◆ How would you describe the expression on the girl's
face? What does her expression tell you?

Unit 1

Introduction

About the Novel

Patty Bergen is the oldest daughter in the only Jewish family in a small Southern town, Jenkinsville, Arkansas. For some reason, her parents don't seem to like her. When her father, Harry Bergen, isn't annoyed with her, he is angry with her. When he is angry enough, he beats her. Patty's mother, Pearl Bergen, doesn't find much to like about her daughter either. She goes out of her way to be insulting to Patty about her appearance and manners.

Twelve-year-old Patty has few acquaintances and no real friends among her schoolmates. As you may imagine, she feels lonely, ugly, and unloved. The one true friend and protector Patty has is Ruth, the Bergen's housekeeper. It is Ruth who provides the only mothering that Patty has ever known.

Summer of My German Soldier is set in 1944 when Hitler's

Germany is on its way to defeat in World War II. German prisoners of war are arriving in the United States in growing numbers. A prisoner-of-war camp is opened outside of Jenkinsville and the first German prisoners arrive. They are put to work picking cotton in the nearby fields.

A group of prisoners is brought to Harry Bergen's store one day to buy field hats for their work in the sun. Among them is a young German named Anton Reiker who speaks English and translates for the others. Patty sells him some pencils and other small articles and they chat. They like one another instantly, and after their brief meeting, Patty hopes she can see him again.

The townspeople consider Anton a dangerous enemy of the United States. And if he shared Hitler's feelings about Jewish people, his friendship with Patty would be very suspicious indeed. But Anton doesn't share Hitler's views. Anton is educated, sensitive, and loving, and he thinks Hitler is a madman.

Patty doesn't see Anton again until he escapes from the prison camp and she accidently finds him by the railroad tracks. She takes him home and hides him in some empty rooms above an unused garage. She and Anton become good friends. He understands Patty and he genuinely likes her.

Patty has put herself in an extremely dangerous situation. Anton is a fugitive who could be shot on sight. To shelter him in wartime is treason. For a Jewish girl to befriend and protect a German soldier is both unbelievable and unthinkable. She risks the anger of the law as well as her father's wrath.

Just before Chapter 11 begins, Anton witnesses Patty's father beating her for a minor disobedience. She has been caught talking to a neighborhood boy she was forbidden to talk to. Anton rushes from his hiding place to help her. But Patty waves him away before he is discovered. Anton can only watch helplessly while Harry Bergen beats Patty unmercifully with his belt.

Ruth is also watching, and she sees Anton rush out. The next morning, Ruth faces Patty with her discovery. She asks Patty to reveal the man's identity, though she has a good idea who he is. Later, Patty and Anton discuss her beating and they try to understand why Patty's father behaves as he does.

What happens after this chapter is at first suspenseful and then painful. Patty's story is not a happy one.

Like Patty, author Bette Greene grew up in a small town in Arkansas. To a large extent, *Summer of My German Soldier* is based on her personal experiences. The novel has won many awards and was made into a television movie starring Kristy McNichol.

After reading the complete novel, you will want to read its sequel, *Morning Is a Long Time Coming*. This book picks up the story of Patty Bergen when she is graduating from high school and facing the question of what to do with her life.

Other books by Bette Greene include *Philip Hall Likes Me, I Reckon Maybe,* and *Get On Out Of Here, Philip Hall.*

About the Lesson

The lesson following the reading selection is about character. Characters are not only people. They can be animals, strange creatures, and even plants, trains, or toys—as in the stories "The Little Fir Tree," "The Little Engine That Could," and "Pinocchio." But the word *character* has another, more important meaning. Character is the complete person—how a person looks, acts, thinks, and feels.

For a story to be believable the author must create characters who are realistic and believable. The technique an author uses to breathe life into characters is called *characterization.* This lesson will point out some of the ways an author accomplishes this very difficult task.

The following questions will help you understand the characters and the author's characterization in the chapter from *Summer of My German Soldier.* Read the chapter carefully and try to answer these questions as you go along:

◆ How does Patty (a character in the story herself) tell you about her father? about Ruth? Freddy?

◆ In a conversation over breakfast, Patty tells Ruth that she is hiding Anton, the German soldier. What does this conversation tell you about both Patty and Ruth?

◆ How does the author make you understand Patty's feelings after she tells Ruth about Anton?

◆ Harry Bergen, Patty's father, is portrayed as mean and cruel in the story. How does the author help you understand the other sides of this man's character?

Creating Characters for a Story

You can better understand what goes into creating a character (characterization) when you create characters of your own. Use your writing notebook or a separate piece of paper and try the following suggestions:

1. Think of a story involving two characters that you would like to write. This can be a true story about two people you know, or a story you will make up.

2. Tell in just a few sentences what your story will be about.

3. Think about your characters. Remember, characters can be animals and things as well as people. Write a sentence or two about each character that tells the following:

   ☐ The characters' names and who they are

   ☐ What the characters are like (loving, mean, brave, intelligent, funny, noble, proud, snooty, dishonest, cowardly, a bully, etc.)

Summer of My German Soldier

by Bette Greene

11

She has to be taking it home with her; I can't think of any other explanation. That kosher salami cost one dollar and ten cents." My mother repeated the price a second time for added emphasis.

I pulled the top sheet over my head to block out the early morning sounds from the kitchen and rolled over a now very warm ice bag and remembered. In another few minutes they would be leaving for the store. Only then would I get out of bed. Just as soon as my mother downs her second cup of coffee and my father finishes his corn flakes. As long as I can remember it has been corn flakes and nothing but corn flakes. He's got the same loyalty towards cars. "I'll buy any kinda car as long as it's a Chevrolet." And cigarettes too. He's never had a cigarette in his mouth that wasn't a Lucky Strike.

"So you'd better talk to her, Harry."

"Talk to who?"

"To Ruth!" Her voice hit a shrill note. "I want to know what's happening to the salami and chicken and all the other food that's been disappearing around here lately."

"Well, how do you know she's taking it home? I don't know what you're talking about. But she'll be coming any minute now, and if you want to fire her it's fine with me. Something about that woman I never liked."

I didn't speak to them, but I didn't want them to suspect either. I yelled out, "I'm sorry about the salami 'cause I ate most of it myself. And about the leftover chicken, Sharon and Sue Ellen ate the last of it."

"Now you see that!" he told her. "Don't ever talk to me again about missing food."

I'll have to say this for him, he's always generous about food, even when we eat in restaurants. Like that Sunday in Memphis not too long ago when we ate at Britlings' and I ordered the chopped sirloin steak and he said, "That's nothing but a hamburger. Wouldn't you like to have a real steak?" My mother didn't like the idea of ordering "an expensive steak that will just go to waste." But my father told her to mind her own business, and that as long as he lived I could eat anything I wanted.

The phrase, "as long as he lived" sounded like a vague prophecy, and I became sorrowful that he might die now that he was being good to me. I became so sorrowful, in fact, that it was Mother's prediction that was soon fulfilled. An expensive steak went to waste.

The familiar sounds of a spiritual—Ruth was passing below my window on her way to the back door. "Morning, folks," she called. "Well, I heard the weatherman say we're gonna get us a little rain by afternoon, enough to cool things off." My mother agreed that a little shower would be very nice. "Is that piece of toast all you've had to eat?" asked Ruth. "That's no kinda breakfast, Miz Bergen. I could make you some hurry-up griddle cakes."

"Griddle cakes are fattening. Besides I have to leave now."

A couple of minutes later the car backed out of the garage, the motor gunned for the two-block trip, and they were gone.

Ruth came into my room, bent over and picked up the flowery chenille bedspread that had fallen to the floor, and asked, "Are you feeling all right?"

I remembered who had brought me the ice bag and

aspirins for my head and the ointment for my legs. "I don't know. I guess I am."

From the other twin bed came a long, low, early morning sound as Sharon flopped over to a better dreaming position.

"Come on into the kitchen," whispered Ruth as she tiptoed out of the room.

The marshmallow slowly began to bleed its whiteness over the steaming cup of chocolate. On the shelf of the breakfast room's built-in cabinet our one surviving goldfish, Goldilocks, began her vigorous after-breakfast swim.

"How come that fish got sense enough to eat her breakfast and you don't?" asked Ruth as she sat down at the table.

I ignored the buttered toast and scrambled egg, but took a long drink of the now lukewarm chocolate. "Don't know except maybe Goldilocks has a better cook that I do."

"Must be the truth," Ruth smiled, showing her left-of-center, solid-gold tooth. "You know what you needs, Honey? One of them fancy Frenchmen who cooks up a fine dinner and jest 'fore serving it, he sets it all afire."

We sat for a while in silence, Ruth taking small now-and-then sips of coffee while I sat stirring my chocolate and watching Goldilocks. Ruth's spoon made an attention getting noise and I saw that those brown eyes were upon me.

"I want you to tell Ruth the truth about something. You hear me talking, girl?" I nodded Yes.

"You tell me who is the man."

"Man?"

"Honey Babe, you can tell Ruth. The man that ran out from the garage. The man that wanted to save you from your daddy."

"That man—the man—the—" My voice was still in some kind of working order even if my brain did just up and die.

How can those eyes that rest so lightly see so deeply? And from them there is nothing in this world to fear. "The man is my friend," I said at last.

"You got him hid up in them rooms over the garage?"

"Yes."

Ruth sighed like she sometimes does before tackling a really big job. "He's not the one the law's after? Not the one from the prison camp?"

"Yes."

Her forehead crinkled up like a washboard. "You telling me, Yes, he's not the one?"

"No, Ruth, I'm telling you Yes. Yes, he's the one."

Ruth's head moved back and forth in a No direction. "Oh, Lord, why are you sending us more, Lord? Don't this child and me have burden enough?"

I stood up and felt this sensation of lightness, near weightlessness, like somebody had just bent down, picked up, and carried away all my trouble. My arm fell across Ruth's shoulder. "Everything'll be all right, honest it will." Beneath my arm, there was no movement, no feeling of life. I squeezed Ruth's shoulder and a hearable breath rushed through her nostrils. "You know how you're all the time helping me because you're my friend? Well, Anton's my friend and I have to help him, you know? Don't you know?"

"I don't know what it is I know," she said in a weighted voice.

In the pantry there was plenty of peanut butter, but the jar of strawberry jam was only fingernail high. I turned on the gas burner under the aluminum percolator. I began to worry that maybe prison camp food was better than this, but at least the loaf of white bread was yesterday fresh.

Ruth followed me into the kitchen. "Honey, them peanut butter and jelly sandwiches ain't no kinda breakfast for no kinda man." She looked up at the kitchen clock. "After I bring Sharon down to Sue Ellen's I'll fix up some hot griddle cakes with maple syrup and a fresh pot of coffee."

I threw my arms as far around Ruth's waist as they would go and tried to lift her up by the pure strength of my will.

"Oh, Ruth, you're good, good, good!"

"Now, girl, don't go 'specting no amount of praise to turn my mind about 'cause my mind ain't come to no clear thought yet. All I knows for sure is that I'm gonna fix up a proper breakfast for you and the man."

"O.K., thanks, but would you mind not calling him the man, 'cause he's my friend, Anton. Mr. Frederick Anton Reiker. You may not know this, but you and Anton are all the friends I've got."

Ruth nodded slowly. "I understands that, Honey."

That understanding made me want to tell her everything all at once. "Ruth, he talks to me and he tells me things because I'm his friend. Ruth, he likes me. He really and truly likes me."

"I knows that too."

My heart swelled up for if Ruth knows it, it must be the truth. "How do you know that? Tell me how you know!"

She gave my arm a couple of short pats before finding my eyes. "That man come a-rushing out from the safety of his hiding 'cause he couldn't stand your pain and anguish no better'n me. That man listens to the love in his heart. Like the Bible tell us, when a man will lay down his life for a friend, well, then there ain't no greater love in this here world than that."

Before I reached the landing I heard his footsteps, and then the door opened. I felt certain he was smiling a welcome, although I was looking past him into the familiar interior of the room much as I would look past the brilliance of the sun.

"How are you?" he asked, making it sound more like an inquiry than a greeting.

"Fine." Cowardliness kept me from looking at him. "Did you sleep O.K.? Were you too hot?" I asked.

"No."

The shortness of his answer frightened me. Maybe it's disgust for what he saw yesterday. My eyes shut in a feeble try at pushing away the memories.

"Sure you're all right?" His eyes were on the red raw stripes that crisscrossed my legs.

I moved quickly to the opposite side of the desk. "Oh, yes, thanks."

"About yesterday—"

"It's O.K."

"No," he said with a force I had never heard him use before. "It's not O.K.! Listen to me, P.B. What happened yesterday bothers me. Tell me if I was in any way responsible." Between his eyebrows there was a deep crease, a mark of concern—for me.

All that painful dabbing of layer after layer of face powder that I subjected my legs to may have been a mistake. Concern might be a little like love.

"It wasn't you," I said. "You weren't responsible."

"Then what? Please tell me what you did to deserve such a beating?"

How could I say in words what I couldn't really understand myself? Sometimes I think it's because I'm bad that my father wants to do the right thing by beating it out of me. And at other times I think he's beating out from my body all his own bad. My head began its confused revolutions.

"Come over to the window," I said finally, pointing toward the tracks. "See over there? The shack with the tin roof? There's a boy who lives there who my father told me I'm not to have anything to do with. Yesterday he saw Freddy sitting next to me on our front steps." I told Anton about sleepy Freddy who cuts grass in his spare time so he can make enough money to sleep during the Saturday matinee. Scholarly Freddy who has been in Miss Bailey's fourth grade for two years because he's finally found, "The one teacher I likes." Fearless Freddy, brave hunter of crawdads. And generous Freddy who once bought me the gift of not quite half of a melted mess of a Hershey bar.

"He sounds perfectly delightful," said Anton with a smile. "But why is your father so opposed to him?"

"Maybe it's because he's so poor, but I'm not sure."

He looked a little perplexed. "Why don't you inquire?"

"I can't inquire." My words had a harshness that I didn't intend. "In my father's vocabulary to ask why is to contradict him."

"I don't like him!" The words seemed to dash out. Then Anton caught my eyes as though asking permission.

"Oh, that's O.K.," I said pleased that Anton was taking my side. "I'll tell you something I've never told anyone before. If he weren't my father, I wouldn't even like him."

"But because he is, you do?"

"Oh, well, I guess I—" Than the image came. The image of his thin, rabid face. "I guess I don't too much. No, I don't like him." That was the first time I had even thought anything like that myself. Funny, but Edna Louise once told me, "Your daddy is so sweet." Probably because every time he sees her he says, "Edna Louise, you sure do look pretty today." To Edna Louise he has to say nice things as if she weren't conceited enough.

"Do you have any idea where your father went—what he did immediately following the beating he gave you?"

"Not exactly, I could guess. He probably went into the house, smoked a Lucky Strike cigarette, washed his hands, and ate a perfectly enormous supper while he listened to the evening news."

"Not true. He stood watching the housekeeper help you into the house. Then he came into the garage and talked to himself. Over and over he kept repeating, 'Nobody loves me. In my whole life nobody has ever loved me.' "

"Anton, it must have been somebody else. That doesn't sound like my father."

"It *was* your father."

"I don't understand. Why? How could he be so mean and then worry that he isn't loved? It doesn't make sense."

Anton shook his head. "I met your father once; I interpreted for some of the prisoners who came into the store."

"I remember! You said the prisoners needed hats to

protect themselves from our formidable Arkansas sun."

Anton smiled, and the smile made him look very young, more like a boy my age than a man. "How could you possibly remember that?"

"Easy. Nobody from around here says things like that. I also remember that he didn't think your remark was very amusing."

"I can believe that because—" Anton paused like he was trying to put some new thoughts into good running order before continuing—"because it seems to me that a man who is incapable of humor is capable of cruelty. If Hitler, for example, had had the ability—the detachment—to observe the absurdity of his own behavior he would have laughed, and today there might not be a madman named Adolph Hitler."

Was he making a comparison between Hitler and my father? "Do you think my father is like that? Like Hitler?"

Anton looked thoughtful. "Cruelty is after all cruelty, and the difference between the two men may have more to do with their degrees of power than their degrees of cruelty. One man is able to affect millions and the other only a few. Would your father's cruelty cause him to crush weak neighboring states? Or would the *Führer's* cruelty cause him to beat his own daughter? Doesn't it seem to you that they both need to inflict pain?"

"I don't know."

Anton smiled. "I don't know either. But you see, the only questions I like to raise are those that are unanswerable. Trying to calculate the different degrees of cruelty is a lot like trying to calculate the different degrees of death."

I laughed, but I knew that tonight while our house slept I would stay awake trying to understand his words. "I'm so glad you're talking to me, teaching me." I heard my enthusiasm running over. "I want you to teach me everything you've learned."

Anton stood, executing a princely bow. "I'm at your service."

"I think I want to be intelligent even more than I want to be pretty."

"You're already intelligent and pretty."

"Me?"

"You. I come from a line of men who have a sure instinct for a woman's beauty. So, P.B., I speak as an expert when I tell you you're going to have it all."

"Well, why hasn't anyone else seen it? That I'm going to have—what you say?"

"They will. Because you are no common garden flower—you are unique."

"Oh."

"I think I'm going to enjoy being your teacher if you'll keep in mind that life produces no maestros, only students of varying degrees of ineptitude. Wait!" said Anton. He jumped from his chair to go rummaging through a GI regulation duffel bag. "Here it is!" He waved a book with a bruised, blue cover. "I checked it out of the prison library the same day I checked myself out. R.W. Emerson. Are you familiar with his work?"

I admitted that I wasn't while I wondered if escaping with a book could be called anything besides stealing. My father would never do anything like that.

Anton asked, "Is something wrong?"

"Uhhh, no. Well, I was wondering how you are going to return the book."

"Oh," he said thoughtfully. "You want to know if I am a thief?"

"Oh, no! I know you're not!"

"In this classroom we call things by their rightful name. I became a thief when I took that book. I couldn't very well pay for it, and I didn't want my brain to starve if I had to go into hiding."

I felt close to laughing. "You're very honest. I mean you don't lie, do you?"

Anton shook his head. "I try never to lie to myself, and I dislike lying to friends." He took a yellow pencil from his hip pocket and made two small check marks in R.W. Emerson's Table of Contents. "Read these essays," he said, like he felt pleased to be making a contribution to my education. "And tomorrow we can start mining the gold."

Then a voice from below us called up, "Come on folks! It's ready." Anton's face was caught in a moment of fear.

"It's all right," I whispered. "That's only Ruth, our house-keeper. She's made griddle cakes for us."

He looked at me. "Why did you—tell?"

He believed—he actually believed—that I would. "But I didn't! Honest! Ruth saw you run out of the garage last night; she saw how you wanted to protect me from my father."

Anton's hand rushed to his forehead. "I came running out of hiding to—My God, I did, didn't I?" His hand dropped to his side, and I could see he was smiling his wonderful glad-to-be-living smile. "After almost two years of being as inconspicuous a coward as possible I had no idea that I would voluntarily risk my life for anyone." He shook his head in disbelief. "But I'm glad I still could."

Character

Creating interesting and believable characters is one of the most important elements of a good story. The better the characters, the better the story. That's why authors work hard to make their characters as realistic as possible. The best characters are those that come alive in the mind of the reader. By the time you have finished reading a good book, the characters are more than words on a page. The author has turned them into real-life acquaintances for you.

Some characters are so believable that they take on a life of their own outside their stories. Tom Sawyer, for instance, will always be *the* example of a boy growing up in Middle America. To many, Sherlock Holmes is a real, living detective. It is easy to forget that these familiar figures came from someone's imagination. But they were, of course, given life by an author. The process by which this is done is called *characterization.*

Authors use the same techniques to create characters that people use to get to know one another in real life. For example, you get to know some people by hearing about them from others. Someone says, "Let me tell you about Alek," and a lively conversation follows in which Alek is described in great detail. In a story, too, description is an important part of developing a character.

Another way you get to know people is by listening to what they say and watching what they do. Once again, authors use a similar method to get you to know their characters. You learn about characters through their words and actions. In a story, what characters say and what they do adds to their characterization.

You don't really know people, however, until you come to understand them. Understanding people can be very difficult. One of the most common expressions you hear from people who disagree is, "Oh, I'll never understand you!" What that means is, "I don't understand how you feel, and I don't understand why you act the way you do."

Here an author of a story has a great advantage. An author can make you understand how a character feels. An author can also make you think about the reasons behind a character's actions.

In this lesson we will look at four ways in which author Bette Greene creates characters and helps you understand them:

1 ◆ Characters are presented by description.

2 ◆ Characters are revealed through dramatic action.

3 ◆ Characters are revealed through their feelings.

4 ◆ Analyzing characters will help you understand them better.

1 ◆ Character and Description

The simplest way for an author to describe a character is to come right out and tell readers what that character is like. Height, weight, eye color, likes, and dislikes are all part of a character description. You may be told about a character's disposition. Is the character brave or timid? generous or spiteful? These are some of the same things you want to find out when you first get to know someone.

An author presents these descriptions in a number of ways. Sometimes the author speaks directly to the readers. This is called a *third-person narration.* Other times, the author has a character give the description, as Patty does in *Summer of My German Soldier.* This is called a *first-person narration.* The author speaks to readers directly through the character.

When Ruth first appeared in the story in an earlier chapter, Patty describes her to readers this way:

> She is the color of hot chocolate before the marshmallow bleeds in. Sometimes I hear my mother telling her to lose weight. . . . But she isn't actually fat; it's just that she has to wear large sizes. I mean it wouldn't be Ruth if she were like my mother. And another thing, a little extra weight keeps a person warm inside.

The author has Patty come right out and tell readers what Ruth is like. Ruth is chocolate brown, large (maybe on the fat side), and she is a warm person. This first impression of Ruth is confirmed by what we see of her as the story goes along.

In Chapter 11, Patty describes her father for you:

> As far as I can remember it has been corn flakes and nothing but corn flakes. He's got the same loyalty towards cars. "I'll buy any kinda car as long as it's a Chevrolet." And cigarettes too. He's never had a cigarette in his mouth that wasn't a Lucky Strike.

That passage is not a description of what Harry Bergen looks like. It is a description of the kind of man he is—a man of habit. Patty suggests that he'll never change. Other passages that show his character also make it clear that he is unreasonably stubborn.

Another way an author describes a character is by showing you a conversation in which the character is discussed. Here Ruth is talking to Patty about Anton. Ruth describes something important about Anton's character for Patty and for readers.

> She gave my arm a couple of pats before finding my eyes. "That man come a-rushing out from the safety of his hiding 'cause he couldn't stand your pain and anguish no better'n me. That man listens to the love in his heart. . . ."

In this short passage, Ruth reveals an important fact about Anton's character. In doing so, she also reveals something about herself. Anton, Ruth says, is the kind of man who "listens to the love in his heart." He can't bear to stand by and watch Patty's suffering. "No better'n me," Ruth says. We learn from Ruth that she, like Anton, is a person who is filled with compassion and love.

1 ♦ Exercise A

Read the following passage and answer the questions about it using what you have learned in this part of the lesson. Use your writing notebook or a separate piece of paper for your answers.

> I told Anton about sleepy Freddy who cuts grass in his spare time so he can make enough money to sleep during the Saturday matinee. Scholarly Freddy who has been in Miss Bailey's fourth grade for two years because he's finally found, "The one teacher I likes." Fearless Freddy, brave hunter of crawdads. And generous Freddy who once brought me the gift of not quite half of a melted mess of a Hershey bar.

1. Patty describes Freddy as "scholarly, fearless, and generous." How do you know that Patty is being humorous and really means the opposite of all these things? Be specific.

2. Patty is making fun of Freddy in this passage. But how would you describe Freddy's character, based on this description?

Now check your answers using the suggestions in the Answer Key starting on page 451. Review this part of the lesson if you don't understand why an answer was wrong.

1♦Writing on Your Own

Look at the sentences you have written for Creating Characters for a Story on page 26. Now do the following:

1. Expand on your character descriptions. Write a paragraph that describes what one of your characters looks like. Make your description as direct as possible, allowing your readers to draw obvious conclusions.

   ☐ For example, if you are describing a bully at school, you might use adjectives such as big, mean, strong, scary, etc.

2. Write a second paragraph that describes what kind of person your character is. In this paragraph, describe your character by referring to his or her behavior. This type of description will allow your readers to draw their own conclusions. Their conclusions, however, will be greatly influenced by your description.

   ☐ For example, if you describe how your bully steals lunch money and beats up the smaller kids, then you expect your readers to conclude that you character is big, mean, strong, and scary.

3. You may want to change and rewrite your paragraphs several times until you are satisfied with your descriptions.

2 ◆ Character and Dramatic Action

Dramatic action is the kind of action you see in a play or movie. The action may be as exciting as a daring rescue. It may be as quiet as a friendly conversation. Sometimes the "action" may simply be a character thinking out loud. Dramatic action is any action or conversation that tells something about a character.

You learn about people in the same way—by watching what they do and listening to what they say. This is also how you learn about characters. Below is an example of dramatic action involving Patty and Ruth. You can learn a great deal about these characters from their conversation.

"I want you to tell Ruth the truth about something. You hear me talking, girl?" I nodded Yes.

"You tell me who is the man."

"Man?"

"Honey Babe, you can tell Ruth. The man that ran out from the garage. The man that wanted to save you from your daddy."

"That man—the man—the—" My voice was still in some kind of working order even if my brain did just up and die. . . .

"The man is my friend," I said at last.

"You got him hid up in them rooms over the garage?"

"Yes."

Ruth sighed like she sometimes does before tackling a really big job. "He's not the one the law's after? Not the one from the prison camp?"

"Yes."

Her forehead crinkled up like a washboard. "You telling me, Yes, he's not the one?"

"No, Ruth, I'm telling you Yes. Yes, he's the one."

Ruth's head moved back and forth in a No direction. "Oh, Lord, why are you sending us more, Lord? Don't this child and me have burden enough?"

I stood up and felt this sensation of lightness, near weightlessness, like somebody had just bent down, picked up, and carried away all my trouble.

For good reason, Patty is weighted down with fears. She fears her mother's next insulting remark. She fears the next beating she may get from her father. Now she is burdened by the worst fear of all. She may be caught hiding a prisoner of war. Ruth has seen Anton and makes Patty confess. With that, Patty feels "like somebody had just bent down, picked up, and carried away" her troubles. Her burden has been lightened.

What does this dramatic action tell readers about Patty and Ruth? It emphasizes the fear that Patty feels all the time. And it shows that in spite of her fear, Patty persists in doing what she feels is right. In this case she feels she must protect Anton, and she does.

We are also shown something about Ruth. She understands Patty's needs and is willing to do what she can to help. She is shown here as being understanding, loving, and courageous. She is also deeply religious and has a thought for her God as she takes up this new burden.

2 ♦ Exercise B

Read the following passage and answer the questions about it using what you have learned in this part of the lesson. Use your writing notebook or a separate piece of paper for your answers.

> "You may not know this, but you and Anton are all the friends I've got."
>
> Ruth nodded slowly. "I understands that, Honey."
>
> That understanding made me want to tell her everything all at once. "Ruth, he talks to me and he tells me things because I'm his friend, Ruth, he likes me. He really and truly likes me."
>
> "I knows that too."

1. How does this passage show that Patty is a lonely person? Find evidence in the story to support your answer.

2. Ruth is shown to be an understanding person. Why is this important in Patty's life? Why might you want to know someone like Ruth?

Now check your answers using the suggestions in the Answer Key starting on page 451. Review this part of the lesson if you don't understand why an answer was wrong.

2 ◆ Writing on Your Own

Look at the sentences you have written for Creating Characters for a Story on page 26. Now do the following:

1. Write a conversation that takes place between your two characters. In the conversation, be sure that different aspects about the personalities of both characters are revealed. Remember, actions and words are a big part of character development. For example:

   ☐ Your first character may be a mean bully who intimidates younger children. Your second character may be a peacemaker intent on putting a stop to the bully's vicious ways.

2. Exchange your writing with a writing partner, or read it to your class or writing circle.

3. Ask your writing partners what they think the conversation tells them about your two characters. Do they see the characters as you intended them to?

4. Write, revise, correct, and rewrite your conversation until it gives the impression you intended.

3 ◆ Character and Feeling

Authors deliberately set out to make you feel differently about each character. You are expected to like Patty, Ruth, and Anton. And you are expected to work up a healthy dislike for Harry Bergen, Patty's father.

Something happens between readers and characters in a well-written story. As the story progresses, you begin to understand the characters' deepest feelings. You come to sympathize with the main characters, and you begin to feel as they do. It is said that you *identify* with these characters. Because you identify with them, you become more involved in the story.

When Ruth discovers Patty's secret, you know exactly how Patty feels. You have probably been in a similar situation yourself. Even if you haven't, the author makes you understand what the feeling is like.

> "That man—the man—the—" My voice was still in some kind of working order even if my brain did just up and die.

How many times have you said: "When they found out, I thought I'd drop dead on the spot!" Because you have felt as Patty does, you understand her situation better. You may also recognize Patty's feeling of relief after confessing to Ruth. And you probably know how Ruth feels as she takes on this new burden.

> I stood up and felt this sensation of lightness, near weightlessness, like somebody had just bent down, picked up, and carried away all my trouble. . . . I squeezed Ruth's shoulder and a hearable breath rushed through her nostrils. "You know how you're all the time helping me because you're my friend? Well, Anton's my friend and I have to help him, you know? Don't you know?"
>
> "I don't know what it is I know," she said in a weighted voice.

Bette Greene has made you feel Patty's sense of relief. You can actually feel the weight flowing from Patty's shoulders. And you know where the burden has gone. It has been transferred to Ruth. Her voice is "weighted" and heavy with concern. You probably know just how she feels as well.

3 ♦ Exercise C

Read the following passage and answer the questions about it using what you have learned in this part of the lesson. Use your writing notebook or a separate piece of paper for your answers.

> [Anton and Patty are talking about Mr. Bergen's dislike of Freddy.]
>
> "But why is you father so opposed to him?"
>
> "Maybe it's because he's so poor, but I'm not sure."
>
> He looked a little perplexed. "Why don't you inquire?"
>
> "I can't inquire." My words had a harshness that I didn't intend. "In my father's vocabulary to ask why is to contradict him."
>
> "I don't like him!" The words seemed to dash out. Then Anton caught my eyes as though asking permission.
>
> "Oh, that's O.K.," I said pleased that Anton was taking my side. "I'll tell you something I've never told anyone before. If he weren't my father, I wouldn't even like him."
>
> "But because he is, you do?"
>
> "Oh, well, I guess I—" Then the image came. The image of his thin, rabid face. "I guess I don't too much. No, I don't like him." That was the first time I had even thought anything like that myself.

1. What does Patty say about Harry Bergen that makes you feel as much dislike for him as Anton and Patty do?

2. Patty says, "If he weren't my father, I wouldn't even like him." You might say this shows that Patty is disloyal and disrespectful to her father. What is your opinion of what Patty says? Give examples from the story to support your answer.

Now check your answers using the suggestions in the Answer Key starting on page 451. Review this part of the lesson if you don't understand why an answer was wrong.

3 ♦ Writing on Your Own

Look at the sentences you have written for Creating Characters for a Story on page 26. Now do the following:

1. Write a paragraph about an action that will make your readers like one of your characters. Here are a few suggestions:

   □ How does the peacemaker feel watching the bully intimidate others?

   □ Why does the peacemaker interfere?

   □ Is he or she nervous or afraid?

2. Then write a paragraph about an action that will make readers *dislike* the same character. Here are a few suggestions:

   □ What motivates your peacemaker to interfere?

   □ Is he or she conceited or pushy?

   □ Does your peacemaker have an ulterior motive?

3. You may want to write, revise, correct, and rewrite your paragraphs until you are satisfied with the results.

4 ◆ Understanding Character

We must all learn to live with other people. Therefore, it is important that we try to understand the actions of others. One technique that you can use to understand another person is called *character analysis*. Through character analysis you try to learn about a character by examining his or her words and actions. Character analysis is what you have been doing in the first three parts of this lesson.

Many people form opinions about others based on their first impressions of that person's appearance. That's why you are careful how you dress and act when you want to impress someone. Or perhaps you may form an early opinion of a person based on what others have told you. In a novel, first impressions usually come from the author's description of a character. You saw how this works in the first part of the lesson.

Your opinions take shape when you see the way characters act and when you listen to what they say. Finally, when you come to understand how the characters feel, you are able to understand why they act and speak as they do.

This is what character analysis is about. It is a process of putting facts and feelings together in order to make a judgment about a person. It is an effort at understanding.

Harry Bergen, Patty's father, is one of the most complicated characters in the story. He is the hardest character to understand. Though you meet him only briefly in Chapter 11, he is the subject of much of the conversation. He has been described for you, and you have been told about some of his vicious actions. Why does he act the way he does? See if you can make a judgment about Mr. Bergen based on the following passage and on what you already know about him. Anton is telling Patty how her father acted after he beat her.

> "Do you have any idea where your father went—what he did immediately following the beating he gave you?"
>
> "Not exactly, I could guess. He probably went into the house, smoked a Lucky Strike cigarette, washed his hands, and ate a perfectly enormous supper while he listened to the evening news."
>
> "Not true. He stood watching the housekeeper help you into the house. Then he came into the garage and talked to himself. Over and over he kept repeating, 'Nobody loves

me. In my whole life nobody has ever loved me.' "

"Anton, it must have been somebody else. That doesn't sound like my father."

"It *was* your father."

"I don't understand. Why? How could he be so mean and then worry that he isn't loved? It doesn't make sense."

This new information forces you to think again about Harry Bergen. You are just as confused as Patty about his unusual actions. You don't like Harry Bergen because of the way he treats Patty. But after listening to Anton in this passage, you probably also feel a little sorry for him. Little by little, you try to put the whole picture of Harry Bergen together.

Harry Bergen is a bitter man. Right or wrong, he feels that no one loves him. He doesn't realize that it is his own fault. Perhaps others have been cruel to him in the past. Being cruel himself may be his only way of releasing his anger.

There are many Harry Bergens in this world. Often they are sweet and charming in society and ogres in their own homes. They are badly disturbed people. Feeling unloved, they strike out at those closest to them. When you learn to analyze and to understand such a character in a novel, you will be able to understand better the same kind of person in life.

4 ◆ Exercise D

Read the following passage and answer the questions about it using what you have learned in this part of the lesson. Use your writing notebook or a separate piece of paper for your answers.

[Anton is talking to Patty about her father.]

". . . it seems to me that a man who is incapable of humor is capable of cruelty. If Hitler, for example, had had the ability—the detachment—to observe the absurdity of his own behavior he would have laughed, and today there might not be a madman named Adolf Hitler.". . .

Anton looked thoughtful. "Cruelty is after all cruelty, and the difference between the two men may have more to do with their degrees of power than their degrees of cruelty. One man is able to affect millions and the other only a few. Would your father's cruelty cause him to crush weak neighboring states? Or would the *Führer's* cruelty cause him to beat his own daughter? Doesn't it seem to you that they both need to inflict pain?"

1. Anton compares Mr. Bergen to Hitler. Is this a valid comparison? What reasons does Anton give to justify his belief?

2. Anton says: "It seems to me that a man who is incapable of humor is capable of cruelty." In your opinion, is it *always* true that a person without a sense of humor is also cruel? And is it possible for a person who has a good sense of humor to be cruel as well?

Now check your answers using the suggestions in the Answer Key starting on page 451. Review this part of the lesson if you don't understand why an answer was wrong.

4♦Writing on Your Own

Look at the sentences you have written for Creating Characters for a Story on page 26. Also, review your writing for the last three Writing On Your Own exercises in this part of the lesson. Now do the following:

1. Choose one of the characters you have written about and write a character analysis. In your analysis try to tell:

   ☐ Why the character is likable or not likable.

   ☐ What you think has caused the character to be the way he or she is.

   ☐ What good points the character has, and what bad points. (There is generally some good in the worst of us and some bad in the best of us. Think about Harry Bergen as an example.)

2. Write, revise, correct, and rewrite your character analysis until you are satisfied with it.

Now go on to Reviewing and Interpreting the Chapter.

Reviewing and Interpreting the Chapter

Answer these questions without looking back at the selection. Choose the best answer to each question and put an *x* in the box beside it, or write your answer on a separate piece of paper.

Remembering Facts

1. There was one thing Harry Bergen was generous with. What was it?

   ☐ a. food

   ☐ b. himself

   ☐ c. money

   ☐ d. his car

2. What was wrong with Patty's legs?

   ☐ a. They were not as pretty as she wanted them to be.

   ☐ b. She had put powder on them to hide a sunburn.

   ☐ c. There was nothing wrong except she imagined they were ugly.

   ☐ d. They had red marks from being beaten.

Following the Order of Events

3. Ruth and Patty had a long talk. When did this occur?

   ☐ a. before Patty knew about Anton

   ☐ b. while Mr. and Mrs. Bergen were having breakfast

   ☐ c. shortly after Mr. and Mrs. Bergen drove away

   ☐ d. after Patty had breakfast with Anton in the garage

4. According to Anton, Patty's father went into the garage and talked to himself. When did this happen?

☐ a. while Patty and Anton were together

☐ b. after Mr. Bergen had beaten Patty

☐ c. while Ruth was watching Anton

☐ d. just before he went to work at the store

Understanding Word Choices

5. "The phrase, 'as long as he lived' sounded like a vague prophecy," according to Patty. *Prophecy* means

☐ a. a threat.

☐ b. a prediction.

☐ c. unclear.

☐ d. silly.

6. The German prisoners needed hats to protect themselves from the "formidable Arkansas sun." The sun was

☐ a. fearfully strong.

☐ b. splendidly bright.

☐ c. beautiful but hot.

☐ d. beautiful in the afternoon.

Understanding Important Ideas

7. What seemed to be Patty's greatest need in life?

☐ a. to rescue a prisoner

☐ b. to have a friend

☐ c. to win her father's love

☐ d. to love Ruth better

8. Anton said Patty's father and Hitler had something in common. What was it?

   ☐ a. They both have a hatred for Jews.

   ☐ b. They both want to be rulers.

   ☐ c. They both seem to need to inflict pain.

   ☐ d. They are both fearful of the future.

Understanding Levels of Meaning
9. Patty says that Ruth has eyes that "see so deeply." This means that Ruth

   ☐ a. has very sharp eyesight.

   ☐ b. sees things she shouldn't see.

   ☐ c. is probably well educated.

   ☐ d. understands Patty's feelings.

10. How were Patty's troubles made lighter?

   ☐ a. by talking to Anton

   ☐ b. by confessing to Ruth

   ☐ c. by fooling her father

   ☐ d. by praying

Understanding Character
11. What can you tell about Harry Bergen from his choices of cereal, cigarettes, and cars?

   ☐ a. He prefers things made in the United States.

   ☐ b. He has a hard time deciding what he likes.

   ☐ c. He really doesn't like anything.

   ☐ d. He forms unshakable habits.

12. How did Ruth show her concern for the physical well-being of others?

☐ a. She prayed a lot.

☐ b. She worried about their eating.

☐ c. She was afraid the police would discover Patty's secret.

☐ d. She sang spirituals.

Understanding Setting

13. The chapter opens with Patty in bed. Which one of the following words goes best with this setting?

☐ a. warm

☐ b. secret

☐ c. alone

☐ d. close

14. In the course of the chapter the action moves from the kitchen to the room over the garage. Which one of the following pairs of words describes Patty's emotions about these settings?

☐ a. warm and friendly

☐ b. tense and worrisome

☐ c. brave and courageous

☐ d. wishful and thankful

Understanding Feelings

15. What was Harry Bergen's secret feeling?

☐ a. He felt unloved.

☐ b. He felt cruel, like Hitler.

☐ c. He had a fear of starving.

☐ d. He secretly admired Patty.

16. Anton had a feeling of relief when he realized that after two years in Hitler's army he could still

☐ a. read a book by Ralph Waldo Emerson.

☐ b. risk his life for someone.

☐ c. be in love with a girl.

☐ d. hate cruelty.

Now check your answers using the Answer Key starting on page 451. Make no mark for right answers. <u>Correct</u> any wrong answers you may have by putting a check mark (✓) in the box next to the right answer. Count the number of questions you answered correctly and plot the total on the Comprehension Scores graph on page 462.

Next, look at the questions you answered incorrectly. What types of questions were they? Count the number you got wrong of each type and enter the numbers in the spaces below.

Remembering Facts   _____

Following the Order of Events   _____

Understanding Word Choices   _____

Understanding Important Ideas   _____

Understanding Levels of Meaning   _____

Understanding Character   _____

Understanding Setting   _____

Understanding Feelings   _____

Now use these numbers to fill in the Comprehension Skills Profile on page 463.

Discussion Guides

The questions below will help you think about the selection and the lesson you have just read. If you don't discuss these questions in class, try to think about them or discuss them with your classmates. Perhaps you will want to write a few paragraphs in answer to the questions.

Discussing Characterization

1. One way authors make characters seem real is by describing small details about their personalities. What small details do you know about the characters in this chapter?

2. Small, unimportant actions help make characters seem real. Point out some of these small actions in the chapter. (For example, at the beginning of the chapter Patty pulls the sheet over her head.)

3. If characterization is done well, you can imagine what the characters sound like when they speak. Try to act out one of the conversations in the story: between Mr. and Mrs. Bergen; Ruth and Patty; Patty and Anton. Read both parts aloud yourself. Allow others to say whether or not your performance has been convincing.

Discussing the Chapter

4. You have read Anton's analysis of Harry Bergen. What is your own analysis?

5. Patty loves Ruth and Anton, and they love her. Considering the time and place of the story, what problems do you foresee in these relationships?

6. Patty says, "If he weren't my father, I wouldn't even like him." How do you feel toward Patty when she says this? Does she seem like a hateful person to you? Why or why not?

Discussing the Author's Work

7. Author Bette Greene says the story is based on a true personal experience. What do you think is true in this chapter? What might be made up? Give reasons for your opinion.

8. Sometimes an author will idealize a character. That is, the character is made to seem better than he or she should be. Does Bette Greene idealize any characters?

9. When she wrote her book, Bette Greene had almost surely read *Anne Frank: The Diary of a Young Girl* (Unit 8). What similarities and differences do you notice between Anne and Patty?

Writing Exercise

Read <u>all</u> the instructions before you begin writing. If you have any questions about how to begin the assignment, review Using the Writing Process beginning on page 439, or confer with your writing coach.

1. At the beginning of the unit you were asked to create two characters for a story. If you haven't done that yet, read the instructions for Creating Characters for a Story on page 26 and create these characters now.

2. If you have done the four Writing on Your Own exercises in the lesson, you can use these to help plan and write the assignment you will do next.

3. Use your story idea and the two characters you have thought of to write a short story. As you write your story

   ◆ Concentrate on the characters more than on the action in the story.

   ◆ Include a conversation between the two characters.

   ◆ Try to make your readers understand how the characters feel.

4. Write, revise, correct, and rewrite your story until you are satisfied with it.

Unit 2   How Authors Use Language

I Know Why the Caged Bird Sings
BY MAYA ANGELOU

About the Illustration

How would you describe the girl's emotions in this scene?
Use details from the illustration to support your response.

Here are some questions to help you think about the
chapter:

◆ What is happening in this scene?

◆ Where do you think this story takes place? Use details
from the illustration to support your response.

Unit 2

Introduction

About the Novel

What was it like to be a young black girl growing up during the 1930s?

In those years, life was hard for people all over the United States. The country was suffering through the Great Depression, and millions of people were out of work.

For black families, life was especially hard. At that time, it was common practice for whites to treat blacks like second-class citizens. In many towns, black residents could only live in certain neighborhoods. They couldn't use public parks or rest rooms. They couldn't attend schools with white students. And most were not treated with the respect and dignity that every human being deserves.

I Know Why the Caged Bird Sings is the true story of a black girl who grew up in the South in the 1930s. The book is Maya Angelou's (Marguerite) *autobiography*—the story of a person's life written by that person. Maya lived in the small town of Stamps, Arkansas, with her brother and her grandmother (called "Momma" in the book). Together, the family ran a general store. Like other black families in town, Maya's family struggled against prejudice and unfair treatment. But even though Maya's life was troubled, she learned the value of caring, humor, and hope.

In this chapter, you will meet Maya and her brother Bailey. You will also meet Momma and Momma's friend Mrs. Flowers. As the chapter begins, Maya is coping with a terrible trauma in her past. Because she is scared and unhappy, she has decided to stop talking in public. The chapter shows how she learns to speak again.

Mrs. Flowers is the person responsible for helping Maya. Because she cares about language, Mrs. Flowers wants to help Maya understand its beauty and importance. And as Maya learns to love the spoken word, she also learns something about dignity and hope.

Maya Angelou was born in 1928 and spent her early years living in California. After her parents separated, she and her brother moved to Arkansas to live with their grandmother. As a teenager, Angelou returned to California, where she studied drama and dance. Eventually she became an actor, a dancer, a teacher, and a writer.

During the 1960s, Angelou became involved in the civil rights movement. She worked closely with Dr. Martin Luther King, Jr., and helped manage a major civil rights organization. At the same time, she used her creative talents to help people understand the importance of racial equality.

Angelou's work is admired by people all over the world. She has received many awards and is respected as an important leader in the black community. In 1993 President Bill Clinton honored Angelou by asking her to speak at his inauguration ceremony.

Maya Angelou has written poetry, screenplays, and television scripts. But she is most famous for her autobiography, which has been published in three separate volumes. *I Know Why the Caged Bird Sings* is the first volume. But if you are interested in learning more about her life, you might also look for *Gather Together in My Name* and *Singin' and Swingin' and Gettin' Merry Like Christmas.*

About the Lesson

The lesson that follows the reading selection looks at how authors use language to make their books interesting and enjoyable. Writers choose language carefully because they want you to understand and appreciate the story.

All books portray experiences in the same way—through *words*. So authors choose words that help you visualize the story. They show you how people really talk. They make comparisons that help you see familiar things in new ways. And they draw your attention to certain important points in the story.

The following questions will help you focus on the way Maya Angelou uses language in *I Know Why the Caged Bird Sings*. Read the story carefully and try to answer these questions as you go along:

◆ What do you learn about the characters from the way they talk? Do all the characters speak in the same way?

◆ Why do some words and phrases seem more interesting and colorful than others? What makes certain words stand out?

◆ What comparisons does Angelou draw between objects? How do those comparisons help you look at things in a new way?

◆ Why does the author use exaggeration? What does it tell you about Maya?

Writing about Your Family

You can understand the importance of language when you write your own description of someone you know very well. Use your writing notebook or a separate piece of paper and try the following suggestions:

1. Think about a person in your family who means a lot to you. You might choose your mother or father, a brother, a sister, even a grandparent or an aunt or uncle.

2. Imagine that person. What makes him or her special? What colors, sounds, shapes, or activities come to mind? How does the person's voice sound? How can you recognize that voice, even when you don't see the person? Make a list of your ideas.

3. Rewrite your list several times until you are satisfied with your character's description.

I Know Why the Caged Bird Sings

by Maya Angelou

15

For nearly a year, I sopped around the house, the Store, the school and the church, like an old biscuit, dirty and inedible. Then I met, or rather got to know, the lady who threw me my first life line.

Mrs. Bertha Flowers was the aristocrat of Black Stamps. She had the grace of control to appear warm in the coldest weather, and on the Arkansas summer days it seemed she had a private breeze which swirled around, cooling her. She was thin without the taut look of wiry people, and her printed voile dresses and flowered hats were as right for her as denim overalls for a farmer. She was our side's answer to the richest white woman in town.

Her skin was a rich black that would have peeled like a plum if snagged, but then no one would have thought of getting close enough to Mrs. Flowers to ruffle her dress, let along snag her skin. She didn't encourage familiarity. She wore gloves too.

I don't think I ever saw Mrs. Flowers laugh, but she smiled often. A slow widening of her thin black lips to show even, small white teeth, then the slow effortless closing. When she chose to smile on me, I always wanted to thank her. The action was so graceful and inclusively benign.

She was one of the few gentlewomen I have ever known,

and has remained throughout my life the measure of what a human being can be.

Momma had a strange relationship with her. Most often when she passed on the road in front of the Store, she spoke to Momma in that soft yet carrying voice, "Good day, Mrs. Henderson." Momma responded with "How you, Sister Flowers?"

Mrs. Flowers didn't belong to our church, nor was she Momma's familiar. Why on earth did she insist on calling her Sister Flowers? Shame made me want to hide my face. Mrs. Flowers deserved better than to be called Sister. Then, Momma left out the verb. Why not ask, "How *are* you, *Mrs*. Flowers?" With the unbalanced passion of the young, I hated her for showing her ignorance to Mrs. Flowers. It didn't occur to me for many years that they were as alike as sisters, separated only by formal education.

Although I was upset, neither of the women was in the least shaken by what I thought an unceremonious greeting. Mrs. Flowers would continue her easy gait up the hill to her little bungalow, and Momma kept on shelling peas or doing whatever had brought her to the front porch.

Occasionally, though, Mrs. Flowers would drift off the road and down to the Store and Momma would say to me, "Sister, you go on and play." As I left I would hear the beginning of an intimate conversation. Momma persistently using the wrong verb, or none at all.

"Brother and Sister Wilcox is sho'ly the meanest—" "Is," Momma? "Is"? Oh, please, not "is," Momma, for two or more. But they talked, and from the side of the building where I waited for the ground to open up and swallow me, I heard the soft-voiced Mrs. Flowers and the textured voice of my grandmother merging and melting. They were interrupted from time to time by giggles that must have come from Mrs. Flowers (Momma never giggled in her life). Then she was gone.

She appealed to me because she was like people I had never met personally. Like women in English novels who walked the moors (whatever they were) with their loyal dogs racing at a respectful distance. Like the women who sat in front of roaring fireplaces, drinking tea incessantly from silver trays full of scones and crumpets. Women who walked over the "heath" and read morocco-bound books and had two last names divided by a hyphen. It would be safe to say that she made me proud to be Negro, just by being herself.

She acted just as refined as whitefolks in the movies and books and she was more beautiful, for none of them could have come near that warm color without looking gray by comparison.

It was fortunate that I never saw her in the company of powhitefolks. For since they tend to think of their whiteness as an evenizer, I'm certain that I would have had to hear her spoken to commonly as Bertha, and my image of her would have been shattered like the unmendable Humpty-Dumpty.

One summer afternoon, sweet-milk fresh in my memory, she stopped at the Store to buy provisions. Another Negro woman of her health and age would have been expected to carry the paper sacks home in one hand, but Momma said, "Sister Flowers, I'll send Bailey up to your house with these things."

She smiled that slow dragging smile, "Thank you, Mrs. Henderson. I'd prefer Marguerite, though." My name was beautiful when she said it. "I've been meaning to talk to her, anyway." They gave each other age-group looks.

Momma said, "Well, that's all right then. Sister, go and change your dress. You going to Sister Flowers's."

The chifforobe was a maze. What on earth did one put on to go to Mrs. Flowers' house? I knew I shouldn't put on a Sunday dress. It might be sacrilegious. Certainly not a house dress, since I was already wearing a fresh one. I chose a school dress, naturally. It was formal without suggesting that going to Mrs. Flowers' house was equivalent to attending church.

I trusted myself back into the Store.

"Now, don't you look nice." I had chosen the right thing, for once.

"Mrs. Henderson, you make most of the children's clothes, don't you?"

"Yes, ma'am. Sure do. Store-bought clothes ain't hardly worth the thread it take to stitch them."

"I'll say you do a lovely job, though, so neat. That dress looks professional."

Momma was enjoying the seldom-received compliments. Since everyone we knew (except Mrs. Flowers, of course) could sew competently, praise was rarely handed out for the commonly practiced craft.

"I try, with the help of the Lord, Sister Flowers, to finish the inside just like I does the outside. Come here, Sister."

I had buttoned up the collar and tied the belt, apronlike, in back. Momma told me to turn around. With one hand she pulled the strings and the belt fell free at both sides of my waist. Then her large hands were at my neck, opening the button loops. I was terrified. What was happening?

"Take it off, Sister." She had her hands on the hem of the dress.

"I don't need to see the inside, Mrs. Henderson, I can tell . . ." But the dress was over my head and my arms were stuck in the sleeves. Momma said, "That'll do. See here, Sister Flowers, I French-seams around the armholes." Through the cloth film, I saw the shadow approach. "That makes it last longer. Children these days would bust out of sheet-metal clothes. They so rough."

"That is a very good job, Mrs. Henderson. You should be proud. You can put your dress back on, Marguerite."

"No, ma'am. Pride is a sin. And 'cording to the Good Book, it goeth before a fall."

"That's right. So the Bible says. It's a good thing to keep in mind."

I wouldn't look at either of them. Momma hadn't thought that taking off my dress in front of Mrs. Flowers would kill me stone dead. If I had refused, she would have thought I was trying to be "womanish" and might have remembered St. Louis. Mrs. Flowers had known that I would be embarrassed and that was even worse. I picked up the groceries and went out to wait in the hot sunshine. It would be fitting if I got a sunstroke and died before they came outside. Just dropped dead on the slanting porch.

There was a little path beside the rocky road, and Mrs. Flowers walked in front swinging her arms and picking her way over the stones.

She said, without turning her head, to me, "I hear you're doing very good school work, Marguerite, but that it's all written. The teachers report that they have trouble getting you to talk in class." We passed the triangular farm on our left and the path widened to allow us to walk together. I hung back in the separate unasked and unanswerable questions.

"Come and walk along with me, Marguerite." I couldn't have refused even if I wanted to. She pronounced my name so nicely. Or more correctly, she spoke each word with such clarity that I was certain a foreigner who didn't understand English could have understood her.

"Now no one is going to make you talk—possibly no one can. But bear in mind, language is man's way of communicating with his fellow man and it is language alone which separates him from the lower animals." That was a totally new idea to me, and I would need time to think about it.

"Your grandmother says you read a lot. Every chance you get. That's good, but not good enough. Words mean more than what is set down on paper. It takes the human voice to infuse them with the shades of deeper meanings."

I memorized the part about the human voice infusing words. It seemed so valid and poetic.

She said she was going to give me some books and that I not only must read them, I must read them aloud. She suggested that I try to make a sentence sound in as many different ways as possible.

"I'll accept no excuse if you return a book to me that has been badly handled." My imagination boggled at the punishment I would deserve if in fact I did abuse a book of Mrs. Flowers'. Death would be too kind and brief.

The odors in the house surprised me. Somehow I had never connected Mrs. Flowers with food or eating or any other common experience of common people. There must have been an outhouse, too, but my mind never recorded it.

The sweet scent of vanilla had met us as she opened the door.

"I made tea cookies this morning. You see, I had planned to invite you for cookies and lemonade so we could have this little chat. The lemonade is in the icebox."

It followed that Mrs. Flowers would have ice on an ordinary day, when most families in our town bought ice late on Saturday only a few times during the summer to be used in the wooden ice-cream freezers.

She took the bags from me and disappeared through the kitchen door. I looked around the room that I had never in my wildest fantasies imagined I would see. Browned photographs leered or threatened from the walls and the white, freshly done curtains pushed against themselves and against the wind. I wanted to gobble up the room entire and take it to Bailey, who would help me analyze and enjoy it.

"Have a seat, Marguerite. Over there by the table." She carried a platter covered with a tea towel. Although she warned that she hadn't tried her hand at baking sweets for some time, I was certain that like everything else around her the cookies would be perfect.

They were flat round wafers, slightly browned on the edges and butter-yellow in the center. With the cold lemonade they were sufficient for childhood's lifelong diet. Remembering my manners, I took nice little lady-like bites off the edges. She said she had made them expressly for me and that she had a few in the kitchen that I could take home to my brother. So I jammed one whole cake in my mouth and the rough crumbs scratched the insides of my jaws, and if I hadn't had to swallow, it would have been a dream come true.

As I ate she began the first of what we later called "my lessons in living." She said that I must always be intolerant of ignorance but understanding of illiteracy. That some people, unable to go to school, were more educated and even more intelligent than college professors. She encouraged me to listen carefully to what country people called mother wit. That in those homely sayings was couched the collective wisdom of generations.

When I finished the cookies she brushed off the table and brought a thick, small book from the bookcase. I had read *A Tale of Two Cities* and found it up to my standards as a romantic novel. She opened the first page and I heard poetry for the first time in my life.

"It was the best of times and the worst of times . . ." Her voice slid in and curved down through and over the words. She was nearly singing. I wanted to look at the pages. Were they the same that I had read? Or were there notes, music, lined on the pages, as in a hymn book? Her sounds began cascading gently. I knew from listening to a thousand preachers that she was nearing the end of her reading, and I hadn't really heard, heard to understand, a single word.

"How do you like that?"

It occurred to me that she expected a response. The sweet vanilla flavor was still on my tongue and her reading was a wonder in my ears. I had to speak.

I said, "Yes, ma'am." It was the least I could do, but it was the most also.

"There's one more thing. Take this book of poems and memorize one for me. Next time you pay me a visit, I want you to recite."

I have tried often to search behind the sophistication of years for the enchantment I so easily found in those gifts.

The essence escapes but its aura remains. To be allowed, no, invited, to share their joys and fears, was a chance to exchange the Southern bitter wormwood for a cup of mead with Beowulf or a hot cup of tea and milk with Oliver Twist. When I said aloud, "It is a far, far better thing that I do, than I have ever done . . ." tears of love filled my eyes at my selflessness.

On that first day, I ran down the hill and into the road (few cars ever came along it) and had the good sense to stop running before I reached the Store.

I was liked, and what a difference it made. I was respected not as Mrs. Henderson's grandchild or Bailey's sister but for just being Marguerite Johnson.

Childhood's logic never asks to be proved (all conclusions are absolute). I didn't question why Mrs. Flowers had singled me out for attention, nor did it occur to me that Momma might have asked her to give me a little talking to. All I cared about was that she had made tea cookies for *me* and read to *me* from her favorite book. It was enough to prove that she liked me.

Momma and Bailey were waiting inside the Store. He said, "My, what did she give you?" He had seen the books, but I held the paper sack with his cookies in my arms shielded by the poems.

Momma said, "Sister, I know you acted like a little lady. That do my heart good to see settled people take to you all. I'm trying my best, the Lord knows, but these days . . ." Her voice trailed off, "Go on in and change your dress."

In the bedroom it was going to be a joy to see Bailey receive his cookies. I said, "By the way, Bailey, Mrs. Flowers sent you some tea cookies—"

Momma shouted, "What did you say, Sister? You, Sister, what did you say?" Hot anger was crackling in her voice.

Bailey said, "She said Mrs. Flowers sent me some—"

"I ain't talking to you, Ju." I heard the heavy feet walk across the floor toward our bedroom. "Sister, you heard me. What's that you said?" She swelled to fill the doorway.

Bailey said, "Momma." His pacifying voice—"Momma, she—"

"You shut up, Ju. I'm talking to your sister."

I didn't know what sacred cow I had bumped, but it was better to find out than to hang like a thread over an open fire. I repeated, "I said, 'Bailey, by the way, Mrs. Flowers sent you—' "

"That's what I thought you said. Go on and take off your dress. I'm going to get a switch."

At first I thought she was playing. Maybe some heavy joke that would end with "You sure she didn't send me something?" but in a minute she was back in the room with a long, ropy, peach-tree switch, the juice smelling bitter at having been torn loose. She said, "Get down on your knees. Bailey, Junior, you come on, too."

The three of us knelt as she began, "Our Father, you know the tribulations of your humble servant. I have with your help raised two grown boys. Many's the day I thought I wouldn't be able to go on, but you gave me the strength to see my way clear. Now, Lord, look down on this heavy heart today. I'm trying to raise my son's children in the way they should go, but, oh, Lord, the Devil try to hinder me on every hand. I never thought I'd live to hear cursing under this roof, what I try to keep dedicated to the glorification of God. And cursing out of the mouths of babes. But you said, in the last days brother would turn against brother, and children against their parents. That there would be a gnashing of teeth and a rendering of flesh. Father, forgive this child, I beg you, on bended knee."

I was crying loudly now. Momma's voice had risen to a shouting pitch, and I knew that whatever wrong I had committed was extremely serious. She had even left the Store untended to take up my case with God. When she finished we were all crying. She pulled me to her with one hand and hit me only a few times with the switch. The shock of my sin and the emotional release of her prayer had exhausted her.

Momma wouldn't talk right then, but later in the evening I found that my violation lay in using the phrase "by the way." Momma explained that "Jesus was the Way, the Truth and the Light," and anyone who says "by the way" is really saying, "by Jesus," or "by God" and the Lord's name would not be taken in vain in her house.

When Bailey tried to interpret the words with: "Whitefolks use 'by the way' to mean while we're on the subject," Momma reminded us that "whitefolks' mouths were most in general loose and their words were an abomination before Christ."

How Authors Use Language

Authors write because they want to share an experience with a reader. They want to project pictures, ideas, and feelings. They want to control what the reader sees and feels.

To create vivid images authors depend on language; they must decide which words will create the images and feelings they want you to experience. They are careful to choose just the right words and phrases to describe the characters. They control the length and sound of the sentences to help support the action in the story. And they combine words in interesting ways to create vivid pictures in your mind.

For example, an author writing a mystery novel wants to frighten you. Notice how Agatha Christie uses words in this sentence to describe a woman who has seen a murder: "Her calm, efficient manner was gone. She sat twisting her hands together, almost weeping, appealing incoherently to Poirot."

The jerky, nervous rhythm of the sentence helps you understand how upset the character is. Words like *twisting, weeping,* and *appealing* also contribute to your picture of the woman. Just reading the sentence makes you wonder what will happen next in the story.

Now compare Christie's sentence with one written by Charles Dickens: "It was the best of times, it was the worst of times, it was the age of wisdom, it was the age of foolishness. . . ." If you read the sentence out loud, it almost sounds like music.

Notice how many words Dickens repeats. The repetition makes the sentence sound like a song. It also shows that words with opposite meanings (like *best* and *worst, wisdom* and *foolishness*) can sound alike. The author wants you to understand that in real life, something can be good and bad or wise and foolish at the same time.

When she was writing *I Know Why the Caged Bird Sings,* Maya Angelou wanted to show you what it was like to be a black girl from a small Arkansas town. She wanted you to experience and to understand her childhood. And like all writers, she had just one tool for the job—words.

Figurative language is the use of words and phrases in unusual ways to create strong vivid images, to focus attention on certain ideas, or to compare dissimilar things. In this lesson we will look at four ways in which Angelou uses figurative language:

1 ◆ She uses *dialect*—the pattern of speech used by people of a certain group or of a particular region.

2 ◆ She chooses words carefully to create pictures and explain ideas.

3 ◆ She uses comparisons to create vivid pictures in the reader's mind.

4 ◆ She uses other figures of speech to focus attention on certain ideas.

1 ♦ Using Dialect

Not everyone who speaks the same language talks in the same way. People from England don't sound like people from the United States. Canadians don't sound like Australians. But all those people are speaking English.

Even within a country, people from different regions speak in different ways. For example, someone who lives in Mississippi doesn't sound much like a person who lives in New York City. But both people are English-speaking Americans.

These differences in speech are called dialect. Dialect is a pattern of speaking that has developed among people of a certain group or a particular region. Authors pay special attention to dialect when they write. They notice interesting words and expressions, unusual pronunciations, and slang. They use dialect to create a picture of people and places.

Maya Angelou uses dialect in her autobiography to give you a vivid picture of the differences between Momma and Mrs. Flowers.

> Momma had a strange relationship with her [Mrs. Flowers]. Most often when she passed on the road in front of the Store, she spoke to Momma in that soft yet carrying voice, "Good day, Mrs. Henderson." Momma responded with "How you, Sister Flowers?"

What do you learn about Mrs. Flowers from the way she greets Momma? You learn that she speaks politely and formally. The author tells you that she has a soft voice. Her words give you a picture of a genteel, well-educated woman.

Now compare Mrs. Flowers' way of speaking with Momma's. Momma says, "How you?" instead of "How are you?". She addresses Mrs. Flowers as *Sister* instead of *Mrs.* The way that Momma uses words hints that she is less educated than her neighbor.

1 ♦ Exercise A

Read the following passage and answer the questions about it using what you have learned in this part of the lesson. Use your writing notebook or a separate piece of paper for your answers.

Occasionally . . . Mrs. Flowers would drift off the road and down to the Store and Momma would say to me, "Sister, you go on and play." As I left I would hear the beginning of an intimate conversation. Momma persistently using the wrong verb, or none at all.

"Brother and Sister Wilcox is sho'ly the meanest—" "Is," Momma? "Is"? Oh, please, not "is," Momma, for two or more. But they talked, and from the side of the building where I waited for the ground to open up and swallow me, I heard the soft-voiced Mrs. Flowers and the textured voice of my grandmother merging and melting.

1. List the words and phrases that show Momma's dialect in this passage.

2. How does Maya feel about the way Momma talks? Why do you think she feels that way?

Now check your answers using the suggestions in the Answer Key starting on page 451. Review this part of the lesson if you don't understand why an answer was wrong.

1 ♦ Writing on Your Own

Look at the list you wrote for Writing about Your Family on page 63. Now do the following:

1. How does your relative sound? What makes the person's speech unique? Does he or she have a Southern accent? A Midwestern accent? A Brooklyn accent? What does that accent sound like? Does the person repeat the same words often? Does he or she say "like" or "uh" in the middle of the sentence? How can you imitate the sound of the person's speech?

2. Imagine that your relative is having a conversation with a salesperson. Write a paragraph that shows the conversation. Remember to pay special attention to your relative's dialect.

3. You may want to change or rewrite your paragraph several times until you are satisfied with the conversation.

2 ♦ Choosing Words Carefully

People enjoy listening to a good speaker. The best teachers have this talent. So do successful politicians and actors. They know how to capture your attention with words. They know how to explain ideas in ways that are easy to understand and remember. They know how to create fresh, interesting pictures in your mind, just by the way they talk.

Good writers also know how to capture your attention with words. They work hard to make their writing interesting and colorful. They choose just the right word to describe their subject. They know that each word, even among synonyms, has its own special meaning.

Think about this sentence: "For nearly a year, I sopped around the house, the Store, the school, and the church. . . ." What picture does the word *sopped* give you? Probably you've heard it most often in the phrase "sopping wet." The word gives you a feeling of dampness. It makes you feel uncomfortable and depressed. And that's exactly the picture Maya Angelou wants you to see. She wants you to understand her own behavior at a time in her life when she was very unhappy.

Angelou also uses the sounds of words to create vivid pictures. Read the following sentence and pay close attention to the way it sounds: "Her voice slid in and curved down through and over the words."

The sentence helps you hear Mrs. Flowers. It lets you imagine that you are listening to the sound of her beautiful voice reading aloud.

How did Maya Angelou create that feeling of sound? Try reading the sentence out loud to learn more about it. Do the words *slid* and *curved* sound smooth or rough? Does the sentence sound best when you read quickly in a nervous voice? Or does it sound better when you read slowly and gently?

Angelou asked herself those same questions as she wrote. She wanted the words to give you a feeling of Mrs. Flowers' gentle, musical voice. So she wrote a gentle, musical sentence about that voice.

2 ♦ Exercise B

Read the following passage and answer the questions about it using what you have learned in this part of the lesson. Use your writing notebook or a separate piece of paper for your answers.

She appealed to me because she was like people I had never met personally. Like women in English novels who walked the moors (whatever they were) with their loyal dogs racing at a respectful distance. Like the women who sat in front of roaring fireplaces, drinking tea incessantly from silver trays full of scones and crumpets. Women who walked over the "heath" and read morocco-bound books and had two last names divided by a hyphen. It would be safe to say that she made me proud to be Negro, just by being herself.

1. List some of the words and phrases that Angelou uses to describe the women in this passage. How do those words make you feel about the women?

2. Why does Angelou compare Mrs. Flowers to women she has never met? What is she trying to tell you?

Now check your answers using the suggestions in the Answer Key starting on page 451. Review this part of the lesson if you don't understand why an answer was wrong.

2 ♦ Writing on Your Own

Look at the list you wrote for Writing about Your Family on page 63. Now do the following:

1. Think about the way the person behaves. For example, what verbs describe the way she climbs a ladder? How does he drink a glass of milk? How does she act when she is very angry? How can you tell if he likes someone?

2. Write a paragraph or two describing how the person would behave if he or she were picked up by an alien spaceship.
   Choose your words and phrases carefully. Try to create descriptions that show the person's unique behavior in this situation.

3. You may want to change and rewrite your paragraphs several times until you are satisfied with your descriptions.

3 ♦ Using Comparisons

Sometimes the best way to describe a thing is to compare it to something else. Imagine you've just come home from school during a snowstorm. Your mother asks, "How's the weather?" And you answer, "It's the North Pole out there!" or "It's as cold as Siberia!" The comparisons you've made give your mother a clear picture of the cold weather.

Authors also use comparisons to create vivid pictures. For example, notice Maya Angelou's description of Mrs. Flowers' skin: "Her skin was a rich black that would have peeled like a plum if snagged." The comparison in that sentence is called a simile.

A *simile* is a direct comparison between unlike things using the word *like, as,* or *resembles* to connect them. Similes help readers look at familiar things in new ways. In the sentence you just read, Angelou compares Mrs. Flowers' skin to a plum. She connects that comparison with the word *like.*

Do you think anyone would mistake a person's skin for a plum? It's not very likely. But the author includes the simile to create a picture. She wants you to imagine the beautiful smooth texture of Mrs. Flowers' skin. She wants you to picture the glossy color of a purple-black plum. Those pictures help you imagine Mrs. Flowers, and they make her an interesting, attractive character.

Angelou also uses another kind of comparison in the chapter. Read the following example: "The chifforobe was a maze." The sentence compares the chifforobe (a combination of a wardrobe and a chest of drawers) to a maze. It uses a comparison called a metaphor.

A *metaphor* is an implied, or suggested, comparison between unlike things. It hints that one thing *is* another. In the sentence you just read, Angelou suggests that a chifforobe is the same thing as a maze. You know that a chifforobe can't really be a maze. A maze is a complicated kind of puzzle, and a chifforobe is a place for storing clothes. But the metaphor helps you picture Maya's confusion as she decides what to wear to Mrs. Flowers' house.

3 ♦ Exercise C

Read the following passages and answer the questions about them using what you have learned in this part of the lesson. Use your writing notebook or a separate piece of paper for your answers.

> For nearly a year, I sopped around the house, the Store, the school, and the church, like an old biscuit, dirty and inedible.

> One summer afternoon, sweet-milk fresh in my memory, she stopped at the Store to buy provisions.

> . . . it was better to find out than to hang like a thread over an open fire.

1. Each sentence contains a comparison. Write down each comparison and identify it as a simile or a metaphor. Then explain your reasoning.

2. Rewrite each sentence, keeping the author's meaning but leaving out the comparison. Does leaving out the comparison change the feeling you get from the sentence? How?

Now check your answers using the suggestions in the Answer Key starting on page 451. Review this part of the lesson if you don't understand why an answer was wrong.

3♦Writing on Your Own

Look at the list you wrote for Writing about Your Family on page 63. Now do the following:

1. Write three similes that describe the person. In each simile, show the person in a different situation. Here are some examples:

☐ Before my Uncle Bill goes out to dinner, he gets dressed up in a plaid suit, and then tops it all off with a hat like an egg carton.

☐ Even in his stocking feet, Uncle Bill stands as tall as Abe Lincoln on stilts.

☐ Whenever his children get sick or hurt, Uncle Bill fusses over them like a kind-hearted grizzly bear.

2. Now write a metaphor about the person. Here's an example:

☐ Uncle Bill, who's a buffalo in the morning, always races down the stairs at fifty miles per hour.

3. You may want to change and rewrite your comparisons several times until you are satisfied with them.

4 ◆ Using Other Figures of Speech

Similes and metaphors are two examples in a long list of techniques called figures of speech. Each figure of speech has its own name and purpose. Authors use them to create strong vivid images, to focus attention on certain ideas, and to compare dissimilar things.

You've already seen how Maya Angelou uses similes and metaphors to help create vivid pictures of characters and situations. Throughout her autobiography, she uses many other figures of speech to tell us more about her childhood. One of them is personification.

Personification is a figure of speech in which an animal, an object, or an idea is described as though it were human. Personification is actually a special kind of metaphor. How does Maya Angelou use personification in this sentence?

> Browned photographs leered or threatened from the walls and the white, freshly done curtains pushed against themselves and against the wind.

The sentence makes the photographs and the curtains seem human. You know that photos can't really threaten or make faces. You know that curtains don't really push and shove against each other. But the author personifies the objects to show you how they made Maya feel when she walked into the room.

Angelou also uses exaggeration in her writing. *Exaggeration* is intentional overstatement to emphasize a point. In this sentence she exaggerates Maya's feelings: "Momma hadn't thought that taking off my dress in front of Mrs. Flowers would kill me stone dead."

Of course, Angelou isn't telling you that Maya really died. She's telling you that Maya was extremely embarrassed about taking off her dress. The exaggeration helps you understand Maya's feelings about the situation.

4 ◆ Exercise D

Read the following passage and answer the questions about it using what you have learned in this part of the lesson. Use your writing notebook or a separate piece of paper for your answers.

Momma said, ". . . See here, Sister Flowers, I French-seams around the armholes." Through the cloth film, I saw the shadow approach. "That makes it last longer. Children these days would bust out of sheet-metal clothes. They so rough."

"That is a very good job, Mrs. Henderson. You should be proud. You can put your dress back on, Marguerite."

. . . I picked up the groceries and went out to wait in the hot sunshine. It would be fitting if I got sunstroke and died before they came outside. Just dropped dead on the slanting porch.

1. Write down the examples of exaggeration in this passage.

2. What does the exaggeration tell you about Momma? What does it tell you about Maya?

Now check your answers using the suggestions in the Answer Key starting on page 451. Review this part of the lesson if you don't understand why an answer was wrong.

4 ◆ Writing on Your Own

Look at the list you wrote for Writing about Your Family on page 63. Now do the following:

1. In the three Writing on Your Own exercises you described your relative in different imaginative ways. You thought about what makes the person special, and you wrote about interesting character traits and behaviors.

   Now imagine the person as the hero of a television comedy show. A comedy takes a person's special character traits and exaggerates them. It makes the person and the situation seem funny.

2. Write a paragraph that describes a funny scene between your relative and a clerk at the grocery store. For example, if your Uncle Bill is allergic to bananas, you might write a scene that includes a clerk who is unpacking bananas in the produce department. He accidentally traps your Uncle Bill in the middle of a stack of banana crates, and Bill starts sneezing. You can guess what happens next!

Concentrate on exaggerating the situation to make the paragraph as funny as you can.

3. You may want to change and rewrite your paragraph several times until you are satisfied with the description of the scene.

Now go on to Reviewing and Interpreting the Chapter.

Reviewing and Interpreting the Chapter

Answer these questions without looking back at the selection. Choose the best answer to each question and put an *x* in the box beside it, or write your answer on a separate piece of paper.

Remembering
Facts

1. Maya's real name is

   ☐ a. Marguerite.

   ☐ b. Bertha.

   ☐ c. Mary.

   ☐ d. Angela.

2. When Mrs. Flowers invites Maya to her house, she serves

   ☐ a. tea and crumpets.

   ☐ b. freshly shelled peas.

   ☐ c. cookies and lemonade.

   ☐ d. peach ice cream.

Following the
Order of Events

3. Before Maya goes to Mrs. Flowers' house, Momma tells her to

   ☐ a. change her dress.

   ☐ b. take Bailey with her.

   ☐ c. borrow some books.

   ☐ d. unpack the groceries.

4. After reading aloud, Mrs. Flowers asks Maya to

    ☐ a. carry a grocery bag.

    ☐ b. memorize a poem.

    ☐ c. learn to sew.

    ☐ d. say hello to Momma.

Understanding
Word Choices
5. "It [the dress] was formal without suggesting that going to Mrs. Flowers' house was <u>equivalent</u> to attending church." What does *equivalent* mean?

    ☐ a. different from

    ☐ b. the same as

    ☐ c. less important than

    ☐ d. most important

6. Maya Angelou tells you that Mrs. Flowers' "printed <u>voile</u> dresses and flowered hats were as right for her as denim overalls for a farmer." What is *voile*?

    ☐ a. a delicate kind of cloth

    ☐ b. a synonym for denim

    ☐ c. a style of hat

    ☐ d. a cheap, untidy dress pattern

Understanding
Important Ideas
7. Mrs. Flowers believes that words

    ☐ a. should not be an important part of life.

    ☐ b. are best when they're written down.

    ☐ c. are most often used to hurt other people.

    ☐ d. should be spoken as well as written.

8. What does Maya value most about Mrs. Flowers?

☐ a. She is well dressed.

☐ b. She cares about Maya.

☐ c. She likes to read aloud.

☐ d. She is Momma's friend.

9. What are Maya's feelings toward her brother?

☐ a. She laughs at him.

☐ b. She is jealous of him.

☐ c. She doesn't think about him.

☐ d. She loves him.

10. At the end of the chapter, Maya is punished because

☐ a. she brings home a gift for Bailey and refuses to share it.

☐ b. Momma is angry with Mrs. Flowers.

☐ c. she doesn't think about words in the same way that Momma does.

☐ d. she talks more than she should.

11. Which word best describes Momma?

☐ a. educated

☐ b. rude

☐ c. lazy

☐ d. strict

12. Mrs. Flowers is

    ☐ a. proud and silent.

    ☐ b. intelligent and caring.

    ☐ c. beautiful and cruel.

    ☐ d. timid and nervous.

Understanding
Setting

13. Why do you think Maya Angelou capitalizes the word *store* in this chapter?

    ☐ a. It tells us that Maya is unhappy at home.

    ☐ b. The word reminds us that Momma is poor.

    ☐ c. The store is a very important place in Maya's life.

    ☐ d. Angelou never forgets that the store is a business.

14. Why is Maya excited to see the inside of Mrs. Flowers' house?

    ☐ a. She thinks she'll learn more about Mrs. Flowers.

    ☐ b. She wants to stare at the photographs.

    ☐ c. She plans to borrow some books and recipes.

    ☐ d. She wants to make Bailey jealous.

Understanding
Feelings

15. How does Momma feel about Mrs. Flowers?

    ☐ a. She is afraid of her.

    ☐ b. She feels comfortable with her.

    ☐ c. She thinks Mrs. Flowers is rude.

    ☐ d. She doesn't think much of her.

16. After spending time with Mrs. Flowers, Maya

☐ a. feels embarrassed about knowing her.

☐ b. thinks that Momma is smarter and more important.

☐ c. likes her even more than she used to.

☐ d. hopes she won't have to visit again.

Now check your answers using the Answer Key starting on page 451. Make no mark for right answers. Correct any wrong answers you may have by putting a check mark (✓) in the box next to the right answer. Count the number of questions you answered correctly and plot the total on the Comprehension Scores graph on page 462.

Next, look at the questions you answered incorrectly. What types of questions were they? Count the number you got wrong of each type and enter the numbers in the spaces below.

Remembering Facts   _____

Following the Order of Events   _____

Understanding Word Choices   _____

Understanding Important Ideas   _____

Understanding Levels of Meaning   _____

Understanding Character   _____

Understanding Setting   _____

Understanding Feelings   _____

Now use these numbers to fill in the Comprehension Skills Profile on page 463.

Discussion Guides

The questions below will help you think about the chapter and the lesson you have just read. If you don't discuss these questions in class, try to think about them or discuss them with your classmates. Perhaps you will want to write a few paragraphs in answer to the questions.

Discussing How Authors Use Language

1. Maya gets angry at Momma about the dialect she uses when she speaks to Mrs. Flowers. Why doesn't that dialect seem to bother Momma or Mrs. Flowers?

2. Maya never heard anyone call Mrs. Flowers by her first name. But if someone had, she says, "my image of her would have been shattered like the unmendable Humpty Dumpty." What picture do you get from that simile? Why do you think Angelou decided to include it?

3. Throughout the chapter, Angelou uses exaggeration to describe Maya's feelings. She "waits for the ground to open up and swallow" her. She believes she will drop "stone dead." And when she visits Mrs. Flowers' house, she wants "to gobble up the room." What does all this exaggeration tell you about Maya? How does she feel about herself? How does she feel about the world around her?

Discussing the Chapter

4. Angelou tells you that Momma and Mrs. Flowers "were as alike as sisters, separated only by formal education." What does she mean by that statement?

5. Why do people treat Mrs. Flowers with respect? Is it because she is beautiful and well educated? Or do people admire her for something more?

6. Momma and Mrs. Flowers both have something to say about the power of words. Compare and contrast their feelings and beliefs.

Discussing the Author's Work

7. A newspaper writer once said that Maya Angelou "makes a story . . . sing." What did the writer mean? Find some examples from the chapter you have read.

8. Angelou is most famous for her autobiography, but she has also written scripts for movies and television. Is it easy to picture this chapter on a movie screen? Why or why not?

9. The need for dignity and respect is an important theme, or underlying idea, in Maya Angelou's work. What do you learn about dignity and respect from this selection?

Writing Exercise

Read all the instructions before you begin writing. If you have any questions about how to begin the writing assignment, review Using the Writing Process, beginning on page 439, or confer with your writing coach.

1. Think of a person who has made a big difference in your life. The person might be a friend, a teacher, or a relative.

    What did the person do? How did the person help you? Why is your life better because of that person?

2. Write a story that describes an important event that you and the person were involved in together. The story can be based on fact, or you can imagine the event. Your story should include the following:

    ☐ dialect

    ☐ colorful descriptions

    ☐ a simile or a metaphor

    ☐ an example of exaggeration

    ☐ an example of personification

    Look back at the selection from *I Know Why the Caged Bird Sings* for some examples of Maya Angelou's use of language. You may also want to review what you wrote for the Writing on Your Own exercises in this lesson.

3. Write, revise, correct, and rewrite your work until you are satisfied with your story.

Unit 3   Setting

Julie of the Wolves
BY JEAN CRAIGHEAD GEORGE

About the Illustration

How do you think the girl in this drawing feels? What might she be thinking about? Point out some details in the drawing to support your response.

Here are some questions to help you think about the chapter:

◆ Where do you think this scene takes place?

◆ What is the man doing?

◆ Would you like to change places with this girl? Why or why not?

Unit 3

Introduction

About the Novel

In *Julie of the Wolves,* you will meet a thirteen-year-old Eskimo girl named Miyax. Miyax is proud of her Eskimo name and enjoys following the "old" Eskimo traditions. Many Eskimos, however, have adopted the "new" ways followed in the white settlements. Miyax—known as Julie in the white settlements—finds herself caught between the two worlds.

As *Julie of the Wolves* opens, Miyax is running away from an arranged marriage to a boy named Daniel, whom she finds hateful. Miyax plans to cross the Arctic plains (the tundra) on foot to Point Hope. At Point Hope she intends to catch a steamer to San Francisco where her pen pal Amy lives. But things don't work out quite as she has planned. She becomes lost in the grassy wilderness, realizes she is walking in circles, and finds herself in danger of starving to death.

Luckily, Miyax had spent a great deal of time watching and listening to her father, Kapugen, when she was growing up. Kapugen was an expert hunter and taught Miyax many of the old Eskimo skills necessary for survival in the harsh northern climate. From Kapugen, she learned that wolves could help a hunter find food. "Wolves are brotherly," he had said. "They love each other, and if you learn to speak to them, they will love you too." The fear that wolves eat people—"That's *gussak* talk. Wolves are brothers," Kapugen had insisted.

Miyax finds herself camped near a den of wolves—several adults and a few pups. She gives them all names, calling the leader Amaroq, and sets about figuring out how to "talk" to them. She wants to show them that she is hungry and needs food. She hopes that somehow she can get the wolves to bring her food as they do for their pups.

Miyax patiently watches the wolves and learns to understand and copy their many signs and actions. She learns the "body language" of the wolves and finds she can communicate with them in this way. Finally, a bond of love and respect develops between Miyax and the wolves.

From that point, the story tells of the adventures of Miyax and her wolf friends as she makes her way to a coastal settlement and civilization. Things go quite well for Miyax as long as she is in the wilderness living close to the land. The most disturbing and heart-stopping moments come as she begins to get close to civilization. And that conflict with civilization gives you a lot to think about. Anyone who likes stories of wilderness adventure will enjoy *Julie of the Wolves*.

In this unit we pick up the story at a point where the wolves have left Miyax to go their own way for a while. She feels abandoned by the wolves. Her loneliness causes her to think back to when she was young and lived in a seal-hunting camp with her father, Kapugen. Her mother had died when she was four, so Miyax had been raised by Kapugen. He took her everywhere with him: to feasts, to seal hunts, and on long walks along the beaches or across the tundra. Her father was both teacher and companion to her and she adored him. But she was forced to leave Kapugen to attend school in a white settlement. Now she thinks Kapugen is dead and she remembers the years she spent with him as the happiest of her life.

About the Lesson

The lesson that follows the reading selection is about setting. The setting of a novel consists of many elements, it is where the action takes place and when the action takes place. But the setting is not limited to time and place. It includes sights, sounds, smells, and feelings. It also includes people, the way they dress, and the way they act. Setting is scenery, animals, objects, and anything else that helps readers understand where they are and what is going on in the story.

The questions below will help you focus on setting in the chapter from *Julie of the Wolves*. Read the chapter carefully and try to answer these questions as you go along:

◆ At the beginning of the selection, you will read about the day Miyax's mother died. How do the descriptions of the setting make you feel at this point?

◆ A little further along in the selection, author Jean Craighead George describes Kapugen's house at seal camp. How does the author make you "really see" the setting?

◆ There is a scene where a whale is caught. How does that scene make you feel about Eskimos and their respect for animals and nature?

◆ Near the end of the reading selection, Miyax's Aunt Martha arrives at seal camp. How does the setting seem to change when she arrives?

Create Your Own Setting

1. Think of an idea for a story you might like to write. For example, what would happen to you if you were stranded on a deserted island? What would you do? How would you survive? Would you live out your remaining days there? Write a few sentences that tell what your story will be about.

2. Make a list of setting elements you will have in the first scene of your story. Include in your list such things as the place, time, scenery, weather, living things, sounds, and smells.

- ◆ **Place.** A country, a town or city, a neighborhood, a school, a house, a farm, a desert, a forest, the ocean, etc.

- ◆ **Time.** The date, a year, a season, the time of day (morning, sunset, midnight, etc.)

- ◆ **Scenery.** Trees, sand, water, mountains, buildings, furniture, furnishings, etc.

- ◆ **Weather.** Sun, rain, wind, clouds, lightning, heat, cold, etc.

- ◆ **Living things.** People, crowds, animals, insects, birds, a baseball team, etc.

- ◆ **Sounds and smells.** Birds singing, music, bells, traffic noise, thunder, cooking odors, flowers, cut grass, a musty cellar, etc.

3. Write one or two sentences that tell how the setting makes you and your readers feel. (Happy, sad, thoughtful, excited, fearful, nervous, etc.)

4. Write a sentence that tells what you think your setting might cause a reader to think about. (The way a game is played, a crime about to be committed, war, a problem in school, a happy event, the danger of an adventure, etc.)

Julie of the Wolves

by Jean Craighead George

The wind, the empty sky, the deserted earth—Miyax had felt the bleakness of being left behind once before.

She could not remember her mother very well, for Miyax was scarcely four when she died, but she did remember the day of her death. The wind was screaming wild high notes and hurling ice-filled waves against the beach. Kapugen was holding her hand and they were walking. When she stumbled he put her on his shoulders, and high above the beach she saw thousands of birds diving toward the sea. The jaegers screamed and the sandpipers cried. The feathered horns of the comical puffins drooped low, and Kapugen told her they seemed to be grieving with him.

She saw this, but she was not sad. She was divinely happy going somewhere alone with Kapugen. Occasionally he climbed the cliffs and brought her eggs to eat; occasionally he took her in his arms and leaned against a rock. She slept at times in the warmth of his big sealskin parka. Then they walked on. She did not know how far.

Later, Kapugen's Aunt Martha told her that he had lost his mind the day her mother died. He had grabbed Miyax up and walked out of his fine house in Mekoryuk. He had left his important job as manager of the reindeer herd, and he had left all his possessions.

"He walked you all the way to seal camp," Martha told her. "And he never did anything good after that."

To Miyax the years at seal camp were infinitely good. The

scenes and events were beautiful color spots in her memory. There was Kapugen's little house of driftwood, not far from the beach. It was rosy-gray on the outside. Inside it was gold-brown. Walrus tusks gleamed and drums, harpoons, and man's knives decorated the walls. The sealskin kayak beside the door glowed as if the moon had been stretched across it and its graceful ribs shone black. Dark gold and soft brown were the old men who sat around Kapugen's camp stove and talked to him by day and night.

The ocean was green and white, and was rimmed by fur, for she saw it through Kapugen's hood as she rode to sea with him on his back inside the parka. Through this frame she saw the soft eyes of the seals on the ice. Kapugen's back would grow taut as he lifted his arms and fired his gun. Then the ice would turn red.

The celebration of the Bladder Feast was many colors—black, blue, purple, fire-red; but Kapugen's hand around hers was rose-colored and that was the color of her memory of the Feast. A shaman, an old priestess whom everyone called "the bent woman," danced. Her face was streaked with black soot. When she finally bowed, a fiery spirit came out of the dark wearing a huge mask that jingled and terrified Miyax. Once, in sheer bravery, she peeked up under a mask and saw that the dancer was not a spirit at all but Naka, Kapugen's serious partner. She whispered his name and he laughed, took off his mask, and sat down beside Kapugen. They talked and the old men joined them. Later that day Kapugen blew up seal bladders and he and the old men carried them out on the ice. There they dropped them into the sea, while Miyax watched and listened to their songs. When she came back to camp the bent woman told her that the men had returned the bladders to the seals.

"Bladders hold the spirits of the animals," she said. "Now the spirits can enter the bodies of the newborn seals and keep them safe until we harvest them again." That night the bent woman seemed all violet-colored as she tied a piece of seal fur and blubber to Miyax's belt. "It's an *i'noGo tied*," she said. "It's a nice little spirit for you."

Another memory was flickering-yellow—it was of the old men beating their drums around Kapugen's stove. She saw them through a scarf of tiny crystals that was her breath on the cold night air inside the house.

Naka and Kapugen were on their hands and knees, prancing lightly, moving swiftly. When Naka tapped Kapugen's chin with his head, Kapugen rose to his knees. He threw back his head, then rocked back on his heels. Naka sat up and together they sang the song of the wolves. When the dance was over the old men cheered and beat their paddle-like drums.

"You are wolves, you are real wolves," they had cried.

After that Kapugen told her about the wolves he had known on the mainland when he went to high school in Nome. He and his joking partner would hunt the wilderness for months, calling to the wolves, speaking their language to ask where the game was. When they were successful, they returned to Nome with sled-loads of caribou.

"Wolves are brotherly," he said. "They love each other, and if you learn to speak to them, they will love you too."

He told her that the birds and animals all had languages and if you listened and watched them you could learn about their enemies, where their food lay and when big storms were coming.

A silver memory was the day when the sun came over the horizon for the first time in winter. She was at the beach, close to Kapugen, helping him haul in a huge gleaming net. In it was a beautiful white whale. Out of sight on the other side of the whale, she could hear the old men as they cheered this gift from the sea.

The whale was a mountain so high she could not see the cliffs beyond, only the sunlit clouds. Kapugen's huge, black, frostbitten hand seemed small as it touched the great body of the whale.

Not far away the bent woman was dancing and gathering

invisible things from the air. Miyax was frightened but Kapugen explained that she was putting the spirit of the whale in her i'noGo tied.

"She will return it to the sea and the whales," he said.

Walking the tundra with Kapugen was all laughter and fun. He would hail the blue sky and shout out his praise for the grasses and bushes. On these trips they ate salmon berries, then lay in the sun watching the birds. Sometimes Kapugen would whistle sandpiper songs and the birds would dip down to see which of their members had gotten lost in the grass. When they saw him and darted away, Kapugen would laugh.

Fishing with Kapugen was murky-tan in her memory, for they would wade out into the river mouth where the stone weirs were built and drive the fish into nets between the walls. Kapugen would spear them or grab them in his hand and throw them to the men in the wooden boats. Occasionally he skimmed after the biggest cod and halibut in his kayak and he would whoop with joy when he caught one and would hold it above his head. It gleamed as it twisted in the sun.

Summers at seal camp were not as beautiful to Miyax as the autumns and winters, for during this season many families from Mekoryuk came to Nash Harbor to hunt and fish and Kapugen was busy. Sometimes he helped people set nets; sometimes he scouted the ocean in his kayak as he searched for seal colonies.

During these hours Miyax was left with the other children on the beach. She played tag and grass ball with them and she pried prickly sea urchins off the rocks, to eat the sweet meat inside. Often she dug for clams and when Kapugen returned he would crack them open and smack his lips as he swallowed them whole.

The Eskimos from Mekoryuk spoke English almost all the time. They called her father Charlie Edwards and Miyax was Julie, for they all had two names, Eskimo and English. Her mother had also called her Julie, so she did not mind her summer name until one day when Kapugen called her that. She stomped her foot and told him her name was Miyax. "I am Eskimo, not a gussak!" she had said, and he had tossed her into the air and hugged her to him.

"Yes, you are Eskimo," he had said. "And never forget it. We live as no other people can, for we truly understand the earth."

But winters always returned. Blizzards came and the temperatures dropped to thirty and forty below zero, and those who stayed at hunting camp spoke only in Eskimo and did only Eskimo things. They scraped hides, mended boots, made boats, and carved walrus tusks. In the evenings Kapugen sang and danced with the old men, and all of their songs and dances were about the sea and the land and the creatures that dwelled there.

One year, probably in September, for the canvas tents were down and the campground almost empty, Kapugen came into the house with a sealskin. It was a harbor seal, but had so few spots that it was a rare prize.

"We must make you a new coat," he had said. "You are getting big. Since your mother is not here to help us, I will do her work. Now watch and learn."

The skin was metallic silver-gold and so beautiful that even the velveteen parkas of the children from Mekoryuk paled by comparison. Miyax stroked it lovingly as Kapugen lay her old coat upon it and began to cut a larger one. As he worked he hummed, and she made up words about the seal who wanted to be a coat. Presently they became aware of the distant throb of a motorboat. The sound grew louder, then shut off at the beach. Footsteps crunched, the cold air rushed in the door, and there was Martha, Kapugen's aunt. She was thin and her face was pinched. Miyax disliked her immediately, but was spared the necessity of speaking nicely to her, for Martha had words only for Kapugen.

She talked swiftly in English, which Miyax barely understood, and she was angry and upset. Martha shook her finger at Kapugen and glanced at Miyax from time to time. The two were arguing very loudly when Martha pulled a sheet of paper from her pocket and showed it to Kapugen.

"No!" he shouted.

"We'll see!" Martha screamed, turned around, and went toward the boat where a white man waited. Kapugen followed her and stood by the boat, talking to the man for a long time.

The next morning Miyax was awakened as Kapugen lifted her up in his arms and held her close. Gently he pushed the hair out of her eyes and, speaking softly in Eskimo, told her she was going to live with Aunt Martha.

"There's a law that says you must go to school . . . and I guess you should. You are nine years old. And I must go to war. The government is fighting somewhere."

Miyax grabbed him around the neck, but did not protest. It never occurred to her that anything that Kapugen decided was not absolutely perfect. She whimpered however.

"Listen closely," he said. "If anything happens to me, and if you are unhappy, when you are thirteen you can leave Aunt Martha by marrying Daniel, Naka's son. Naka is going to Barrow on the Arctic Ocean. I shall make arrangements with him. He is like me, an old-time Eskimo who likes our traditions. He will agree."

Miyax listened carefully, then he put her down and hastily packed her bladder-bag, wrapped her in an oilskin against the wild spray of the sea, and carried her to the boat. She sat down beside Martha and stared bravely at Kapugen. The motor started and Kapugen looked at her until the boat moved, then he turned his back and walked quickly away. The launch sped up a huge wave, slammed down into a foaming trough, and Kapugen was no longer visible.

With that Miyax became Julie. She was given a cot near the door in Martha's little house and was soon walking to school in the darkness. She liked to learn the printed English words in books, and so a month passed rather happily.

One morning when the air was cold and the puddles around the house were solid ice, an old man from seal camp arrived at the door. He spoke softly to Martha, then pulled his hood tightly around his face and went away. Martha came to Miyax's bed.

"Your father," she said, "went seal hunting in that ridiculous kayak. He has been gone a month this day. He will not be back. Bits of his kayak washed up on the shore." Martha stumped to the fire and turned her back.

Julie ran out of the house into the dark morning. She darted past the store, the reindeer-packing house, the church. She did not stop until she came to the beach. There she crouched among the oil drums and looked out on the sea.

The wind blew across the water, shattering the tips of the waves and shooting ice-sparklets north with the storm. "Kapugen!" she called. No one answered. Kapugen was gone. The earth was empty and bleak.

Setting

Everyone is familiar with the cry of the director who is about to shoot a scene for a new movie: "Quiet on the set!" is the command. When all is ready, the next order is "Action!" Then the actors begin to play their roles in the setting that has been made for them.

Before they get to the "Action" command, however, great pains have been taken to set the scene just the way the director wants it. The reason such care is taken to set a scene is that the setting must create a certain image for the viewer.

Think for a moment about a movie or television show you have seen recently. As soon as the show begins, you get some very distinct impressions. From the way people dress, the way they live, and the vehicles they ride in, you know at once where you are and if the story takes place in the present or in the past. If it's a bright, sunny day in a park, you will tend to feel bright and sunny yourself. But if dark clouds are looming over an old cemetery, you will probably scrunch down and get set for a good scare. If you are shown a luxurious mansion in Texas, you will imagine what it's like to be rich. If the setting is a city slum, you will think about the problems of the poor.

So the setting does a number of things. Most important, it creates a realistic scene. You believe you are really seeing a certain place at a certain time. The setting also prepares you for the action that will take place. And because the setting makes you feel a certain way, you will be in the proper mood to appreciate the action. Setting also helps you think about important ideas that are presented in the movie.

The setting of a novel must also create those same feelings. Actually, every movie, TV show, or stage play begins as a written story. The director must read the story and translate the settings into something you can hear and see. The difference when you read rather than view a story is that the sounds and settings must be projected in your mind rather than on a screen.

Setting is very important in understanding *Julie of the Wolves*. Julie's world is vastly different from the world most of us know. And before we can appreciate what is going on in her world, we must somehow be brought into that world. Author Jean George uses setting very skillfully to do just that.

In this lesson, we will look at how the author uses setting in four different ways:

1 ♦ Setting is used to make you feel a certain way about Julie's world.

2 ♦ Setting is used to make you feel as if you are really on the scene.

3 ♦ Setting is used to present ideas that are important in the story.

4 ♦ Setting can help you understand and share in the action that takes place.

1 ◆ Setting and Feelings

Settings can affect your feelings, and your feelings can affect the way you view a setting. It works both ways. For example, you might look at a lake ringed by pine trees and say, "I just love the peaceful beauty of this place!"

But what if you had just seen someone drown in the lake? Then your feelings would likely create a totally different view of the setting: "The somber pine trees stared down on the murky waters where my friend died."

In *Julie of the Wolves* Miyax often has different feelings about the Arctic wilderness. In the following passages, Miyax is recalling the time when her mother died and she and Kapugen were left alone. Notice here how the setting is used to emphasize Kapugen's feelings. Later, you will see how Miyax's feelings can affect, even change, your view of the somber Arctic setting.

> The wind, the empty sky, the deserted earth—Miyax had felt the bleakness of being left behind once before.
>
> She could not remember her mother very well, for Miyax was scarcely four when she died, but she did remember the day of her death. The wind was screaming wild high notes and hurling ice-filled waves against the beach. Kapugen was holding her hand and they were walking. When she stumbled he put her on his shoulders, and high above the beach she saw thousands of birds diving toward the sea. The jaegers screamed and the sandpipers cried. The feathered horns of the comical puffins drooped low, and Kapugen told her they seemed to be grieving with him.

How lonely this setting makes you feel: "The wind, the empty sky, the deserted earth." It is a barren scene. And the barrenness matches the barrenness felt by Kapugen over the loss of his wife.

Notice that sounds are an important part of the setting too. The wind is screaming; the birds are screaming and crying. Kapugen knows they are grieving with him, and we feel that way too.

As you become more aware of setting in your reading, you will see that there is more than scenery in a good setting. People can be part of a setting, and even smells and clothing are important.

Setting is also viewed differently by different people. So you, as the reader, may have many different feelings about a particular setting. For example, Miyax was only four when her mother died. So her feelings give an entirely different view of the Arctic setting in the passage in Exercise A.

1◆Exercise A

Read the following passage and answer the questions about it using what you have learned in this part of the lesson. Use your writing notebook or a separate piece of paper for your answers.

> She [Miyax] saw this [Kapugen's grief], but she was not sad. She was divinely happy going somewhere alone with Kapugen. Occasionally he climbed the cliffs and brought her eggs to eat; occasionally he took her in his arms and leaned against a rock. She slept at times in the warmth of his big sealskin parka. Then they walked on. She did not know how far.

1. What feature of the landscape are part of the setting? How has Miyax's feelings changed your view of the Arctic setting? Be specific.

2. The setting is still the cold, barren, Arctic wilderness that Kapugen grieves in. Yet Miyax's view is quite different from Kapugen's. Describe how Miyax feels. Why does she feel this way? Is she wrong to feel this way?

Now check your answers using the suggestions in the Answer Key starting on page 451. Review this part of the lesson if you don't understand why an answer was wrong.

1◆Writing on Your Own

Review your story idea and list of setting elements that you made for Create Your Own Setting on page 99. Now do the following:

1. Write an opening paragraph for your story. Use some of the setting elements you listed and expand on the feelings created by your setting.

☐ Perhaps as a lone inhabitant of a deserted island you are frightened by your surroundings.

☐ Maybe you are delighted to find yourself alone on a peaceful tropical island.

2. In a separate sentence, explain how you expect your readers to feel when they read your paragraph. Will they be envious of your luck, or fear for your safety?

3. Read your paragraph to others and ask them:

☐ What feeling do you get from my paragraph?

☐ What setting elements help convey this feeling?

4. If your paragraph does not affect others the way you think it should, try rewriting it until you get the effect you want.

2 ♦ Setting and the Sense of Really Being There

In a novel, just as in a movie, you must be able to "see" the place where the action occurs. It makes no difference that in movies you see with your eyes and in novels or stories you see with your "mind's eye." The important thing is that you get the sense, the feeling, of really being where the action is.

Setting helps put you right in the middle of the action. An author often describes sights, sounds, smells, and textures in great detail. As the details pile up, you get a clearer picture or feeling for where you are. Then, if the vision becomes strong enough in your mind, the author has succeeded in placing you within the setting. This is one mark of a good story.

In the preceding passages you stood on a cold Arctic seashore. Now you will visit Kapugen's house and attend a feast with him and Miyax. Notice how many details are provided to give you a sense of really being there.

> To Miyax the years at seal camp were infinitely good. The scenes and events were beautiful color spots in her memory. There was Kapugen's little house of driftwood, not far from the beach. It was rosy-gray on the outside. Inside, it was gold-brown. Walrus tusks gleamed and drums, harpoons, and man's knives decorated the walls. The sealskin kayak beside the door glowed as if the moon had been stretched across it and its graceful ribs shone back. Dark gold and soft brown were the old men who sat around Kapugen's camp stove and talked to him by day and night.

That description is in technicolor: rosy-gray, dark gold, soft brown. In a way it gives a clearer feeling of "really being there" than you could get from seeing Kapugen's house on a movie screen. A camera might just "pan" or sweep across the scene very quickly. Here you linger and see the details through Miyax's eyes. And as in the other passages you've read, you begin to feel and see the setting from the description.

Notice how people become a part of the setting. It is not important who the old men are. But for Miyax, and for the reader, they supply the golds and browns in the setting.

People and colors become even more important in placing the reader at the scene in the passage in Exercise B.

2 ♦ Exercise B

Read the following passage and answer the questions about it using what you have learned in this part of the lesson. Use your writing notebook or a separate piece of paper for your answers.

> The celebration of the Bladder Feast was many colors—black, blue, purple, fire-red; but Kapugen's hand around hers was rose-colored and that was the color of her memory of the Feast. A shaman, an old priestess whom everyone called "the bent woman," danced. Her face was streaked with black soot. When she finally bowed, a fiery spirit came out of the dark wearing a huge mask that jingled and terrified Miyax. Once, in sheer bravery, she peeked up under a mask and saw that the dancer was not a spirit at all but Naka, Kapugen's serious partner. She whispered his name and he laughed. . . .

1. Miyax and Kapugen are the main characters in this scene. There are two other people, but they are used as part of the setting. Who are they and what do they contribute to the setting?

2. Author Jean George's use of color to describe setting takes a reader from the black-and-white print on the book page right into the scene at the seal camp. List the colors she uses and how they add to the setting. What colors would you use to describe your home, your school, the library, a park, a street, or a neighborhood?

Now check your answers using the suggestions in the Answer Key starting on page 451. Review this part of the lesson if you don't understand why an answer was wrong.

2 ♦ Writing on Your Own

Review the story idea and the list of setting elements that you made for Create a Setting of Your Own on page 99. Now do the following:

1. Write a paragraph that describes a scene from your story.

   □ Perhaps you are captured by natives who take you to meet their leader.

   □ Maybe a storm strikes your island and you are forced to seek out shelter.

2. Pack as much descriptive detail into your scene as you can so that your reader gets the sense of really being there. Here are a few suggestions:

   □ Describe the natives, their customs, their speech, their dress, and so on.

   □ What type of storm strikes the island? How do the animals respond? Describe the changing colors of the sky.

3. You may want to change and rewrite your paragraph several times until you are satisfied with your scene.

3 ◆ Setting and Ideas

When you ask someone why they liked a novel, they will probably say it was exciting, or sad, or funny, or romantic, or a great adventure. But if a story is interesting, it is usually because of the ideas it presents.

An author introduces ideas into a story in many different ways. Ideas can be presented in the dialogue between characters. The way the characters act in a story may also give readers some ideas to think about. Or the author may pause in telling the story to present an idea directly to the readers. Setting is another technique authors use to express ideas.

One of the important ideas in *Julie of the Wolves* has to do with the relationship between the Eskimos and nature. Those Eskimos who follow the old traditions survive off the land and find comfort in its awesome beauty. That special relationship between Eskimo and nature can be seen in the description below.

> A silver memory was the day when the sun came over the horizon for the first time in winter. She [Miyax] was at the beach, close to Kapugen, helping him haul in a huge gleaming net. In it was a beautiful white whale. Out of sight on the other side of the whale, she could hear the old men as they cheered this gift from the sea.
>
> The whale was a mountain so high she could not see the cliffs beyond, only the sunlit clouds. Kapugen's huge, black, frostbitten hand seemed small as it touched the great body of the whale.

Two cherished gifts of nature are described—the sun and the whale. Remember that the sun doesn't shine for months on end during an Arctic winter. So the sun peeking over the horizon is always a welcome sight.

Capturing a whale was considered a blessing. It would provide food, clothing, heat, and light for an entire village. It is described as "this gift from the sea." Generally we think of hunting as taking from nature. But that is not always true. The Eskimos are hunters, but they think of their catch as a gift from nature that will allow them to live.

Notice in the second paragraph how author Jean Craighead George shows you the clouds, Kapugen's hand, and the whale all together. She seems to be saying that all are a part of one nature. The

Eskimos respect nature, and others can learn from that respect.

A lighter side of the same idea is presented in the passage in Exercise C.

3 ♦ Exercise C

Read the following passage and answer the questions about it using what you have learned in this part of the lesson. Use your writing notebook or a separate piece of paper for your answers.

> Walking the tundra [Arctic plains] with Kapugen was all laughter and fun. He would hail the blue sky and shout out his praise for the grasses and bushes. On these trips they ate salmon berries, then lay in the sun watching the birds. Sometimes Kapugen would whistle sandpiper songs and the birds would dip down to see which of their members had gotten lost in the grass. When they saw him and darted away, Kapugen would laugh.

1. Kapugen rejoices in the beauty of his world. Do you agree or disagree with this statement? Give reasons to support your answer.

2. Walking the tundra was all laughter and fun. Why was this simple activity so enjoyable? Be specific. Can you think of a simple pastime that gives you a great deal of pleasure?

Now check your answers using the suggestions in the Answer Key starting on page 451. Review this part of the lesson if you don't understand why an answer was wrong.

3 ♦ Writing on Your Own

Review the story idea and the list of setting elements that you made for Create a Setting of Your Own on page 99. Now do the following:

1. Write one sentence that tells about an idea you would like to communicate to your readers in your story. You may want to develop your idea from the scene you described in 2 ♦ Writing on Your Own.

☐ By experiencing a new culture, maybe you have developed a sense of respect for those whose culture and ideas are different from yours.

☐ The powerful storm may have taught you a valuable lesson about the importance of respecting nature.

2. Write a paragraph for your story that explains your idea and the lesson you have learned. Try to use elements of setting to help explain the idea to your readers.

3. You may want to change and rewrite your paragraph several times until you are satisfied with your idea.

4 ◆ Setting and Action

An author takes great care to see that what is happening in a story fits the setting where that action takes place. This connection between setting and actions is easily seen in some cases. For example, you would not expect action set on the Arctic tundra to include a cops-and-robbers car chase. Miyax's adventures are much more appropriate for an Arctic setting.

There are also small details of setting that an author must choose to go with a particular action. These details often add to the action by making readers more clearly aware of what is going on. For example, by adding a detail or two in the setting, an author can hint that something new is about to happen. The change in setting indicates a change in the action. A happy scene may turn suddenly tense. A calm scene can become chaotic or terrifying.

Think of a group of happy people having a picnic beside a lake. The sun is shining and the birds are singing. Then the sky grows dark. There is a rumbling followed by a low growl. The gaiety turns to fear and panic as the water on the lake churns and froths and a monster rises from the deep. The changing weather warns us that the circumstances are about to change for the worse.

In the following passage, the change in setting is a change of sounds. See if you can spot the place where the setting and the action change together.

One year, probably in September, for the canvas tents were down and the campground almost empty, Kapugen came into the house with a sealskin. . . .

"We must make you a new coat," he had said. . . .

The skin was metallic silver-gold and so beautiful that even the velveteen parkas of children from Mekoryuk paled by comparison. Miyax stroked it lovingly as Kapugen lay her old coat upon it and began to cut a larger one. As he worked he hummed, and she made up words about the seal who wanted to be a coat. Presently they became aware of the distant throb of a motorboat. The sound grew louder, then shut off at the beach. Footsteps crunched, the cold air rushed in the door, and there was Martha, Kapugen's aunt. She was thin and her face was pinched. Miyax disliked her immediately, but was spared the necessity of speaking nicely to her, for Martha had words only for Kapugen.

The scene begins as a happy one. Kapugen is making Miyax a new coat. She is delighted and strokes the fur lovingly. Kapugen hums a tune and Miyax makes up a song to it. This is a happy sound that matches the happy action.

But then there is the distant throb of a motorboat. A detail in the setting has changed and the action is about to change. Notice also that there is a change from old Eskimo ways—the seal catch and the home-made coat—to the new ways of the white settlements—the motorboat. The sound grows louder, then stops. We wait anxiously to see what will happen next. Thus, the detail of setting is helping to move the action.

What happens next is unpleasant, exactly what the author has prepared us for by changing small details of setting. And there is a larger change going on that will come later in the story. With the intrusion of the motorboat and its foreign sound, and of Aunt Martha with her foreign ways, Julie is about to begin a new part of her life, living in white society.

You should be able to match action and setting in the passage in Exercise D. As you read, remember that Julie and Miyax are the same person.

4 ♦ Exercise D

Read the following passage and answer the questions about it using what you have learned in this part of the lesson. Use your writing notebook or a separate piece of paper for your answers.

Martha came to Miyax's bed.

"Your father," she said, "went seal hunting in that ridiculous kayak. He has been gone a month this day. He will not be back. Bits of his kayak washed up on the shore." Martha stumped to the fire and turned her back.

Julie ran out of the house into the dark morning. She darted past the store, the reindeer-packing house, the church. She did not stop until she came to the beach. There she crouched among the oil drums and looked out to sea.

The wind blew across the water, shattering the tips of the waves and shooting ice-sparklets north with the storm.

"Kapugen!" she called. No one answered. Kapugen was gone. The earth was empty and bleak.

1. Julie (Miyax) runs from the white world to the Eskimo world to call to Kapugen. Describe the change in scenery between the two worlds.

2. The plot or action in this part of the novel tells you that: Kapugen is gone and Julie is left alone with Martha. How do the following three sentences work together to emphasize Miyax's loneliness? "Martha stumped to the fire and turned her back. . . . The wind blew across the water. . . . The earth was empty and bleak."

Now check your answers using the suggestions in the Answer Key starting on page 451. Review this part of the lesson if you don't understand why an answer was wrong.

4◆Writing on Your Own

Review the story idea and the list of setting elements that you made for Create a Setting of Your Own on page 99. Now do the following:

1. Select one or more setting elements from your list that might be used to bring about a change in the action of your story.

2. Write a short paragraph in which the setting hints that a change in action is about to occur. Here are some suggestions:

   ☐ Perhaps the natives are making preparations for a feast in your honor.

   ☐ The warmth of the sun returns and the awakening sounds of the wildlife announce an end to the terrifying storm.

3. You may want to change and rewrite your paragraph several times until you are satisfied with the setting and action.

Now go on to Reviewing and Interpreting the Chapter.

Reviewing and Interpreting the Chapter

Answer these questions without looking back at the selection. Choose the best answer to each question and put an *x* in the box beside it, or write your answer on a separate piece of paper.

Remembering Facts

1. When her mother died, Miyax was
   - ☐ a. an infant not yet two.
   - ☐ b. a young teenager.
   - ☐ c. about four years old.
   - ☐ d. at least ten.

2. Who was "the bent woman"?
   - ☐ a. a shaman or religious leader
   - ☐ b. Kapugen's sister
   - ☐ c. Kapugen's aunt
   - ☐ d. a fire spirit

Following the Order of Events

3. Immediately after her mother died, Miyax
   - ☐ a. went to live with Aunt Martha.
   - ☐ b. went off to school.
   - ☐ c. was promised to Daniel as a wife.
   - ☐ d. spent some years at a seal camp.

4. The bladder feast took place
   - ☐ a. when Kapugen died.
   - ☐ b. to honor Miyax's mother.
   - ☐ c. after the seal hunt.
   - ☐ d. after the whale was caught.

Understanding
Word Choices
5. Miyax became angry when Kapugen called her Julie. She said: "I am Eskimo, not a <u>gussak</u>!" A *gussak* is probably a
   - ☐ a. white person.
   - ☐ b. member of another tribe.
   - ☐ c. baby.
   - ☐ d. pet seal.

6. The words *bleak* and *bleakness* are used twice in the chapter, once at the beginning and once at the end. *Bleak* can mean several things:
   - ☐ a. angry, upset, and tearful.
   - ☐ b. barren, cold, and gloomy.
   - ☐ c. flat, dry, and empty.
   - ☐ d. hard, rough, and ugly.

Understanding
Important Ideas
7. Which of these quotations tells an important idea presented in the story?
   - ☐ a. "Often she dug for clams . . . and he would crack them open."
   - ☐ b. " 'We must make you a new coat,' he had said."
   - ☐ c. " 'We live as no other people can, for we truly understand the earth.' "
   - ☐ d. " 'We'll see!' Martha screamed, turned around, and went toward the boat. . . ."

8. Miyax and Kapugen are also called Julie and Charlie Edwards. What do these changes in their names represent?

   ☐ a. their lives as children and their lives as adults

   ☐ b. Eskimo old ways and Eskimo new ways

   ☐ c. their first names and last names

   ☐ d. life on the coast and life on the tundra

Understanding
Levels of
Meaning
9. The seal camp was very rough and primitive. Still, Miyax enjoyed the years she spent there. Why?

   ☐ a. She loved Kapugen and the things he did.

   ☐ b. She felt she was safe from Aunt Martha.

   ☐ c. She knew someday she would be a seal hunter too.

   ☐ d. It was the place her mother had liked best.

10. The Eskimos hunted and fished. Judging from what you have read, what would you say is a good word to describe their attitude toward wildlife?

   ☐ a. fearful

   ☐ b. cruel

   ☐ c. soft-hearted

   ☐ d. respectful

11. The day her mother died, Miyax went off with
Kapugen and "she was divinely happy." What
does this say about Miyax?

☐ a. She only cared for herself and Kapugen.

☐ b. She was too young to understand and was
happy to be with Kapugen.

☐ c. She loved the outdoors and wanted to learn
the ways of her people.

☐ d. She loved the birds and other wildlife on the
tundra.

12. When Miyax's mother died, Kapugen left his job,
his home, and all his possessions and walked all
the way to seal camp. Why did he act that way?

☐ a. He was crazy, as Aunt Martha said.

☐ b. He yearned to be hunting again.

☐ c. The fire spirit was in him.

☐ d. He was overcome by grief.

13. Miyax's memories are often connected with
colors. The memory of the old men around
Kapugen's stove was "flickering yellow." Why
flickering yellow?

☐ a. The old men's faces were yellowed with age.

☐ b. The memory was as bright in her mind as
the sun.

☐ c. It was probably the flickering yellow flames
of the fire.

☐ d. It was a wolf dance, and wolves eyes are
yellow.

14. Much of the Arctic is empty and bleak as Miyax twice felt it to be. It did *not* seem empty and bleak to her when

    ☐ a. people came from Mekoryuk in the summer.

    ☐ b. Miyax was with Kapugen.

    ☐ c. Miyax ran from Aunt Martha's home.

    ☐ d. she felt like an Eskimo.

Understanding Feelings 15. Kapugen said, "wolves are brotherly," and "birds and animals all had languages." What do these phrases tell you about Kapugen's feelings toward animals?

    ☐ a. Kapugen enjoyed teasing Miyax with animal stories.

    ☐ b. Kapugen was superstitious about animals.

    ☐ c. Kapugen was really afraid of animals and said those things to calm his fear.

    ☐ d. Kapugen seemed to feel a kinship with animals.

16. According to the story, being left alone is bleak. Why?

    ☐ a. Being left alone is often peaceful and relaxing.

    ☐ b. Being left alone often makes you feel empty inside.

    ☐ c. Being left alone is always pleasant.

    ☐ d. Being left alone gives you a feeling of danger lurking everywhere.

Now check your answers using the Answer Key starting on page 451. Make no mark for right answers. Correct any wrong answers you may have by putting a check mark (✓) in the box next to the right answer. Count the number of questions you answered correctly and plot the total on the Comprehension Scores graph on page 462.

Next, look at the questions you answered incorrectly. What types of questions were they? Count the number you got wrong of each type and enter the numbers in the spaces below.

Remembering Facts _____

Following the Order of Events _____

Understanding Word Choices _____

Understanding Important Ideas _____

Understanding Levels of Meaning _____

Understanding Character _____

Understanding Setting _____

Understanding Feelings _____

Now use these numbers to fill in the Comprehension Skills Profile on page 463.

Discussion Guides

The questions below will help you think about the selection and the lesson you have just read. If you don't discuss these questions in class, try to think about them or discuss them with your classmates. Perhaps you will want to write a few paragraphs in answer to the questions.

Discussing Setting

1. "The wind, the empty sky, the deserted earth. . . ." How are these words important in the story?

2. There are three dance scenes in the reading selection: one at the Bladder Feast, one at the death of the whale, and one at night at Kapugen's house. What purposes do the dance scenes serve in the story?

3. When Julie heard Kapugen was missing and thought to be dead, she ran to the beach, crouched among oil drums there, and looked out to sea. What meaning would the beach, the oil drums, and the sea have for Julie at that time?

Discussing the Chapter

4. How would you describe Aunt Martha? Is she entirely good or evil? Give reasons for your answer.

5. Are the old ways of the Eskimos better than the new ways, or just the opposite? Give reasons for your opinion.

6. Miyax seemed to admire Kapugen and everything he did. Give examples of how you admire someone in your family or among your friends. Compare your examples with the way Miyax acted in the story.

Discussing the Author's Work

7. The author uses colors a great deal in her descriptions. Find a place in the story where a color is used in a description. Read the passage aloud. Then tell how the color affects your feelings about that scene.

8. The name of the book is *Julie of the Wolves*. Why do you think the author used "Julie" in the title rather than "Miyax"?

9. Jean George dedicated the book this way: "To Luke George who loves wolves and the Eskimos of Alaska." Why is this an appropriate way to dedicate *Julie of the Wolves*?

Writing Exercise

Read all the instructions before you begin writing. If you have any questions about how to begin the writing assignment, review Using the Writing Process beginning on page 439, or confer with your writing coach.

1. Write a "short short" story based on the story idea you thought of at the beginning of the lesson. If you haven't developed a story idea yet and a list of setting elements to go with it, turn to Create a Setting of Your Own on page 99 and do it now. (If you have developed a story idea but would like to change your mind at this point and write about something else, that's okay too.)

2. Use as many setting details in your story as you can. Help your readers understand feelings, ideas, and the action through the setting.

   If you have done the four Writing on Your Own exercises throughout the lesson you can use these to help you write your story.

3. Write, revise, correct, and rewrite your story until you are satisfied with it.

Unit 4   Tone and Mood

To Kill a Mockingbird
BY HARPER LEE

About the Illustration

Describe what is happening in this scene. Use details from the illustration to support your response.

Here are some questions to help you think about the chapter:

◆ What time of day is it in the scene?

◆ What mood does the picture create?

◆ Who do you think the main characters will be in the chapter?

Unit 4

Introduction

About the Novel

To Kill a Mockingbird is about eight-year-old Jean Louise (Scout) Finch, her twelve-year-old brother Jem, their father Atticus Finch, and the people of Maycomb County, Alabama. The children's mother died when they were small. In her place there are two women: Calpurnia, who is the cook and nurse to the children; and Atticus's sister, Aunt Alexandra. The story takes place between 1933 and 1935.

Two parts of the story come together in the chapter you will read. One part involves Arthur (Boo) Radley, a next-door neighbor who is never seen. When he was a teenager, Boo got into some small trouble with the law. To keep him from the disgrace of jail, his father shut him up in the house. As far as anyone knows, Boo has never been out of the house in twenty-five years.

The children believe Boo is some sort of monster. Stories told about him say that he goes out at night peeking in windows and killing animals to eat raw. The Radley house, then, is something that children and many adults fear.

One summer Scout, Jem, and a friend named Dill decide they are going to be daring enough to get a look at Boo Radley. Making swift raids up to the Radley house becomes a game with them. Once they are even bold enough to try to peek through a window. They never do get to see Boo, but Boo Radley is watching them.

The other part of the story deals with Tom Robinson, a black man who has been wrongly accused of raping and beating a white woman, Mayella Ewell. Atticus Finch, who is a lawyer, is given the job of defending Tom. In court Atticus proves that the girl was not raped, and that it was the girl's father, Bob Ewell—and not Tom—who beat her.

Bob Ewell, a mean and treacherous man, swears he will get Atticus Finch for shaming him in public. But Ewell is a coward. In a drunken rage he goes instead after Atticus's children, Scout and Jem.

Chapter 28 begins with Jem and Scout walking to a Halloween pageant being held in the school auditorium. The school is just around the corner from their house (past the Radley house) and across the schoolyard. Scout will be in the pageant dressed as a smoked ham, one of the products of Maycomb County. Her costume is made from chicken wire. The wire is bent in the shape of a ham, wide and round at the bottom and narrow at the top where the bone, or hock, is. The whole thing is covered with brown cloth.

What happens before, during, and after the pageant is the subject of this chapter. You will meet Mrs. Merriweather, a town busybody who is in charge of the pageant. Atticus Finch appears in the last part of the chapter, and in the last few pages you will meet Dr. Reynolds and Sheriff Heck Tate.

One other character appears. He is described only as a "countryman" whom Scout has never seen before. He is the one who saves the children's lives when they are attacked. It will be up to you to figure out who he could be.

You will notice a reference to a mockingbird (a "mocker") early in the chapter. A mockingbird is a plain gray-and-white songbird that imitates the songs of other birds. It is one of the most delightful birds to listen to as it goes through its repertoire, or list, of songs it has learned from other birds.

The point is made in the novel that people sometimes kill these lovely songbirds for no other reason than they are small, weak, and defenseless. This mean streak in people is beyond explanation or understanding. The author uses this point to show how people sometimes kill other people in the same senseless way. Just as they might kill a mockingbird, the strong people in society will mistreat or even kill other people for no other reason than they are weak and defenseless.

To Kill a Mockingbird by Harper Lee was published in 1960 and has been a best seller ever since. Lee, who was born in 1926, grew up in Monroeville, Alabama, during the Depression years. *To Kill a Mockingbird* is also set during the Depression, and the town of Maycomb is, in fact, based on Lee's hometown of Monroeville. Her father was a lawyer there, and he served as a model for Atticus Finch. *To Kill a Mockingbird,* Lee's first and only novel, won a Pulitzer Prize in 1961. It was made into a movie starring Gregory Peck as Atticus and often replays on television. The movie is also available on videotape.

About the Lesson

This lesson is about tone and mood. When you think of tone you probably think of a sound. A bell has a certain tone. Your voice has a tone when you speak or sing. You can change the tone of your voice to match your feelings. You shout when you are angry. You speak softly in a romantic mood.

Writing has tone as well, even if there is no sound. It shows up as a feeling. It can be said that a piece of writing has a sad tone, an angry tone, a sarcastic tone, a happy tone, and so on.

Mood is a feeling too. Moods carry the same names as tone: happiness, sorrow, despair, excitement, boredom. You know what moods are because you have experienced them all yourself.

Tone and mood are closely related, but sometimes it's hard to tell which comes first. Tones create moods, and moods create tones. As a writer writes, he or she is in a certain mood. The author has certain feelings and attitudes about the subject matter and the characters. This mood is reflected in the writing as tone. You can also detect the moods of the characters. And as a reader you notice the tone and adopt a mood to match it.

The following questions will help you focus on tone and mood in the chapter from *To Kill a Mockingbird*. Read the chapter carefully and try to answer these questions as you go along:

◆ Tone and mood constantly change in a story. Where are there changes of tone and mood in the chapter? Mark them as you find them. Try to label them as funny, tense, exciting, calm, frightening, or whatever you think they are.

◆ How does the setting in the dark schoolyard affect the tone of the story, the mood of the characters, and your mood as a reader?

◆ Special tones and moods may be associated with people you know. Tones and moods are also associated with characters in a novel. What tone and what mood do you sense when you read about Mrs. Merriweather? What tones are connected with other characters?

◆ Authors create tone and mood with words and with the way they put words together. What words or expressions can you find in the story that seem to create a special tone or mood? Mark them as you find them.

Creating Tone and Mood in a Story

One way that people communicate their moods is through the tone they use. Tone is created by voice and by actions—facial expressions, movements, gestures, attitudes, and so on. The setting, or where you happen to be, also influences the tone of what is said or what is happening.

Authors create tone and communicate moods by describing actions and settings in their stories. Experiment with creating tones and moods with the following exercise:

1. Read this sentence: "You have to see that movie."

2. Now read the sentence in different ways to your class, a friend, your family, or your writing partner. Create a different mood each time you speak the sentence by varying the tone. Here are some examples:

□ Emphasize different words each time you read—**You** have to see that movie. You **have** to see that movie. You have **to see** that movie. You have to see that **movie**. Explain how the tone and mood change each time you say the sentence. How does the meaning of the sentence change each time?

□ Read the sentence loudly, angrily, softly, sarcastically, comically.

□ Read the sentence looking your friend straight in the eye. Read it as you look around the room. Read it while you emphasize certain words with your hands. How does the tone and mood change with the setting?

□ Speak the sentences as if you were saying them in private, in a crowded hallway, in the library, at your house.

□ Use this same exercise and try other sentences. You might try "Yes, I like you"; "You are a nice person"; "Pass the salt." You'll be surprised by how many meanings you can make from one short sentence.

3. Now write about two people who are talking to each other. Tell a little about the people, where they are, how they feel, and what they say and how they say it. For example, you could have your characters say the line you have been practicing, "You have to see that movie," and describe *how* the words were spoken.

4. Let others read what you have written. Ask them how the writing sounds (the tone) and how they think the characters feel (the mood).

To Kill a Mockingbird

by Harper Lee

28.

The weather was unusually warm for the last day of October. We didn't even need jackets. The wind was growing stronger, and Jem said it might be raining before we got home. There was no moon.

The street light on the corner cast sharp shadows on the Radley house. I heard Jem laugh softly. "Bet nobody bothers them tonight," he said. Jem was carrying my ham costume, rather awkwardly, as it was hard to hold. I thought it gallant of him to do so.

"It is a scary place though, ain't it?" I said. "Boo doesn't mean anybody any harm, but I'm right glad you're along."

"You know Atticus wouldn't let you go to the schoolhouse by yourself," Jem said.

"Don't see why, it's just around the corner and across the yard."

"That yard's a mighty long place for little girls to cross at night," Jem teased. "Ain't you scared of haints?"

We laughed. Haints, Hot Steams, incantations, secret signs, had vanished with our years as mist with sunrise. "What was that old thing," Jem said, "Angel bright, life-in-death; get off the road, don't suck my breath."

"Cut it out, now," I said. We were in front of the Radley Place.

Jem said, "Boo must not be at home. Listen."

High above us in the darkness a solitary mocker poured out his repertoire in blissful unawareness of whose tree he sat in, plunging from the shrill kee, kee of the sunflower bird to the irascible qua-ack of a bluejay, to the sad lament of Poor Will, Poor Will, Poor Will.

We turned the corner and I tripped on a root growing in the road. Jem tried to help me, but all he did was drop my costume in the dust. I didn't fall, though, and soon we were on our way again.

We turned off the road and entered the schoolyard. It was pitch black.

"How do you know where we're at, Jem?" I asked, when we had gone a few steps.

"I can tell we're under the big oak because we're passin' through a cool spot. Careful now, and don't fall again."

We had slowed to a cautious gait, and were feeling our way forward so as not to bump into the tree. The tree was a single and ancient oak; two children could not reach around its trunk and touch hands. It was far away from teachers, their spies, and curious neighbors: it was near the Radley lot, but the Radleys were not curious. A small patch of earth beneath its branches was packed hard from many fights and furtive crap games.

The lights in the high school auditorium were blazing in the distance, but they blinded us, if anything. "Don't look ahead, Scout," Jem said. "Look at the ground and you won't fall."

"You should have brought the flashlight, Jem."

"Didn't know it was this dark. Didn't look like it'd be this dark earlier in the evening. So cloudy, that's why. It'll hold off a while, though."

Someone leaped at us.

"God amighty!" Jem yelled.

A circle of light burst in our faces, and Cecil Jacobs jumped in glee behind it. "Ha-a-a, gotcha!" he shrieked. "Thought you'd be comin' along this way!"

"What are you doin' way out here by yourself, boy? Ain't you scared of Boo Radley?"

Cecil had ridden safely to the auditorium with his

parents, hadn't seen us, then had ventured down this far because he knew good and well we'd be coming along. He thought Mr. Finch'd be with us, though.

"Shucks, ain't much but around the corner," said Jem. "Who's scared to go around the corner?" We had to admit that Cecil was pretty good, though. He *had* given us a fright, and he could tell it all over the schoolhouse, that was his privilege.

"Say," I said, "ain't you a cow tonight? Where's your costume?"

"It's up behind the stage," he said. "Mrs. Merriweather says the pageant ain't comin' on for a while. You can put yours back of the stage by mine, Scout, and we can go with the rest of 'em."

This was an excellent idea, Jem thought. He also thought it a good thing that Cecil and I would be together. This way, Jem would be left to go with people his own age.

When we reached the auditorium, the whole town was there except Atticus and the ladies worn out from decorating, and the usual outcasts and shut-ins. Most of the county, it seemed, was there: the hall was teeming with slicked-up country people. The high school building had a wide downstairs hallway; people milled around booths that had been installed along each side.

"Oh Jem, I forgot my money," I sighed, when I saw them.

"Atticus didn't," Jem said. "Here's thirty cents, you can do six things. See you later on."

"Okay," I said, quite content with thirty cents and Cecil. I went with Cecil down to the front of the auditorium, through a door on one side, and backstage. I got rid of my ham costume and departed in a hurry, for Mrs. Merriweather was standing at a lectern in front of the first row of seats making last-minute, frenzied changes in the script.

"How much money you got?" I asked Cecil. Cecil had thirty cents, too, which made us even. We squandered our first nickels on the House of Horrors, which scared us not at all; we entered the black seventh-grade room and were led around by the temporary ghoul in residence and were made to touch several objects alleged to be component parts of a human being. "Here's his eyes," we were told when we touched two peeled grapes on a saucer. "Here's his heart," which felt like raw liver. "These are his innards," and our hands were thrust into a plate of cold spaghetti.

Cecil and I visited several booths. We each bought a sack of Mrs. Judge Taylor's homemade divinity. I wanted to bob for apples, but Cecil said it wasn't sanitary. His mother said he might catch something from everybody's heads having been in the same tub. "Ain't anything around town now to catch," I protested. But Cecil said his mother said it was unsanitary to eat after folks. I later asked Aunt Alexandra about this, and she said people who held such views were usually climbers.

We were about to purchase a blob of taffy when Mrs. Merriweather's runners appeared and told us to go backstage, it was time to get ready. The auditorium was filling with people; the Maycomb County High School band had assembled in front below the stage; the stage footlights were on and the red velvet curtain rippled and billowed from the scurrying going on behind it.

Backstage, Cecil and I found the narrow hallway teeming with people: adults in homemade three-corner hats, Confederate caps, Spanish-American War hats, and World War helmets. Children dressed as various agricultural enterprises crowded around the one small window.

"Somebody's mashed my costume," I wailed in dismay. Mrs. Merriweather galloped to me, reshaped the chicken wire, and thrust me inside.

"You all right in there, Scout?" asked Cecil. "You sound so far off, like you was on the other side of a hill."

"You don't sound any nearer," I said.

The band played the national anthem, and we heard the audience rise. Then the bass drum sounded. Mrs. Merriweather, stationed behind her lectern beside the band, said: "Maycomb County: Ad Astra Per Aspera." The bass drum boomed again. "That means," said Mrs. Merriweather, translating for the rustic elements, "from the mud to the stars." She added, unnecessarily, it seemed to me, "A pageant."

"Reckon they wouldn't know what it was if she didn't tell 'em," whispered Cecil, who was immediately shushed.

"The whole town knows it," I breathed.

"But the country folks've come in," Cecil said.

"Be quiet back there," a man's voice ordered, and we were silent.

The bass drum went boom with every sentence Mrs. Merriweather uttered. She chanted mournfully about Maycomb County being older than the state, that it was a part of the Mississippi and Alabama Territories, that the first white man to set foot in the virgin forests was the Probate Judge's great-grandfather five times removed, who was never heard of again. Then came the fearless Colonel Maycomb, for whom the county was named.

Andrew Jackson appointed him to a position of authority, and Colonel Maycomb's misplaced self-confidence and slender sense of direction brought disaster to all who rode with him in the Creek Indian Wars. Colonel Maycomb persevered in his efforts to make the region safe for democracy, but his first campaign was his last. His orders, relayed to him by a friendly Indian runner, were to move south. After consulting a tree to ascertain from its lichen which way was south, and taking no lip from the subordinates who ventured to correct him, Colonel Maycomb set out on a purposeful journey to rout the enemy and entangled his troops so far northwest in the forest primeval that they were eventually rescued by settlers moving inland.

Mrs. Merriweather gave a thirty-minute description of Colonel Maycomb's exploits. I discovered that if I bent my knees I could tuck them under my costume and more or less sit. I sat down, listened to Mrs. Merriweather's drone and the bass drum's boom and was soon fast asleep.

They said later that Mrs. Merriweather was putting her all into the grand finale, that she had crooned, "Po-ork," with a confidence born of pine trees and butterbeans entering on cue. She waited a few seconds, then called, "Po-ork?" When nothing materialized, she yelled, "Pork!"

I must have heard her in my sleep, or the band playing *Dixie* woke me, but it was when Mrs. Merriweather triumphantly mounted the stage with the state flag that I chose to make my entrance. Chose is incorrect: I thought I'd better catch up with the rest of them.

They told me later that Judge Taylor went out behind the auditorium and stood there slapping his knees so hard Mrs. Taylor brought him a glass of water and one of his pills.

Mrs. Merriweather seemed to have a hit, everybody was cheering so, but she caught me backstage and told me I had ruined her pageant. She made me feel awful, but when Jem came to fetch me he was sympathetic. He said he couldn't see my costume much from where he was sitting. How he could tell I was feeling bad under my costume I don't know, but he said I did all right, I just came in a little late, that was all. Jem was becoming almost as good as Atticus at making you feel right when things went wrong. Almost—not even Jem could make me go through that crowd, and he consented to wait backstage with me until the audience left.

"You wanta take it off, Scout?" he asked.

"Naw, I'll just keep it on," I said. I could hide my mortification under it.

"You all want a ride home?" someone asked.

"No sir, thank you," I heard Jem say. "It's just a little walk."

"Be careful of haints," the voice said. "Better still, tell the haints to be careful of Scout."

"There aren't many folks left now," Jem told me. "Let's go."

We went through the auditorium to the hallway, then

down the steps. It was still black dark. The remaining cars were parked on the other side of the building, and their headlights were little help. "If some of 'em were goin' in our direction we could see better," said Jem. "Here Scout, let me hold onto your—hock. You might lose your balance."

"I can see all right."

"Yeah, but you might lose your balance." I felt a slight pressure on my head, and assumed that Jem had grabbed that end of the ham. "You got me?"

"Uh huh."

We began crossing the black schoolyard straining to see our feet. "Jem," I said, "I forgot my shoes, they're back behind the stage."

"Well let's go get 'em." But as we turned around the auditorium lights went off. "You can get 'em tomorrow," he said.

"But tomorrow's Sunday," I protested as Jem turned me homeward.

"You can get the Janitor to let you in . . . Scout?"

"Hm?"

"Nothing."

Jem hadn't started that in a long time. I wondered what he was thinking. He'd tell me when he wanted to, probably when we got home. I felt his fingers press the top of my costume, too hard, it seemed. I shook my head. "Jem, you don't hafta—"

"Hush a minute, Scout," he said, pinching me.

We walked along silently. "Minute's up," I said. "Whatcha thinkin' about?" I turned to look at him, but his outline was barely visible.

"Thought I heard something," he said. "Stop a minute."

We stopped.

"Hear anything?" he asked.

"No."

We had not gone five paces before he made me stop again.

"Jem, are you tryin' to scare me? You know I'm too old—"

"Be quiet," he said, and I knew he was not joking.

The night was still. I could hear his breath coming easily beside me. Occasionally there was a sudden breeze that hit my bare legs, but it was all that remained of a promised windy night. This was the stillness before a thunderstorm. We listened.

"Heard an old dog just then," I said.

"It's not that," Jem answered. "I hear it when we're walkin' along, but when we stop I don't hear it."

"You hear my costume rustlin'. Aw, it's just Halloween got you. . . ."

I said it more to convince myself than Jem, for sure enough, as we began walking, I heard what he was talking about. It was not my costume.

"It's just old Cecil," said Jem presently. "He won't get us again. Let's don't let him think we're hurrying."

We slowed to a crawl. I asked Jem how Cecil could follow us in this dark, looked to me like he'd bump into us from behind.

"I can see you, Scout," Jem said.

"How? I can't see you."

"Your fat streaks are showin'. Mrs. Crenshaw painted 'em with some of that shiny stuff so they'd show up under the footlights. I can see you pretty well, an' I expect Cecil can see you well enough to keep his distance."

I would show Cecil that we knew he was behind us and we were ready for him. "Cecil Jacobs is a big wet he-en!" I yelled suddenly, turning around.

We stopped. There was no acknowledgment save he-en bouncing off the distant schoolhouse wall.

"I'll get him," said Jem. *"He-y!"*

Hay-e-hay-e-hay-ey, answered the schoolhouse wall.

It was unlike Cecil to hold out for so long; once he pulled a joke he'd repeat it time and again. We should have been leapt at already. Jem signaled for me to stop again.

He said softly, "Scout, can you take that thing off?"

"I think so, but I ain't got anything on under it much."

"I've got your dress here."

"I can't get it on in the dark."

"Okay," he said, "never mind."

"Jem, are you afraid?"

"No. Think we're almost to the tree now. Few yards from that, an' we'll be to the road. We can see the street light then." Jem was talking in an unhurried, flat toneless voice. I wondered how long he would try to keep the Cecil myth going.

"You reckon we oughta sing, Jem?"

"No. Be real quiet again, Scout."

We had not increased our pace. Jem knew as well as I that it was difficult to walk fast without stumping a toe, tripping on stones, and other inconveniences, and I was barefooted. Maybe it was the wind rustling the trees. But there wasn't any wind and there weren't any trees except the big oak.

Our company shuffled and dragged his feet, as if wearing heavy shoes. Whoever it was wore thick cotton pants; what I thought were trees rustling was the soft swish of cotton on cotton, wheek, wheek, with every step.

I felt the sand go cold under my feet and I knew we were near the big oak. Jem pressed my head. We stopped and listened.

Shuffle-foot had not stopped with us this time. His trousers swished softly and steadily. Then they stopped. He was running, running toward us with no child's steps.

"Run, Scout! Run! Run!" Jem screamed.

I took one giant step and found myself reeling: my arms useless, in the dark, I could not keep my balance.

"Jem, Jem, help me, Jem!"

Something crushed the chicken wire around me. Metal ripped on metal and I fell to the ground and rolled as far as I could, floundering to escape my wire prison. From somewhere near by came scuffling, kicking sounds, sounds of shoes and flesh scraping dirt and roots. Someone rolled against me and I felt Jem. He was up like lightning and pulling me with him but, though my head and shoulders were free, I was so entangled we didn't get very far.

We were nearly to the road when I felt Jem's hand leave me, felt him jerk backwards to the ground. More scuffling, and then came a dull crunching sound and Jem screamed.

I ran in the direction of Jem's scream and sank into a flabby male stomach. Its owner said, "Uff!" and tried to catch my arms, but they were tightly pinioned. His stomach was soft but his arms were like steel. He slowly squeezed the breath out of me. I could not move. Suddenly he was jerked backwards and flung on the ground, almost carrying me with him. I thought, Jem's up.

One's mind works very slowly at times. Stunned, I stood there dumbly. The scuffling noises were dying; someone wheezed and the night was still again.

Still but for a man breathing heavily, breathing heavily and staggering. I thought he went to the tree and leaned against it. He coughed violently, a sobbing, bone-shaking cough.

"Jem?"

There was no answer but the man's heavy breathing.

"Jem?"

Jem didn't answer.

The man began moving around, as if searching for something. I heard him groan and pull something heavy along the ground. It was slowly coming to me that there were now four people under the tree.

"Atticus . . . ?"

The man was walking heavily and unsteadily toward the road.

I went to where I thought he had been and felt frantically along the ground, reaching out with my toes. Presently I touched someone.

"Jem?"

My toes touched trousers, a belt buckle, buttons, something I could not identify, a collar, and a face. A prickly stubble on the face told me it was not Jem's. I smelled stale whiskey.

I made my way along in what I thought was the direction of the road. I was not sure, because I had been turned around so many times. But I found it and looked down to the street light. A man was passing under it. The man was walking with the staccato steps of someone carrying a load too heavy for him. He was going around the corner. He was carrying Jem. Jem's arm was dangling crazily in front of him.

By the time I reached the corner the man was crossing our front yard. Light from our front door framed Atticus for an instant; he ran down the steps, and together, he and the man took Jem inside.

I was at the front door when they were going down the hall. Aunt Alexandra was running to meet me. "Call Dr. Reynolds!" Atticus's voice came sharply from Jem's room. "Where's Scout?"

"Here she is," Aunt Alexandra called, pulling me along with her to the telephone. She tugged at me anxiously. "I'm all right, Aunty," I said, "you better call."

She pulled the receiver from the hook and said, "Eula May, get Dr. Reynolds, quick!"

"Agnes, is your father home? Oh God, where is he? Please tell him to come over here as soon as he comes in. Please, it's urgent!"

There was no need for Aunt Alexandra to identify herself; people in Maycomb knew each other's voices.

Atticus came out of Jem's room. The moment Aunt Alexandra broke the connection, Atticus took the receiver from her. He rattled the hook, then said, "Eula May, get me the sheriff, please."

"Heck? Atticus Finch. Someone's been after my children. Jem's hurt. Between here and the schoolhouse. I can't leave my boy. Run out there for me, please, and see if he's still around. Doubt if you'll find him now, but I'd like to see him if you do. Got to go now. Thanks, Heck."

"Atticus, is Jem dead?"

"No, Scout. Look after her, sister," he called, as he went down the hall.

Aunt Alexandra's fingers trembled as she unwound the crushed fabric and wire from around me. "Are you all right, darling?" she asked over and over as she worked me free.

It was a relief to be out. My arms were beginning to tingle, and they were red with small hexagonal marks. I rubbed them, and they felt better.

"Aunty, is Jem dead?"

"No—no, darling, he's unconscious. We won't know how badly he's hurt until Dr. Reynolds gets here. Jean Louise, what happened?"

"I don't know."

She left it at that. She brought me something to put on, and had I thought about it then, I would have never let her forget it: in her distraction, Aunty brought me my overalls. "Put these on, darling," she said, handing me the garments she most despised.

She rushed back to Jem's room, then came to me in the hall. She patted me vaguely, and went back to Jem's room.

A car stopped in front of the house. I knew Dr. Reynolds's step almost as well as my father's. He had brought Jem and me into the world, had led us through every childhood disease known to man including the time Jem fell out of the treehouse, and he had never lost our friendship. Dr. Reynolds said if we had been boil-prone things would have been different, but we doubted it.

He came in the door and said, "Good Lord." He walked toward me, said, "You're still standing," and changed his course. He knew every room in the house. He also knew that if I was in bad shape, so was Jem.

After ten forevers Dr. Reynolds returned. "Is Jem dead?" I asked.

"Far from it," he said, squatting down to me. "He's got a bump on the head just like yours, and a broken arm.

Scout, look that way—no, don't turn your head, roll your eyes. Now look over yonder. He's got a bad break, so far as I can tell now it's in the elbow. Like somebody tried to wring his arm off . . . now look at me."

"Then he's not dead?"

"No-o!" Dr. Reynolds got to his feet. "We can't do much tonight," he said, "except try to make him as comfortable as we can. We'll have to X-ray his arm—looks like he'll be wearing his arm 'way out by his side for a while. Don't worry, though, he'll be as good as new. Boys his age bounce."

While he was talking, Dr. Reynolds had been looking keenly at me, lightly fingering the bump that was coming on my forehead. "You don't feel broke anywhere, do you?"

Dr. Reynolds's small joke made me smile. "Then you don't think he's dead, then?"

He put on his hat. "Now I may be wrong, of course, but I think he's very alive. Shows all the symptoms of it. Go have a look at him, and when I come back we'll get together and decide."

Dr. Reynolds's step was young and brisk. Mr. Heck Tate's was not. His heavy boots punished the porch and he opened the door awkwardly, but he said the same thing Dr. Reynolds said when he came in. "You all right, Scout?" he added.

"Yes sir, I'm goin' in to see Jem. Atticus'n'them's in there."

"I'll go with you," said Mr. Tate.

Aunt Alexandra had shaded Jem's reading light with a towel, and his room was dim. Jem was lying on his back. There was an ugly mark along one side of his face. His left arm lay out from his body; his elbow was bent slightly, but in the wrong direction. Jem was frowning.

"Jem . . . ?"

Atticus spoke. "He can't hear you, Scout, he's out like a light. He was coming around, but Dr. Reynolds put him out again."

"Yes sir." I retreated. Jem's room was large and square. Aunt Alexandra was sitting in a rocking-chair by the fireplace. The man who brought Jem in was standing in a corner, leaning against the wall. He was some country-man I did not know. He had probably been at the pageant, and was in the vicinity when it happened. He must have heard our screams and come running.

Atticus was standing by Jem's bed.

Mr. Heck Tate stood in the doorway. His hat was in his hand, and a flashlight bulged from his pants pocket. He was in his working clothes.

"Come in, Heck," said Atticus. "Did you find anything? I can't conceive of anyone low-down enough to do a thing like this, but I hope you found him."

Mr. Tate sniffed. He glanced sharply at the man in the corner, nodded to him, then looked around the room—at Jem, at Aunt Alexandra, then at Atticus.

"Sit down, Mr. Finch," he said pleasantly.

Atticus said, "Let's all sit down. Have that chair, Heck. I'll get another one from the livingroom."

Mr. Tate sat in Jem's desk chair. He waited until Atticus returned and settled himself. I wondered why Atticus had not brought a chair for the man in the corner, but Atticus knew the ways of country people far better than I. Some of his rural clients would park their long-eared steeds under the chinaberry trees in the back yard, and Atticus would often keep appointments on the back steps. This one was probably more comfortable where he was.

"Mr. Finch," said Mr. Tate, "tell you what I found. I found a little girl's dress—it's out there in my car. That your dress, Scout?"

"Yes sir, if it's a pink one with smockin'," I said. Mr. Tate was behaving as if he were on the witness stand. He liked to tell things his own way, untrammeled by state or defense, and sometimes it took him a while.

"I found some funny-looking pieces of muddy-colored cloth—"

"That's m'costume, Mr. Tate."

Mr. Tate ran his hands down his thighs. He rubbed his left arm and investigated Jem's mantelpiece, then he seemed to be interested in the fireplace. His fingers sought his long nose.

"What is it, Heck?" said Atticus.

Mr. Tate found his neck and rubbed it. "Bob Ewell's lyin' on the ground under that tree down yonder with a kitchen knife stuck up under his ribs. He's dead, Mr. Finch."

Tone and Mood

People turn to entertainment mostly to change their moods. Say you feel bored. That is your mood of the moment. Seeking a change of mood, you decide to read or to watch television. Now you are faced with a choice. "What am I in the mood for?" you ask yourself.

What you really mean is, "What mood would I like to be in?" If you want to be put in a lighthearted mood, you choose something funny, a comedy or a humorous book. There's soap opera or romance or tragic drama if you want a good cry. There's sports or adventure if you want to be lifted out of your seat.

A mood is the way you feel. The moods of a book are the way the characters feel and the way they make you feel in turn as a reader. Joy, anger, sorrow, fear, excitement—all of these and more are moods. What is tone? Tone is what carries the mood to you. A comedy is funny because it has a comic tone. A drama may be sad because it has a tragic tone. In a mystery, the tone is mysterious or ghostly or suspenseful. You respond, or the characters in the story respond, with a mood that is fearful or expectant.

Tone and mood work very closely together. The tone of a church is awe-inspiring. That tone may put you in a thoughtful or prayerful mood. The tone at a ball game is exciting. It puts you in a happy or eager mood. The tone at a funeral is quiet and mournful. Accordingly, your mood is sad.

But mood can create tone also. In a classroom, an angry teacher can create a tone that is tense. One person's sour mood at a party can set a tone that is strained and unhappy for everyone.

In any case, the difference between tone and mood is this: tone is a manner or an attitude that carries—or *conveys*—a feeling. Mood, on the other hand, is the feeling itself. Or sometimes it is a state of mind.

Tone and mood work together in novels as they do everywhere else. The author is always in control of what is going on. It is the author who creates the tone and tells you about the moods of the characters. The writer deliberately creates tone and mood for a number of purposes.

First, the author wants to show the characters in all the different moods we expect from people in real life. So you may expect that moods will change. Second, the author usually has a feeling or attitude toward the characters in the novel and toward the subject matter of the story. By using tone carefully, a good author can communicate that attitude to readers and even make them feel the same way. Thus, you always know when to cheer the hero and hiss at the villain. You can usually tell from the tone how the author feels in any passage. If there is a revolution, for example, you can tell at once from the tone which side the author is on.

Finally, the author wants you to be entertained. To be sure that you are, the author has to make certain that you are responding properly to the events of the story. Your mood can be controlled most easily, then, by the author's use of exactly the right tone.

We will look at four ways in which author Harper Lee creates tone and mood:

1 ♦ Tone and mood are changed to make the story more entertaining and lifelike.

2 ♦ Setting is used to convey tone and mood.

3 ♦ Tone and mood are used to let us know what we should feel about a certain character.

4 ♦ Tone and mood are created by carefully choosing different kinds of language.

1 ◆ Changing Tones and Moods

No one is happy all the time. Everyone has bad moments and good moments. You may be laughing one minute and ready to cry the next. Some part of your day will be exciting. The rest may be boring or neither very good nor very bad. Moods change.

Tones also change. Think of a beautiful forest, for example. By day it might seem peaceful and put you in the mood for a quiet rest beside a stream. But on a pitch-black night, branches seem to reach out like claws, and every sound sends a shiver down your spine. It's the same forest, but a changed tone puts you into an entirely different mood.

Changes in tone and mood occur all the time in a novel. These changes make the book more true to life. They also provide variety in your reading. Often, then, an author will use one kind of tone to emphasize an opposite tone. For example, a serious event will seem more serious to you if something funny has happened just before it.

To Kill a Mockingbird treats some very serious attitudes: hate and prejudice. But Harper Lee has Scout tell the story as an eight-year-old girl would. Events in the story can seem more amusing than they would if they were told by an older person. Because Scout is telling the story, the tone often seems naive, or innocent, to us in the same way that small children often seem innocent.

But events in the book often get deadly serious. And at these places, the tone becomes serious, frightening, or even sickening. The author has very clear feelings about what goes on in the story. She lets you know exactly how she feels through changes in tone.

Notice how tone and mood change from funny to quiet to something more serious in these passages. In the first example, Scout makes a late appearance onstage in her ham costume and ruins Mrs. Merriweather's pageant.

> I must have heard her in my sleep, or the band playing *Dixie* woke me, but it was when Mrs. Merriweather triumphantly mounted the stage with the state flag that I chose to make my entrance. . . .
> They told me later that Judge Taylor went out behind the auditorium and stood there slapping his knees so hard Mrs. Taylor brought him a glass of water and one of his pills.

Scout has fallen asleep and missed her cue. The "ham" appears late, just when the program is most dramatic. The audience collapses in laughter and for a moment Scout thinks she is the hit of the evening—which in one way she is. The author has created a light, humorous tone for this scene. The audience is having a good time and readers are provided with a good chuckle. Everyone is in a good mood at this point. But the tone changes as Jem and Scout start home across the dark schoolyard.

> It was still black dark. The remaining cars were parked on the other side of the building, and their headlights were little help. . . . "Here Scout, let me hold onto your—hock. You might lose you balance."
> "I can see all right."
> . . . I felt a slight pressure on my head, and assumed that Jem had grabbed the end of the ham. "You got me?"
> "Uh huh."

This is a quieter tone. There is still a hint of the humor of the previous scene: Jem has to grab Scout's "hock." But it's dark now. And there is always a more somber tone in darkness. Then the tone changes once more.

> I felt his fingers press the top of my costume, too hard, it seemed. I shook my head. "Jem, you don't hafta—"
> "Hush a minute, Scout," he said, pinching me. . . .
> "Thought I heard something," he said. "Stop a minute."
> We stopped.
> "Hear anything?" he asked.
> "No."
> We had not gone five paces before he made me stop again.
> "Jem, are you tryin' to scare me? You know I'm too old—"
> "Be quiet," he said, and I knew he was not joking.

The tone is now tense and threatening. What is the mood of the children? Plainly they are frightened. Readers become tense and expectant. Perhaps this is another one of Cecil Jacobs' Halloween pranks. But somehow, from the tone of things, you get the feeling that this time it's something more serious. In the space of a little more than a page, the author has changed the tone three times. The moods of characters and readers also change.

1 ✦ Exercise A

Read the following passage and answer the questions about it using what you have learned in this part of the lesson. Use your writing notebook or a separate piece of paper for your answers.

> "Sit down, Mr. Finch," he [Sheriff Tate] said pleasantly.
> Atticus said, "Let's all sit down. Have that chair, Heck. I'll get another one from the livingroom." . . .
> "Mr. Finch," said Mr. Tate, "tell you what I found. I found a little girl's dress—it's out there in my car. That your dress, Scout?"
> "Yes sir, if it's a pink one with smockin'," I said. Mr. Tate was behaving as if he were on the witness stand. He liked to tell things his own way . . . and sometimes it took him a while. . . .
> Mr. Tate ran his hands down his thighs. He rubbed his left arm and investigated Jem's mantelpiece. . . . His fingers sought his long nose.
> "What is it, Heck?" said Atticus.
> Mr. Tate found his neck and rubbed it. "Bob Ewell's lyin' on the ground under that tree down yonder with a kitchen knife stuck up under his ribs. He's dead, Mr. Finch."

1. A short sentence in the passage tells you that Atticus Finch has caught Sheriff Tate's somber mood and realizes that something is very wrong. Write the short sentence and explain how Atticus's mood has changed.

2. What body language does the author describe that tells you Sheriff Tate is nervous and upset? Think of people you know. How can you tell their mood just by looking at them and reading their body language?

Now check your answers using the suggestions in the Answer Key starting on page 451. Review this part of the lesson if you don't understand why your answer was wrong.

1♦Writing on Your Own

In the writing exercise Creating Tone and Mood in a Story on page 138 you experimented with creating different tones and moods. Then you wrote about two people who are having a conversation. Now do the following:

1. Write another version of the conversation and change the tone and mood. You may want to use the sentence you worked on and include it in your dialogue. For example, if one person says, "You have to see that movie," vary the tone. If it was said cheerfully, you may want your character to say it sarcastically. That change in tone will also change the overall mood.

2. After you have finished your writing, answer these questions:

   ◆ How are the tone and mood different from the first conversation?

   ◆ What did you do to make the tone and mood different?

3. You may want to rewrite your conversation several times until you are satisfied with the tone and mood.

2 ◆ Tone, Mood, and Setting

Early in the lesson it was pointed out that different places have a certain tone about them. A church, a ball park, a funeral home—each has its own tone and creates its own mood in people. In describing a setting, authors try to do more than just tell you what the place looks like. They try to give you a sense of the tone of the place. Once you feel the tone of the story, you know how the author feels, how the characters must feel, and how you, as a reader, are supposed to feel. The author has established the mood.

If setting a scene were just a matter of describing the time and place, Harper Lee could have done something like this:

> Time: October
> Place: The schoolyard behind the Radley house. You can
>   see a single street light.
> Characters: Enter Jem and Scout

But the author does much more than give you a time, place, and character names. She establishes a tone in the beginning of the chapter. From the tone, you catch the mood of the characters. And you are ready for what happens as the story moves along.

> The weather was unusually warm for the last day of October. We didn't even need jackets. The wind was growing stronger, and Jem said it might be raining before we got home. There was no moon.
>
> The street light on the corner cast sharp shadows on the Radley house. I heard Jem laugh softly. "Bet nobody bothers them tonight," he said. . . .
>
> "It is a scary place though, ain't it?" I said. "Boo doesn't mean anybody any harm, but I'm right glad you're along."
>
> "You know Atticus wouldn't let you go to the schoolhouse by yourself," Jem said.
>
> "Don't see why, it's just around the corner and across the yard."
>
> "That yard's a mighty long place for little girls to cross at night," Jem teased. "Ain't you scared of haints?"
>
> We laughed. Haints, Hot Steams, incantations, secret signs, had vanished with our years as mist with sunrise.

It is the last day of October—Halloween. Though it is still warm in Alabama, it is a windy night. Windy nights are always a bit scary, especially when there in no moon. It is dark, and rain is threatening. The single street light is making sharp shadows on the Radley house. This place is frightening for children even in daytime. But the children are too old to believe in ghosts (haints). Jem is joking and teasing.

The whole passage creates an uneasy feeling. There is nothing frightening—yet. But you can't help feeling that maybe something *might* happen. And of course the author has set the scene up that way to prepare you for what will happen at the end of the chapter. Harper Lee will return to this tone later and develop it into something terrifying.

But before that happens, there are several other scenes, each with its own tone and mood. Read the passage in Exercise B that describes events just before the pageant begins.

2 ◆ Exercise B

Read the following passage and answer the questions about it using what you have learned in this part of the lesson. Use your writing notebook or a separate piece of paper for your answers.

> The auditorium was filling with people; the Maycomb County High School band had assembled in front below the stage; the stage footlights were on and the red velvet curtain rippled and billowed from the scurrying going on behind it.
>
> Backstage, Cecil and I found the narrow hallway teeming with people. . . . Children dressed as various agricultural enterprises crowded around the one small window.
>
> "Somebody's mashed my costume," I wailed in dismay. Mrs. Merriweather galloped to me, reshaped the chicken wire, and thrust me inside.

1. Pick out at least two phrases from this setting that give the impression of crowding and confusion. What mood has the author created with this scene?

2. How is Mrs. Merriweather affected by this setting? What gives this

scene in the story a true-to-life feeling? You have probably been in a setting like this one yourself—a program in the school auditorium or a play you may have been in. How did you feel?

Now check your answers using the suggestions in the Answer Key starting on page 451. Review this part of the lesson if you don't understand why your answer was wrong.

2♦Writing on Your Own

1. Part of developing tone and mood is creating a setting that reflects or adds to the feelings of the characters. In a paragraph describe a setting in which the tone provides readers with one of the following feelings (or choose any other feeling you want to describe):

   ☐ excitement

   ☐ horror

   ☐ sentimentality

   ☐ disappointment

2. Now describe a setting in which the feeling is the *opposite* of what you have created above. Here are a few examples of opposite emotions: excitement/boredom, horror/calm, sentimentality/cold-heartedness, disappointment/satisfaction or pleasure.

3. You may want to change and rewrite your two paragraphs until you are satisfied with the tone of each.

3 ◆ Tone, Mood, and Character

You can usually tell what an author thinks of a character by the tone that is used whenever that character appears. The author likes Scout. You can be sure something funny or endearing is going to happen when she's around. You like Scout because the author likes Scout. When Atticus is around, the tone is comfortable and secure.

How does the author feel, and how do you feel, about Mrs. Merriweather in these passages?

> The bass drum went boom with every sentence Mrs. Merriweather uttered. She chanted mournfully about Maycomb County being older than the state, that it was a part of Mississippi and Alabama Territories, that the first white man to set foot in the virgin forests was the Probate Judge's great-grandfather five times removed, who was never heard of again. Then came the fearless Colonel Maycomb, for whom the county was named. . . .
>
> Mrs. Merriweather gave a thirty-minute description of Colonel Maycomb's exploits. . . . I sat down, listened to Mrs. Merriweather's drone and the bass drum's boom and was soon fast asleep.

Who wouldn't fall asleep? Mrs. Merriweather is boring. She is long-winded. She is full of her own cleverness and importance. But she is neither clever nor very important. Because of the author's language, you can tell how she feels about Mrs. Merriweather. The reader knows this because of the tone the author creates whenever Mrs. Merriweather appears.

What mood does Mrs. Merriweather inspire in readers and other characters in the story? We snicker at her. We can't wait for an excuse to laugh out loud at her. And that is exactly what Judge Taylor does when Scout marches onstage at the wrong time and breaks up Mrs. Merriweather's performance.

3 ◆ Exercise C

Read the following passages and answer the questions about them using what you have learned in this part of the lesson. Use your writing notebook or a separate piece of paper for your answers.

> I knew Dr. Reynolds's step almost as well as my father's.
> He had brought Jem and me into the world, had led us
> through every childhood disease known to man including
> the time Jem fell out of the treehouse, and he had never lost
> our friendship.

1. By her tone, the author tells us that Dr. Reynolds is a man to be
   trusted. What makes you feel that Dr. Reynolds is well liked and
   respected by Scout and Jem? Explain your answer.

> Dr. Reynolds's step was young and brisk. Mr. Heck
> Tate's was not. His heavy boots punished the porch and
> he opened the door awkwardly, but he said the same
> thing Dr. Reynolds had said when he came in. "You all
> right, Scout?" he added.
> "Yes sir, I'm goin' in to see Jem. Atticus'n'them's in
> there."
> "I'll go with you," said Mr. Tate.

2. Heck Tate's "heavy boots punished the porch." If that were the one
   sentence that described the sheriff, you might feel he was clumsy,
   awkward, and heavy-footed. What follows in the passage that
   makes Sheriff Tate seem like a gentle and caring man?

Now check your answers using the suggestions in the Answer Key
starting on page 451. Review this part of the lesson if you don't
understand why your answer was wrong.

3 ♦ Writing on Your Own

1. Write two short conversations:

   ☐ The characters in the first conversation are you and a good friend.

   ☐ The characters in the second conversation are you and your
   friend's father or mother.

2. Reread and rewrite the conversations until you are satisfied with the
   tone of each.

3. Discuss with your class or a writing partner how the tone of the each conversation is different. Why does a change of characters change the tone of the conversations?

4 ◆ Tone, Mood, and Language

In a conversation you can tell the attitude, or tone, of the speakers from several things. You listen to the words used. Are they harsh or friendly? You watch facial expressions, listen to how the words are spoken, and notice body movements and hand gestures. By watching people and listening to them, you can understand how they feel.

But in a book there are only words. Readers have to imagine the rest. Providing just the right tone through words is one of the arts of expert writing. What the author has to do is select just the right words and put them together in just the right way to achieve a desired effect. Let's look at some examples.

In the last section of the lesson you saw how Mrs. Merriweather was presented as a tiresome bore. Harper Lee didn't say, "She spoke sadly." The words chosen were, "She chanted mournfully." From that word choice you can imagine what it was like listening to this lady. Her speech had the tone of a funeral. Even the sentences describing her are long and tiresome—just like the woman herself. By contrast, people weren't just moving around backstage. They were "scurrying." That one word makes you feel the hustle and bustle and confusion.

Words are chosen for their sound and their shades of meaning. "He *raced*" sounds faster than "he *ran*." "The bells *tinkled merrily*" puts you in a different mood from "the bells *rang*." "I heard *the sweet song of the birds*" has a different tone from "the birds *sang*."

It makes a difference, too, if sentences are long or short, straightforward or roundabout. It is much funnier to hear in a long sentence that Judge Taylor slapped his knees and had to take a pill than to be told simply that he laughed heartily. Short sentences are frequently used in action scenes to build suspense and excitement. Long sentences are often used in describing calm, peaceful scenes. Try to see how some of these choices about language are used in the passage in Exercise D.

4 ◆ Exercise D

Read the following passage and answer the questions about it using what you have learned in this part of the lesson. Use your writing notebook or a separate piece of paper for your answers.

Maybe it was the wind rustling the trees. But there wasn't any wind and there weren't any trees except the big oak.

Our company shuffled and dragged his feet, as if wearing heavy shoes. Whoever it was wore thick cotton pants; what I thought were trees rustling was the soft swish of cotton on cotton, wheek, wheek, with every step.

I felt the sand go cold under my feet and I knew we were near the big oak. Jem pressed my head. We stopped and listened.

Shuffle-foot had not stopped with us this time. His trousers swished softly and steadily. Then they stopped. He was running, running toward us with no child's steps.

"Run, Scout! Run! Run!" Jem screamed.

1. In this scene it is very dark. The author sets the tone and mood of the passage by describing sounds. Write down at least two phrases from the passage that describe sounds. Do you think the author's choice of words helps create a threatening tone?

2. What tone do the sounds give this passage? What is the mood of the children? What sounds can you think of that put you in a good mood? a bad mood?

Now check your answers using the suggestions in the Answer Key starting on page 451. Review this part of the lesson if you don't understand why an answer was wrong.

4♦Writing on Your Own

1. Imagine that you are walking in the woods with a young friend or a younger sister or brother.

2. Rewrite the following sentences, choosing words that provide a tone and mood for your walk. The first one has been done for you.

  a. We walked along the path.
     We tread cautiously along the narrow, twisting trail.

  b. There were shadows in the woods.

  c. Branches hung over the path.

d. The path went deep into the woods.

e. My friend spoke to me.

3. Now rewrite each sentence a second time, choosing words that change the tone and mood. For example, your first sentence might now read like this:

a. We walked along the path.
   We ran laughing down the broad, cool, woodland path.

Now go on to Reviewing and Interpreting the Chapter.

Answer these questions without looking back at the selection. Choose the best answer to each question and put an *x* in the box beside it, or write your answer on a separate piece of paper.

Remembering Facts

1. It was October. The weather was
   - ☐ a. very hot and humid.
   - ☐ b. chilly and damp.
   - ☐ c. wet, cold, and windy.
   - ☐ d. warm, with rain threatening.

2. What did Scout and Cecil Jacobs do while waiting for the pageant to begin?
   - ☐ a. They fell asleep behind the stage.
   - ☐ b. They fussed with Mrs. Merriweather.
   - ☐ c. They tried the games and shows.
   - ☐ d. They played in the schoolyard.

Following the Order of Events

3. When did Cecil Jacobs frighten Jem and Scout?
   - ☐ a. as they were crossing the schoolyard
   - ☐ b. while everyone was waiting for the pageant to begin
   - ☐ c. when they were crossing the schoolyard on the way to the pageant
   - ☐ d. just before Jem and Scout were attacked

4. Following the attack, when did Scout arrive at the house?

☐ a. before anyone else did

☐ b. after Jem and the man carrying him

☐ c. at the same time as Dr. Reynolds

☐ d. before Dr. Reynolds but after Heck Tate

Understanding
Word Choices

5. "We had slowed to a cautious gait, and were feeling our way forward so as not to bump into the tree." The word *gait* means

☐ a. crawl.

☐ b. gallop.

☐ c. dance.

☐ d. manner of walking.

6. Atticus was a lawyer. "Some of his rural clients would park their long-eared steeds in the backyard." What are *long-eared steeds*?

☐ a. mules

☐ b. cars

☐ c. horses

☐ d. wagons

Understanding
Important Ideas

7. Two people saved Scout from harm. Who were they?

☐ a. Atticus and Heck Tate

☐ b. Jem and the man

☐ c. Jem and Aunt Alexandra

☐ d. Jem and Sheriff Tate

8. When Dr. Reynolds arrived, Scout said: "He also knew that if I was in bad shape, so was Jem." What does that mean?

☐ a. Scout and Jem were always getting injured.

☐ b. When it comes to getting into trouble, Scout and Jem are like twins.

☐ c. Jem wouldn't let Scout get hurt without putting up a good fight.

☐ d. If Scout had been punished for something, Jem had been too.

Understanding Levels of Meaning

9. After the attack was over, Scout says: "It was slowly coming to me that there were now four people under the tree." Who were the four people?

☐ a. Jem, Atticus, Sheriff Tate, Cecil

☐ b. Bob Ewell, Jem, Scout, the man who saved the children

☐ c. Sheriff Tate, Scout, Dr. Reynolds, Atticus

☐ d. Scout, Jem, Bob Ewell, Heck Tate

10. After the attack, Scout felt about with her toes. She "touched trousers, a belt buckle, buttons, *something I could not identify,* a collar, and a face." At the end of the chapter, Sheriff Tate lets us know what the "something" was. It was

☐ a. heavy boots.

☐ b. a large flashlight.

☐ c. a kitchen knife.

☐ d. a hairy fist.

11. Jem's conduct during this chapter was

    ☐ a. childish and panicky.

    ☐ b. foolish and risky.

    ☐ c. cocky and assured.

    ☐ d. frightened but controlled.

12. How did Jem act toward Scout?

    ☐ a. protective

    ☐ b. annoyed

    ☐ c. bossy

    ☐ d. uncaring

13. The children were attacked

    ☐ a. next to the street light.

    ☐ b. near the auditorium.

    ☐ c. near the tree.

    ☐ d. outside the Radley house.

14. Some of the settings in the story represent safety and some represent danger. What two ideas does the author contrast to make us see the difference between the two settings?

    ☐ a. school means safety; schoolyard means danger

    ☐ b. sheriff means safety; Bob Ewell means danger

    ☐ c. light means safety; dark means danger

    ☐ d. home means safety; auditorium means danger

15. How would you say Aunt Alexandra was feeling
when Scout came home?

   ☐ a. She was furious with the children for getting into trouble.

   ☐ b. She was trembling with concern over what
had happened.

   ☐ c. Like Atticus, she was angry but calm.

   ☐ d. She was not alarmed by what had
happened.

16. How did Sheriff Tate seem to feel about finding
Bob Ewell's body?

   ☐ a. He didn't feel very different.

   ☐ b. He was proud of himself.

   ☐ c. He was upset.

   ☐ d. He was calm and relieved.

Now check your answers using the Answer Key starting on page 451. Make no mark for right answers. Correct any wrong answers you may have by putting a check mark (✓) in the box next to the right answer. Count the number of questions you answered correctly and plot the total on the Comprehension Scores graph on page 462.

Next, look at the questions you answered incorrectly. What types of questions were they? Count the number you got wrong of each type and enter the numbers in the spaces below.

Remembering Facts   _____

Following the Order of Events   _____

Understanding Word Choices   _____

Understanding Important Ideas   _____

Understanding Levels of Meaning   _____

Understanding Character   _____

Understanding Setting   _____

Understanding Feelings   _____

Now use these numbers to fill in the Comprehension Skills Profile on page 463.

Discussion Guides

The questions below will help you think about the selection and the lesson you have just read. If you don't discuss these questions in class, try to think about them or discuss them with your classmates. Perhaps you will want to write a few paragraphs in answer to the questions.

Discussing Tone and Mood

1. Think of yourself as a writer who is working on the novel *To Kill a Mockingbird*. What do you think you have to do to create tones and moods in your story?

2. Tone reflects the author's attitude. Judging from the tone, how do you think Harper Lee feels about Jem?

3. When the sheriff appears, you are told about him directly: "Mr. Heck Tate stood in the doorway. His hat was in his hand, and a flashlight bulged from his pants pocket. He was in his working clothes." This description sets a serious tone for the sheriff's visit. How does it put you in a mood to expect trouble?

Discussing the Chapter

4. Describe a time when you were in a play or a pageant. How was it like the pageant that Scout was in?

5. Jem, Scout, and other people were nervous about the Radley house. Most people know a place that makes them nervous. Tell about a place that seems scary or unnerving to you.

6. Bob Ewell was an evil man. He attacked the children in darkness and someone killed him. It was not legal to kill Bob Ewell. Was it right or wrong? Is there ever a difference between what is legal and what is right? Should there be a difference? Explain your opinions.

Discussing the Author's Work

7. The author tells the story thinking back to the time when she was eight. Find passages that sound as if they were told by an eight-year-old. Find other passages that sound as if they were told by an adult. What is it that makes one passage sound childish and the other adultlike?

8. *To Kill a Mockingbird* is written in the first-person point of view.

Scout is a character in the story and she looks back at her childhood and tells the story as she experienced or understood it. The author has Scout use the "I" vantage point to tell what happens. Several of the stories in this text are also written in the first-person point of view. *Summer of My German Soldier* (Unit 1) is one. How are the two stories alike or different? How would the stories be different if they were told from a third-person point of view?

9. Harper Lee makes fun of the "glorious" history of Maycomb County. Find a place in the chapter where she does that. Explain how she makes fun while appearing to be serious.

Writing Exercise

Read <u>all</u> the instructions before you begin writing. If you have any questions about how to begin the writing assignment, review Using the Writing Process beginning on page 439, or confer with your writing coach.

1. At the beginning of the unit you were asked to say the sentence, "You have to see that movie" in different ways so that the tone changed each time. If you haven't done that yet, read the directions for Creating Tone and Mood in a Story on page 138, and do that exercise now.

2. Choose one of the sentences you used for Creating Tone and Mood in a Story as a title for your short story. For example, if you used the sentence, "Yes, I like you," that would become the title of your story.

    Create a tone for your story that lets readers know exactly how they should feel about the character and the words that character speaks. Keep these ideas in mind when you write your story:

    ☐ character   ☐ setting   ☐ situation   ☐ language

    All these elements combine to create tone and mood. Will these elements combine to make your character sarcastic, tender, sweet, harsh?

3. Write, revise, correct, and rewrite your story until you are satisfied with the tone and mood it creates.

Unit 5   Theme

The Westing Game
BY ELLEN RASKIN

About the Illustration

What do you think the people in the illustration are talking about? Point out some of the details in the drawing to support your response.

Here are some questions to help you think about the chapter:

◆ What is the man pointing to?

◆ Do you think the house on the hill will figure in the story?

◆ What is the expression on the girl's face?

Unit 5

Introduction

About the Novel

Sam Westing, a millionaire businessman, is found dead in his mansion. He leaves behind sixteen heirs . . . and a very strange will.

The will asks the heirs to take part in a contest. According to the rules of the contest, the heirs must work in assigned pairs, and each pair receives clues to a puzzle. But what's the point of the puzzle? Is it to win the inheritance? Or is it something more?

As the heirs race to solve the puzzle, they learn some interesting secrets about one another. And they also begin to suspect that one of them has murdered Samuel Westing. But which one?

The selection you will read includes the first three chapters from *The Westing Game*. And once you read these chapters, you'll want to finish the rest of the book. The novel is a murder mystery, but it's also a game. Author Ellen Raskin includes all the clues, and it's up to you to solve the puzzle before the characters do.

Ellen Raskin was born in Milwaukee, Wisconsin, in 1928. She grew up during the Depression, a time when many people struggled hard to make ends meet. But Raskin didn't let money troubles make her angry or depressed. She later said, "Those were hard times, the Depression years; they made me a humorist. Just about anything is funny after that."

Raskin attended the University of Wisconsin planning to major in journalism. But she soon switched to fine arts and concentrated on sculpture and painting. After she graduated, she moved to New York City to look for a job. Before long, she was working as an illustrator, drawing thousands of pictures and designing many book jackets.

Raskin's illustrations won awards, but she wasn't comfortable working as an artist. So she decided to try her hand at writing. In 1966 she published her first children's book, *Nothing Ever Happens on My Block.*

Raskin's books were successful right from the start. She tried to write funny, unusual books that caught a reader's attention. She once said, "In their letters to me, kids usually tell me, 'This is the first book I've read all the way through.' I know I reached a certain group of readers. . . . I got who I wanted: the kids who were just like me."

Ellen Raskin died in 1984. But her books continue to be popular with readers of all ages. *The Westing Game,* which won a Newbery Medal, is one of her most famous. If you like that book, you might also want to read *Figgs and Phantoms* and *The Tattooed Potato and Other Clues.*

About the Lesson

This lesson is about theme. In literature, *theme* is the underlying message or meaning of a story. An author often uses a theme to share his or her insights about life.

The theme of a novel is a very important part of the book. Through theme, an author connects the book to real life. He or she uses theme to help you understand problems or ideas that everyone must deal with.

When she wrote *The Westing Game,* Ellen Raskin wanted to create an exciting mystery story. But she also wanted you to think about some important ideas. The following questions will help you focus on the theme of *The Westing Game.* Read the selection carefully and try to answer these questions as you go along:

◆ What do you learn about Sydelle Pulaski from her actions? How do those actions help you understand the theme of the novel?

◆ Why are the characters so different from one another? How does that difference support the novel's theme?

◆ Think about the conversation between Angela, Mrs. Wexler, and Turtle. What does that conversation tell you about the theme?

◆ Which characters do you like? Which characters do you dislike? How do your feelings about the characters relate to the novel's theme?

Developing a Theme

You can understand the importance of theme when you think about ideas in your own writing. Use your writing notebook or a separate piece of paper and try the following suggestions:

1. Choose one of the following ideas for a story, or think of an idea of your own:

   □ You get a part-time job working at a local store. Before long, you notice that one of the clerks is taking money out of the cash register. You know the clerk is very poor.

   □ You go on a camping trip with your family. A bear invades your camp, and your mother shoots and kills it. You later find out that the bear was protecting its cubs.

   □ Your best friend is elected class president. After winning the contest, your friend starts hanging out with the popular kids in class and doesn't answer your phone calls.

2. How do you feel about this situation? How do you feel about the people involved? How do you feel about your own behavior? Make a list of your feelings.

3. Rewrite your list several times until you are satisfied with the ideas.

The Westing Game

by Ellen Raskin

1. SUNSET TOWERS

The sun sets in the west (just about everyone knows that), but Sunset Towers faced east. Strange!

Sunset Towers faced east and had no towers. This glittery, glassy apartment house stood alone on the Lake Michigan shore five stories high. Five empty stories high.

Then one day (it happened to be the Fourth of July), a most uncommon-looking delivery boy rode around town slipping letters under the doors of the chosen tenants-to-be. The letters were signed *Barney Northrup*.

The delivery boy was sixty-two years old, and there was no such person as Barney Northrup.

. . . .

Dear Lucky One:

Here it is—the apartment you've always dreamed of, at a rent you can afford, in the newest, most luxurious building on Lake Michigan:

SUNSET TOWERS

- Picture windows in every room
- Uniformed doorman, maid service
- Central air conditioning, hi-speed elevator
- Exclusive neighborhood, near excellent schools
- Etc., etc.

You have to see it to believe it. But these unbelievably elegant apartments will be shown by appointment only. So hurry, there are only a few left!!! Call me now at 276-7474 for this once-in-a-lifetime offer.

Your servant,
Barney Northrup

P.S. I am also renting ideal space for:
- Doctor's office in lobby
- Coffee shop with entrance from parking lot
- Hi-class restaurant on entire top floor

. . . .

Six letters were delivered, just six. Six appointments were made, and one by one, family by family, talk, talk, talk, Barney Northrup led the tours around and about Sunset Towers.

"Take a look at all that glass. One-way glass," Barney Northrup said. "You can see out, nobody can see in."

Looking up, the Wexlers (the first appointment of the day) were blinded by the blast of morning sun that flashed off the face of the building.

"See those chandeliers? Crystal!" Barney Northrup said, slicking his black moustache and straightening his hand-painted tie in the lobby's mirrored wall. "How about this carpeting? Three inches thick!"

"Gorgeous," Mrs. Wexler replied, clutching her husband's arm as her high heels wobbled in the deep plush pile. She, too, managed an approving glance in the mirror before the elevator door opened.

"You're really in luck," Barney Northrup said. "There's only one apartment left, but you'll love it. It was meant for you." He flung open the door to 3D. "Now, is that breathtaking, or is that breathtaking?"

Mrs. Wexler gasped; it was breathtaking, all right. Two walls of the living room were floor-to-ceiling glass. Following Barney Northrup's lead, she ooh-ed and aah-ed her joyous way through the entire apartment.

Her trailing husband was less enthusiastic. "What's this, a bedroom or a closet?" Jake Wexler asked, peering into the last room.

"It's a bedroom, of course," his wife replied.

"It looks like a closet."

"Oh Jake, this apartment is perfect for us, just perfect," Grace Wexler argued in a whining coo. The third bedroom was a trifle small, but it would do just fine for Turtle. "And think what it means having your office in the lobby, Jake; no more driving to and from work, no more mowing the lawn or shoveling snow."

"Let me remind you," Barney Northrup said, "the rent here is cheaper than what your old house costs in upkeep."

How would he know that, Jake wondered.

Grace stood before the front window where, beyond the road, beyond the trees, Lake Michigan lay calm and glistening. A lake view! Just wait until those so-called friends of hers with their classy houses see this place. The furniture would have to be reupholstered; no, she'd buy new furniture—beige velvet. And she'd have stationery made—blue with a deckle edge, her name and fancy address in swirling type across the top: *Grace Windsor Wexler, Sunset Towers on the Lake Shore.*

Not every tenant-to-be was quite as overjoyed as Grace Windsor Wexler. Arriving in the late afternoon, Sydelle Pulaski looked up and saw only the dim, warped reflections of tree-tops and drifting clouds in the glass face of Sunset Towers.

"You're really in luck," Barney Northrup said for the sixth and last time. "There's only one apartment left, but you'll love it. It was meant for you." He flung open the door to a one-bedroom apartment in the rear. "Now, is that breathtaking or is that breathtaking?"

"Not especially," Sydelle Pulaski replied as she blinked into the rays of the summer sun setting behind the parking lot. She had waited all these years for a place of her own, and here it was, in an elegant building where rich people lived. But she wanted a lake view.

"The front apartments are taken," Barney Northrup said. "Besides, the rent's too steep for a secretary's salary. Believe me, you get the same luxuries here at a third of the price."

At least the view from the side window was pleasant. "Are you sure nobody can see in?" Sydelle Pulaski asked.

"Absolutely," Barney Northrup said, following her suspicious stare to the mansion on the north cliff. "That's just the old Westing house up there; it hasn't been lived in for fifteen years."

"Well, I'll have to think it over."

"I have twenty people begging for this apartment," Barney Northrup said, lying through his buckteeth. "Take it or leave it."

"I'll take it."

Whoever, whatever else he was, Barney Northrup was a good salesman. In one day he had rented all of Sunset Towers to the people whose names were already printed on the mailboxes in an alcove off the lobby:

OFFICE ☐ *Dr. Wexler*
LOBBY ☐ *Theodorakis Coffee Shop*
2C ☐ *F. Baumbach*
2D ☐ *Theodorakis*
3C ☐ *S. Pulaski*
3D ☐ *Wexler*
4C ☐ *Hoo*
4D ☐ *J. J. Ford*
5 ☐ *Shin Hoo's Restaurant*

Who were these people, these specially selected tenants? They were mothers and fathers and children. A dressmaker, a secretary, an inventor, a doctor, a judge. And, oh yes, one was a bookie, one was a burglar, one was a bomber, and one was a mistake. Barney Northrup had rented one of the apartments to the wrong person.

2. GHOSTS' OR WORSE

On September first the chosen ones (and the mistake) moved in. A wired fence had been erected along the north side of the building; on it a sign warned:

NO TRESPASSING—*Property of the Westing estate.*

The newly paved driveway curved sharply and doubled back on itself rather than breach the city-county line. Sunset Towers stood at the far edge of town.

On September second Shin Hoo's Restaurant, specializing in authentic Chinese cuisine, held its grand opening. Only three people came. It was, indeed, an exclusive neighborhood; too exclusive for Mr. Hoo. However, the less expensive coffee shop that opened on the parking lot was kept busy serving breakfast, lunch, and dinner to tenants "ordering up" and to workers from nearby Westingtown.

Sunset Towers was a quiet, well-run building, and (except for the grumbling Mr. Hoo) the people who lived there seemed content. Neighbor greeted neighbor with "Good morning" or "Good evening" or a friendly smile, and grappled with small problems behind closed doors.

The big problems were yet to come.

Now it was the end of October. A cold, raw wind whipped dead leaves about the ankles of the four people grouped in the Sunset Towers driveway, but not one of them shivered. Not yet.

The stocky, broad-shouldered man in the doorman's uniform, standing with feet spread, fists on hips, was Sandy McSouthers. The two slim, trim high-school seniors, shielding their eyes against the stinging chill, were Theo Theodorakis and Doug Hoo. The small, wiry man pointing to the house on the hill was Otis Amber, the sixty-two-year-old delivery boy.

They faced north, gaping like statues cast in the moment of discovery, until Turtle Wexler, her kite tail of a braid flying behind her, raced her bicycle into the driveway. "Look! Look, there's smoke—there's smoke coming from the chimney of the Westing house."

The others had seen it. What did she think they were looking at anyway?

Turtle leaned on the handlebars, panting for breath. (Sunset Towers was near excellent schools, as Barney Northrup had promised, but the junior high was four miles away.) "Do you think—do you think old man Westing's up there?"

"Naw," Otis Amber, the old delivery boy, answered. "Nobody's seen him for years. Supposed to be living on a private island in the South Seas, he is; but most folks say he's dead. Long-gone dead. They say his corpse is still up there in that big old house. They say his body is sprawled out on a fancy Oriental rug, and his flesh is rotting off those mean bones, and maggots are creeping in his eye sockets and crawling out his nose holes." The delivery boy added a high-pitched he-he-he to the gruesome details.

Now someone shivered. It was Turtle.

"Serves him right," Sandy said. At other times a cheery fellow, the doorman often complained bitterly about having been fired from his job of twenty years in the Westing paper mill. "But somebody must be up there. Somebody alive, that is." He pushed back the gold-braided cap and squinted at the house through his steel-framed glasses as if expecting the curling smoke to write the answer in the autumn air. "Maybe it's those kids again. No, it couldn't be."

"What kids?" the three kids wanted to know.

"Why, those two unfortunate fellas from Westingtown."

"What unfortunate fellas?" The three heads twisted from the doorman to the delivery boy. Doug Hoo ducked Turtle's whizzing braid. Touch her precious pigtail, even by accident, and she'll kick you in the shins, the brat. He couldn't chance an injury to his legs, not with the big meet coming. The track star began to jog in place.

"Horrible, it was horrible," Otis Amber said with a shudder that sent the loose straps of his leather aviator's helmet swinging about his long, thin face. "Come to think of it, it happened exactly one year ago tonight. On Halloween."

"What happened?" Theo Theodorakis asked impatiently. He was late for work in the coffee shop.

"Tell them, Otis," Sandy urged.

The delivery boy stroked the gray stubble on his pointed chin. "Seems it all started with a bet; somebody bet them a dollar they couldn't stay in that spooky house five minutes. One measly buck! The poor kids hardly got through those French doors on this side of the Westing house when they came tearing out like they was being chased by a ghost. Chased by a ghost—or worse."

Or worse? Turtle forgot her throbbing toothache. Theo Theodorakis and Doug Hoo, older and more worldly-wise, exchanged winks but stayed to hear the rest of the story.

"One fella ran out crazy-like, screaming his head off. He never stopped screaming 'til he hit the rocks at the bottom of the cliff. The other fella hasn't said but two words since. Something about purple."

Sandy helped him out. "Purple waves."

Otis Amber nodded sadly. "Yep, that poor fella just sits in the state asylum saying, 'Purple waves, purple waves' over and over again, and his scared eyes keep staring at his hands. You see, when he came running out of the Westing house, his hands was dripping with warm, red blood."

Now all three shivered.

"Poor kid," the doorman said. "All that pain and suffering for a dollar bet."

"Make it two dollars for each minute I stay in there, and you're on," Turtle said.

Someone was spying on the group in the driveway.

From the front window of apartment 2D, fifteen-year-old Chris Theodorakis watched his brother Theo shake hands (it must be a bet) with the skinny, one-pigtailed girl and rush into the lobby. The family coffee shop would be busy now; his brother should have been working the counter half an hour ago. Chris checked the wall clock. Two more hours before Theo would bring up his dinner. Then he would tell him about the limper.

Earlier that afternoon Chris had followed the flight of a purple martin *(Progne subis)* across the field of brambles, through the oaks, but something else caught his eye. Someone (he could not tell if the person was a man or a woman) came out of the shadows on the lawn, unlocked the French doors, and disappeared into the Westing house. Someone with a limp. Minutes later smoke began to rise from the chimney.

Once again Chris turned toward the side window and scanned the house on the cliff. The French doors were closed; heavy drapes hung full against the seventeen windows he had counted so many times.

They didn't need drapes on the special glass windows here in Sunset Towers. He could see out, but nobody could see in. Then why did he sometimes feel that someone was watching him? Who could be watching him? God? If God was watching, then why was he like this?

The binoculars fell to the boy's lap. His head jerked, his body coiled, lashed by violent spasms. Relax, Theo will come soon. Relax, soon the geese will be flying south in a V. Canada goose *(Branta canadensis)*. Relax. Relax and watch the wind tangle the smoke and blow it toward Westingtown.

3. TENANTS IN AND OUT

Upstairs in 3D Angela Wexler stood on a hassock as still and blank-faced as a store-window dummy. Her pale blue eyes stared unblinkingly at the lake.

"Turn dear," said Flora Baumbach, the dressmaker, who lived and worked in a smaller apartment on the second floor.

Angela pivoted in a slow quarter turn. "Oh!"

Startled by the small cry, Flora Baumbach dropped the pin from her pudgy fingers and almost swallowed the three in her mouth.

"Please be careful, Mrs. Baumbach; my Angela has very delicate skin." Grace Windsor Wexler was supervising the fitting of her daughter's wedding dress from the beige velvet couch. Above her hung the two-dozen framed flower prints she had selected and arranged with the greatest of taste and care. She could have been an interior decorator, a good one, too, if it wasn't for the pressing demands of so on and so forth.

"Mrs. Baumbach didn't prick me, mother," Angela said evenly. "I was just surprised to see smoke coming from the Westing house chimney."

Crawling with slow caution on her hands and knees, Flora Baumbach paused in the search for the dropped pin to peer up through her straight gray bangs.

Mrs. Wexler set her coffee cup on the driftwood coffee table and craned her neck for a better view. "We must have new neighbors; I'll have to drive up there with a house-warming gift; they may need some decorating advice."

"Hey, look! There's smoke coming from the Westing house!" Again Turtle was late with the news.

"Oh, it's you." Mrs. Wexler always seemed surprised to see her other daughter, so unlike golden-haired, angel-faced Angela.

Flora Baumbach, about to rise with the found pin, quickly sank down again to protect her sore shin in the shag carpeting. She had pulled Turtle's braid in the lobby yesterday.

"Otis Amber says that old man Westing's stinking corpse is rotting on an Oriental rug."

"My, oh my," Flora Baumbach exclaimed, and Mrs. Wexler clicked her tongue in an irritated "tsk."

Turtle decided not to go on with the horror story. Not that her mother cared if she got killed or ended up a raving lunatic. "Mrs. Baumbach, could you hem my witch's costume? I need it for tonight."

Mrs. Wexler answered. "Can't you see she's busy with Angela's wedding dress? And why must you wear a silly costume like that? Really, Turtle, I don't know why you insist on making yourself ugly."

"It's no sillier than a wedding dress," Turtle snapped back. "Besides, nobody gets married anymore, and if they do, they don't wear silly wedding dresses." She was close to a tantrum. "Besides, who would want to marry that stuck-up-know-it-all-marshmallow-face-doctor-denton . . . ?"

"That's enough of your smart mouth!" Mrs. Wexler leaped up, hand ready to strike; instead she straightened a framed flower print, patted her fashionable honey-blonde hairdo, and sat down again. She had never hit Turtle, but one of these days—besides, a stranger was present. "Doctor Deere is a brilliant young man," she explained for Flora Baumbach's ears. The dressmaker smiled politely. "Angela will soon be Angela Deere; isn't that a precious name?" The dressmaker nodded. "And then we'll have two doctors in the family. Now where do you think you're going?"

Turtle was at the front door. "Downstairs to tell daddy about the smoke coming from the Westing house."

"Come back this instant. You know your father operates in the afternoon; why don't you go to your room and work on stock market reports or whatever you do in there."

"Some room, it's even too small for a closet."

"I'll hem your witch's costume, Turtle," Angela offered.

Mrs. Wexler beamed on her perfect child draped in white. "What an angel."

Crow's clothes were black; her skin, dead white. She looked

severe. Rigid, in fact. Rigid and righteously severe. No one could have guessed that under that stern facade her stomach was doing flip-flops as Doctor Wexler cut out a corn.

Staring down at the fine lines of pink scalp that showed through the podiatrist's thinning light brown hair did nothing to ease her queasiness; so, softly humming a hymn, she settled her gaze on the north window. "Smoke!"

"Watch it!" Jake Wexler almost cut off her little toe along with the corn.

Unaware of the near amputation, the cleaning woman stared at the Westing house.

"If you will just sit back," Jake began, but his patient did not hear him. She must have been a handsome woman at one time, but life had used her harshly. Her faded hair, knotted in a tight bun on the nape of her gaunt neck, glinted gold-red in the light. Her profile was fine, marred only by the jut of her clenched jaw. Well, let's get on with it, Friday was his busy day, he had phone calls to make. "Please sit back, Mrs. Crow. I'm almost finished."

"What?"

Jake gently replaced her foot on the chair's pedestal. "I see you've hurt your shin."

"What?" For an instant their eyes met; then she looked away. A shy creature (or a guilty one), Crow averted her face when she spoke. "Your daughter Turtle kicked me," she muttered, staring once again at the Westing house. "That's what happens when there is no religion in the home. Sandy says Westing's corpse is up there, rotting away on an Oriental rug, but I don't believe it. If he's truly dead, then he's roasting in hell. We are sinners, all."

"What do you mean his corpse is rotting on an Oriental rug, some kind of Persian rug, maybe a Chinese rug." Mr. Hoo joined his son at the glass sidewall of the fifth floor restaurant. "And why were you wasting precious time listening to an overaged delivery boy with an overactive imagination when you should have been studying." It was not a question; Doug's father never asked questions. "Don't shrug at me, go study."

"Sure, dad." Doug jogged off through the kitchen; it was no use arguing that there was no school tomorrow, just track practice. He jogged down the back stairs; no matter what excuse he gave, "Go study," his father would say, "go study." He jogged into the Hoos' rear apartment, stretched out on the bare floor and repeated "Go study" to twenty sit-ups.

Only two customers were expected for the dinner hour (Shin Hoo's Restaurant could seat one hundred). Mr. Hoo slammed the reservations book shut, pressed a hand against the pain in his ample stomach, unwrapped a chocolate bar and devoured it quickly before acid etched another ulcer. Back home again, is he. Well, Westing won't get off so easy this time, not on his life.

A small, delicate woman in a long white apron stood in silence before the restaurant's east window. She stared longingly into the boundless gray distance as if far, far on the other side of Lake Michigan lay China.

Sandy McSouthers saluted as the maroon Mercedes swung around the curved driveway and came to a stop at the entrance. He opened the car door with a ceremony reserved only for Judge J. J. Ford. "Look up there, judge. There's smoke coming from the Westing house."

A tall black woman in a tailored suit, her short-clipped hair touched with gray, slipped out from behind the wheel, handed the car keys to the doorman, and cast a disinterested glance at the house on the hill.

"They say nobody's up there, just the corpse of old man Westing rotting away on an Oriental rug," Sandy reported as he hoisted a full briefcase from the trunk of the car. "Do you believe in ghosts, judge?"

"There is certain to be a more rational explanation."

"You're right, of course, judge." Sandy opened the heavy

glass door and followed on the judge's heels through the lobby. "I was just repeating what Otis Amber said."

"Otis Amber is a stupid man, if not downright mad." J. J. Ford hurried into the elevator. She should not have said that, not her, not the first black, the first woman, to have been elected to a judgeship in the state. She was tired after a trying day, that was it. Or was it? So Sam Westing has come home at last. Well, she could sell the car, take out a bank loan, pay him back—in cash. But would he take it? "Please don't repeat what I said about Otis Amber, Mr. McSouthers."

"Don't worry, judge." The doorman escorted her to the door of apartment 4D. "What you tell me is strictly confidential." And it was. J. J. Ford was the biggest tipper in Sunset Towers.

"I saw someb-b-b . . ." Chris Theodorakis was too excited to stutter out the news to his brother. One arm shot out and twisted up over his head. Dumb arm.

Theo squatted next to the wheelchair. "Listen, Chris, I'll tell you about that haunted castle on the hill." His voice was soothing and hushed in mystery. "Somebody is up there, Chris, but nobody is there, just rich Mr. Westing, and he's dead. Dead as a squashed June bug and rotting away on a moth-eaten Oriental rug."

Chris relaxed as he always did when his brother told him a story. Theo was good at making up stories.

"And the worms are crawling in and out of the dead man's skull, in and out of his ear holes, his nose holes, his mouth holes, in and out of all his holes."

Chris laughed, then quickly composed his face. He was supposed to look scared.

Theo leaned closer. "And high above the putrid corpse a crystal chandelier is tinkling. It tinkles and twinkles, but not one breath of air stirs in that gloomy tomb of a room."

Gloomy tomb of a room—Theo will make a good writer someday, Chris thought. He wouldn't spoil this wonderful, spooky Halloween story by telling him about the real person up there, the one with the limp.

So Chris sat quietly, his body at ease, and heard about ghosts and ghouls and purple waves, and smiled at his brother with pure delight.

"A smile that could break your heart," Sydelle Pulaski, the tenant in 3C, always said. But no one paid any attention to Sydelle Pulaski.

Sydelle Pulaski struggled out of the taxi, large end first. She was not a heavy woman, just wide-hipped from years of secretarial sitting. If only there was a ladylike way to get out of a cab. Her green rhinestone-studded glasses slipped down her fleshy nose as she grappled with a tall triangular package and a stuffed shopping bag. If only that lazy driver would lend her a hand.

Not for a nickel tip, he wouldn't. The cabbie slammed the back door and sped around the curved driveway, narrowly missing the Mercedes that Sandy was driving to the parking lot.

At least the never-there-when-you-need-him doorman had propped open the front door. Not that he ever helped her, or noticed her, for that matter.

No one ever noticed. Sydelle Pulaski limped through the lobby. She could be carrying a high-powered rifle in that package and no one would notice. She had moved to Sunset Towers hoping to meet elegant people, but no one had invited her in for so much as tea. No one paid any attention to her, except that poor crippled boy whose smile could break your heart, and that bratty kid with the braid—she'll be sorry she kicked her in the shin.

Juggling her load, earrings jingling and charm bracelet jangling, Sydelle Pulaski unlocked the several locks to apartment 3C and bolted the door behind her. There'd be fewer burglaries around here if people listened to her about putting in dead-bolt locks. But nobody listened. Nobody cared.

On the plastic-covered dining table she set out the contents of the shopping bag: six cans of enamel, paint thinner, and brushes. She unwrapped the long package and leaned four wooden crutches against the wall. The sun was setting over the parking lot, but Sydelle Pulaski did not look out her back window. From the side window smoke could be seen rising from the Westing house, but Sydelle Pulaski did not notice.

"No one ever notices Sydelle Pulaski," she muttered, "but now they will. Now they will."

Theme

Authors write books to express ideas. Sometimes the ideas are stated directly, and they are easy to find in the text. For example, a nonfiction book about astronomy might get you to think about the relationship between planets, stars, and other objects in space. That relationship is the theme of the book. The author explains the theme by using examples—solar systems, star clusters, and galaxies. Those examples all support the theme of the book.

But a novel is different. An author can't directly say, "The theme of this story is greed." Such a statement would interrupt the action, and it would make the story seem heavy and dull. So instead the author must *suggest* the themes. He or she must let them emerge as part of the story.

A novel usually has several themes. A major theme is one of the most important ideas in the story. The author emphasizes a major theme over and over again. Minor themes are ideas that are less important. The author may emphasize them now and again, but they are not a key part of the book.

In *The Westing Game* author Ellen Raskin asks you to think about people. What judgments do we make about people who are different from us? What roles do we expect certain kinds of people to play? Those ideas are major themes of the novel. And along the way, Raskin adds some minor themes that tell us more about individual people.

The theme of a novel can be expressed in several ways. In this lesson we will look at four ways in which Ellen Raskin expresses the theme of *The Westing Game*:

1 ◆ She uses action and the events in the story to suggest themes.

2 ◆ She uses the characters to point out themes.

3 ◆ She includes thoughts and conversations that tell you more about themes.

4 ◆ She emphasizes themes by controlling the way you feel.

1 ◆ Theme and Action

People often express their ideas and feelings through their actions. For example, a hug expresses love and affection. Starting an argument expresses anger or frustration.

Novels also express ideas and feelings through action. Authors carefully choose actions and events that express important ideas. What theme does Ellen Raskin emphasize in the following paragraph? How do Sydelle Pulaski's actions help you understand that theme?

> Juggling her load, earrings jingling and charm bracelet jangling, Sydelle Pulaski unlocked the several locks to apartment 3C and bolted the door behind her. There'd be fewer burglaries around here if people listened to her about putting in dead-bolt locks. But nobody listened. Nobody cared.
>
> On the plastic-covered dining table she set out the contents of the shopping bag: six cans of enamel, paint thinner, and brushes. She unwrapped the long package and leaned four wooden crutches against the wall. The sun was setting over the parking lot, but Sydelle did not look out her back window. From the side window smoke could be seen rising from the Westing house, but Sydelle did not notice.
>
> "No one ever notices Sydelle Pulaski," she muttered, "but now they will. Now they will."

You learn one very important point from Sydelle's actions—she wants attention. She is hurt that no one cares about her, and she seems determined to change their feelings. But at the same time, the author makes it clear that Sydelle doesn't notice what's going on around her. She doesn't pay any attention to the smoke rising from the Westing house.

What important ideas have you learned from the paragraph? You've learned that people want to be liked and appreciated. But you've also learned that people can sometimes think too much about themselves. Those ideas help to express the theme of *The Westing Game.*

1♦Exercise A

Read the following passage and answer the questions about it using what you have learned in this part of the lesson. Use your writing notebook or a separate piece of paper for your answers.

> Sandy McSouthers saluted as the maroon Mercedes swung around the curved driveway and came to a stop at the entrance. He opened the car door with a ceremony reserved only for Judge J. J. Ford. "Look up there, judge. There's smoke coming from the Westing house."
>
> A tall black woman in a tailored suit, her short-clipped hair touched with gray, slipped out from behind the wheel, handed the car keys to the doorman, and cast a disinterested glance at the house on the hill.
>
> "They say nobody's up there, just the corpse of old man Westing rotting away on an Oriental rug," Sandy reported as he hoisted a full briefcase from the trunk of the car. "Do you believe in ghosts, judge?"
>
> "There is certain to be a more rational explanation."
>
> "You're right, of course, judge." Sandy opened the heavy glass door and followed on the judge's heels through the lobby.

1. How does Sandy behave toward Judge Ford? How does Judge Ford behave toward Sandy?

2. What is the author asking you to think about in this passage? What do you learn about the way certain people relate to each other?

Now check your answers using the suggestions in the Answer Key starting on page 451. Review this part of the lesson if you don't understand why an answer was wrong.

1♦Writing on Your Own

Look at the list you wrote for Developing a Theme on page 185. Now do the following:

1. Think about the action in your story (stealing money, shooting the

bear, or being ignored). How do you feel when that action takes place? Why?

2. Write a paragraph or two that shows the action taking place in your story. As you show the action, try to let the reader know how you feel about the event. Here's an example:

> Grandpa broke two eggs on the edge of the frying pan and dropped them into the sizzling oil. As he carried the carton back to the refrigerator, I noticed that his hands were shaking. My heart sank.
>
> "Grandpa, are you sure you feel OK?" I asked. I couldn't stand to watch his hands shake. It made me feel sad and sick inside.
>
> He laughed a little and pretended he didn't know what I was talking about.

3. You may want to change and rewrite your paragraphs several times until you are satisfied with the action and the theme.

2 ◆ Theme and Character

You may know someone who is mean and stingy. Perhaps that person is so stingy that whenever you think of stinginess, you think of that person.

In Charles Dickens's book *A Christmas Carol,* there is a mean, stingy character named Scrooge. Through Scrooge's character, Dickens presents the theme of his book—greed and meanness. Dickens did such a good job that, for many people, the name Scrooge now stands for greed and meanness.

You've probably read stories where a character was linked with good or evil. Maybe you've read a book in which an animal character stood for love and faithfulness. The authors of those books used the characters to discuss themes. Perhaps the theme of one story was the triumph of good over evil. Perhaps another one pointed out the value of love and loyalty.

What do you learn from the description of the character in the following passage?

> Crow's clothes were black; her skin, dead white. She looked severe. Rigid, in fact. Rigid and righteously severe. No one could have guessed that under that stern facade her stomach was doing flip-flops as Doctor Wexler cut out a corn.
> . . . "If you will just sit back," Jake began, but his patient did not hear him. She must have been a handsome woman at one time, but life had used her harshly. Her faded hair, knotted in a tight bun on the nape of her gaunt neck, glinted red-gold in the light. Her profile was fine, marred only by the jut of her clenched jaw.

You learn that Crow dresses in dark, severe clothes. She's not very attractive now, but she might have been once. She pretends to be stern, but underneath she is nervous and scared.

In fact, you learn that Crow is not the person that she appears to be on the surface. The description of Crow supports Raskin's theme. The author wants you to remember that people are individual and unique. We shouldn't judge them by the way they look or behave.

2 ◆ Exercise B

Read the following passage and answer the questions about it using what you have learned in this part of the lesson. Use your writing notebook or a separate piece of paper for your answers.

> Only two customers were expected for the dinner hour (Shin Hoo's Restaurant could seat one hundred). Mr. Hoo slammed the reservations book shut, pressed a hand against the pain in his ample stomach, unwrapped a chocolate bar and devoured it quickly before acid etched another ulcer. Back home again, is he. Well, Westing won't get off so easy this time, not on his life.
>
> A small, delicate woman in a long white apron stood in silence before the restaurant's east window. She stared longingly into the boundless gray distance as if far, far on the other side of Lake Michigan lay China.

1. What do you learn about Mr. Hoo in this passage? What kind of person is he?

2. The woman is Mr. Hoo's wife. How is her character different from Mr. Hoo's? How does that difference support the theme?

Now check your answers using the suggestions in the Answer Key starting on page 451. Review this part of the lesson if you don't understand why an answer was wrong.

2 ◆ Writing on Your Own

Look at the list you wrote for Developing a Theme on page 185. Now do the following:

1. How would you describe the main character of your story (the clerk, your mother, or your best friend)? What words or phrases come to mind? Do those words also express your own feelings about the character?

2. Write a paragraph or two describing the main character of your story. Try to let your reader know how you feel about the character. Here's an example:

> Grandpa was tall and thin, with a thick white mustache that hung down over the sides of his mouth. He'd worked in the steel mill all his life, and his arms were veined with scars and burns from the hot steel. He'd always been a strong man. But now, after the operation, he shuffled a little, as if he couldn't quite find the floor beneath his feet. He pretended that nothing was wrong. But he knew—and I knew—that this might be our last summer together.

3. You may want to change and rewrite your paragraph several times until you are satisfied with your character.

3 ◆ Themes, Thoughts, and Conversations

A careful writer has a good reason for including each detail in a novel. The author makes sure that the book contains no wasted information. Every action or description moves the story along, explains a character, or develops a theme.

Thoughts and conversations work in the same way. Author Ellen Raskin uses them to advance the plot, but she also uses them to discuss the theme. What do you learn about the novel's theme from Grace Wexler's thoughts?

> Grace stood before the front window where, beyond the road, beyond the trees, Lake Michigan lay calm and glistening. A lake view! Just wait until those so-called friends of hers with their classy houses see this place. The furniture would have to be reupholstered; no, she'd buy new furniture—beige velvet. And she'd have stationery made—blue with a deckle edge, her name and fancy address in swirling type across the top: *Grace Windsor Wexler, Sunset Towers on the Lake Shore.*

Mrs. Wexler is very proud of her new apartment. But why? She's proud because she thinks it will impress her friends. All her plans—showing off the view, buying new furniture, choosing her stationery—have to do with making herself appear rich and important.

The author uses Mrs. Wexler's thoughts to support the novel's theme. Those thoughts tell us that Mrs. Wexler cares about appearances. She thinks that the way things look is more important than the way they really are. Appearances versus reality is an important theme of the novel. As the author keeps reminding us, we shouldn't make judgments that are based on appearance.

3 ◆ Exercise C

Read the following passage and answer the questions about it using what you have learned in this part of the lesson. Use your writing notebook or a separate piece of paper for your answers.

"Please be careful, Mrs. Baumbach; my Angela has very

delicate skin." Grace Windsor Wexler was supervising the fitting of her daughter's wedding dress from the beige velvet couch. . . .

"Mrs. Baumbach didn't prick me, mother," Angela said evenly. "I was just surprised to see smoke coming from the Westing house chimney." . . .

Mrs. Wexler set her coffee cup on the driftwood coffee table and craned her neck for a better view. "We must have new neighbors; I'll have to drive up there with a house-warming gift; they may need some decorating advice."

"Hey, look! There's smoke coming from the Westing house!" Again Turtle was late with the news.

"Oh, it's you." Mrs. Wexler always seemed surprised to see her other daughter, so unlike golden-haired, angel-faced Angela.

1. How does Mrs. Wexler feel about her daughters? What clues can you find in this conversation?

2. How does the conversation support the theme of the novel?

Now check your answers using the suggestions in the Answer Key starting on page 451. Review this part of the lesson if you don't understand why an answer was wrong.

3 ◆ Writing on Your Own

Look at the list you wrote for Developing a Theme on page 185. Now do the following.

1. Imagine a conversation between yourself and the main character of your story (the clerk, your mother, or your best friend). How can you use that conversation to show your feelings about the event the character was involved in?

2. Write a dialogue between yourself and your main character. Try to let your reader understand how you are feeling about the character and the situation. Here's an example:

> "Kid," said Grandpa, "you worry too much. It must be

from your father's side. *My* family never worried like that."

"Grandpa, I'm not just worrying." I tried to sound serious and grown up. "You have to stop pretending you're twenty-five. You're not. You're eighty-five. And you're sick."

He looked at me and then looked away. "No one asked your opinion," he said, but his voice wasn't angry. It was just quiet.

"Oh, Grandpa," I said. I felt the tears rising, and I couldn't say anything more.

3. You may want to change and rewrite your dialogue several times until you are satisfied with it.

4 ◆ Themes and Feelings

Writers use theme to teach us a lesson about life. So they guide our feelings as we read to make sure we understand that lesson.

Ellen Raskin wants us to think about different kinds of people. She wants us to understand that we can't always judge them by the way they look or behave. She reminds us that each person is an individual.

But the lesson the author teaches wouldn't be very effective if she didn't guide our feelings. How does the author control the way you feel about Chris Theodorakis in the following passage?

> They didn't need drapes on the special glass windows here in Sunset Towers. He [Chris] could see out, but nobody could see in. Then why did he sometimes feel that someone was watching him? Who could be watching him? God? If God was watching, then why was he like this?
>
> The binoculars fell to the boy's lap. His head jerked, his body coiled, lashed by violent spasms. Relax, Theo will come soon. Relax, soon the geese will be flying south in a V. Canada goose *(Branta canadensis)*. Relax. Relax and watch the wind tangle the smoke and blow it toward Westingtown.

The author wants you to sympathize with Chris. She wants you to understand how hard it is to live with a disability. By guiding your feelings about Chris, she reminds you not to judge a person by the way he or she looks. She uses your feelings about Chris to reinforce the theme of the novel.

4 ◆ Exercise D

Read the following passage and answer the questions about it using what you have learned in this part of the lesson. Use your writing notebook or a separate piece of paper for your answers.

> [Barney Northrup is showing an apartment to the Wexlers.]
>
> "Gorgeous," Mrs. Wexler replied, clutching her husband's arm as her high heels wobbled in the deep plush pile. She,

too, managed an approving glance in the mirror before the elevator door opened.

"You're really in luck," Barney Northrup said. "There's only one apartment left, but you'll love it. It was meant for you." He flung open the door to 3D. "Now, is that breathtaking, or is that breathtaking?"

Mrs. Wexler gasped; it was breathtaking, all right. . . . Following Barney Northrup's lead, she ooh-ed and aah-ed her joyous way through the entire apartment. . . .

"Oh, Jake, this apartment is perfect for us, just perfect," Grace Wexler argued in a whining coo.

1. How does the author want you to feel about Grace Wexler? How can you tell?

2. How does the passage support the theme of the novel?

Now check your answers using the suggestions in the Answer Key starting on page 451. Review this part of the lesson if you don't understand why an answer was wrong.

4♦Writing on Your Own

Look at the list you wrote for Developing a Theme on page 185. Now do the following:

1. Reread the paragraphs you wrote for the three Writing on Your Own exercises in this lesson. What feelings do those paragraphs express? How do you feel about the character? How do you feel about the character's actions?

2. What can you learn from those feelings? What ideas do they express? What lessons do they teach about yourself or other people? In other words, what is the theme?

3. In a sentence or two, write the theme or themes you have explored in your writing exercises.

Now go on to Reviewing and Interpreting the Chapter.

Reviewing and Interpreting the Chapter

Answer these questions without looking back at the selection. Choose the best answer to each question and put an *x* in the box beside it, or write your answer on a separate piece of paper.

Remembering Facts

1. The sun sets in the west, but Sunset Towers faces
   - ☐ a. west.
   - ☐ b. south.
   - ☐ c. east.
   - ☐ d. north.

2. Who shows the apartments to the new tenants?
   - ☐ a. Otis Amber
   - ☐ b. Barney Northrup
   - ☐ c. Sandy McSouthers
   - ☐ d. Turtle Wexler

Following the Order of Events

3. Turtle arrives on her bike
   - ☐ a. after Doug and Theo see the smoke.
   - ☐ b. before she meets her neighbors.
   - ☐ c. at the same time as Doug.
   - ☐ d. before she moves into the apartment.

4. When people pull Turtle's braid, she

    ☐ a. laughs.

    ☐ b. bursts into tears.

    ☐ c. kicks them.

    ☐ d. starts an argument.

Understanding
Word Choices

5. "A shy creature (or a guilty one), Crow <u>averted</u> her face when she spoke." The word *averted* suggests that Crow

    ☐ a. looked straight ahead.

    ☐ b. smiled and laughed.

    ☐ c. looked annoyed.

    ☐ d. looked away.

6. Sydelle Pulaski's glasses "slipped down her fleshy nose as she <u>grappled</u> with a tall triangular package and a stuffed shopping bag." *Grappled* means

    ☐ a. struggled.

    ☐ b. whistled.

    ☐ c. stole.

    ☐ d. broke.

Understanding
Important Ideas

7. In *The Westing Game,* the characters are

    ☐ a. all murderers.

    ☐ b. not what they appear to be.

    ☐ c. predictable and dull.

    ☐ d. exactly the same as each other.

8. The characters in this novel

   □ a. don't seem to know very much about each other.

   □ b. seem like a close, happy family.

   □ c. are not interested in the Westing fortune.

   □ d. have lived in Sunset Towers for many years.

Understanding
Levels of
Meaning

9. You can probably guess that Angela is

   □ a. not an important character in the story.

   □ b. really a statue.

   □ c. not related to Mrs. Wexler.

   □ d. more interesting than she appears.

10. Sydelle Pulaski

   □ a. will probably move out of the building.

   □ b. could not have murdered Samuel Westing.

   □ c. has a plan to get people to notice her.

   □ d. is actually the doorman in disguise.

Understanding
Character

11. Which word best describes Mrs. Wexler?

   □ a. shy

   □ b. vain

   □ c. depressed

   □ d. intelligent

12. Turtle Wexler is
    - ☐ a. sweet, pretty, and kind.
    - ☐ b. quiet but friendly.
    - ☐ c. smart and annoying.
    - ☐ d. a whiny coward.

Understanding Setting 13. Sunset Towers is located near
    - ☐ a. Shin Hoo's restaurant.
    - ☐ b. the Westing estate.
    - ☐ c. a large field.
    - ☐ d. Lake Ontario.

14. Why did the author choose an apartment house as the setting for her mystery novel?
    - ☐ a. Apartments sometimes have elevators and stores.
    - ☐ b. Many of her readers live in apartment buildings.
    - ☐ c. The story takes place in New York City.
    - ☐ d. She wanted all the characters to live in the same place.

Understanding Feelings 15. When Sydelle Pulaski talks about Chris, she mentions "a smile that could break your heart." In that sentence she lets you know that
    - ☐ a. she doesn't like Chris.
    - ☐ b. Chris is a friendly person.
    - ☐ c. she feels sorry for Chris.
    - ☐ d. Chris feels sorry for himself.

16. How does Judge J. J. Ford feel about Sam Westing's return?

☐ a. excited

☐ b. worried

☐ c. angry

☐ d. indifferent

Now check your answers using the Answer Key starting on page 451. Make no mark for right answers. Correct any wrong answers you may have by putting a check mark (✓) in the box next to the right answer. Count the number of questions you answered correctly and plot the total on the Comprehension Scores graph on page 462.

Next, look at the questions you answered incorrectly. What types of questions were they? Count the number you got wrong of each type and enter the numbers in the spaces below.

Remembering Facts	_____
Following the Order of Events	_____
Understanding Word Choices	_____
Understanding Important Ideas	_____
Understanding Levels of Meaning	_____
Understanding Character	_____
Understanding Setting	_____
Understanding Feelings	_____

Now use these numbers to fill in the Comprehension Skills Profile on page 463.

Discussion Guides

The questions below will help you think about the selection and the lesson you have just read. If you don't discuss these questions in class, try to think about them or discuss them with your classmates. Perhaps you will want to write a few paragraphs in answer to the questions.

Discussing Theme

1. In *The Westing Game,* the author asks you to think about the problems that result when we make judgments based on the way people look or behave. Is that theme related to real life? How?

2. *The Westing Game* is a mystery novel. Do you think the theme (appearance versus reality) is also an important part of the plot? Explain your answer.

3. Later in the novel, the author develops the theme of family relationships. You've already met three families: the Wexlers, the Hoos, and the Theodorakis brothers. How are these families similar? How are they different? What ideas does the author want you to think about?

Discussing the Chapter

4. At the beginning of *The Westing Game,* you meet the character Barney Northrup, who shows apartments to the future tenants of Sunset Towers. But the author says, "There was no such person as Barney Northrup." What does she mean?

5. Why do you think Turtle Wexler is so mean to other people?

6. In the selection you just read, you met almost all the important characters in the novel. Which character do you think will solve the mystery? Why?

Discussing the Author's Work

7. When Raskin was young, she spent much of her time inventing characters. "My sister and I would spend weeks at a time acting out the lives of at least ten characters." How do you think that childhood experience affected *The Westing Game?*

8. Raskin believed that it is "very important for young people who want to write to read." Why do you think reading helps a person write better?

9. During the Depression, Shirley Temple was a popular child actress. Many people loved her dimples and curls, but Ellen Raskin didn't like her at all. Raskin once said, "Now any goody-goody darling that dares enter my books will end up the villain. Or the bomber. Or at least get pimples." Does that statement give you any clue about future events in *The Westing Game*?

Writing Exercise

Read all the instructions before you begin writing. If you have any questions about how to begin the writing assignment, review Using the Writing Process, beginning on page 439, or confer with your writing coach.

1. Choose one of the themes from the following list:

   ☐ selfishness   ☐ kindness

   ☐ bravery   ☐ greed

   ☐ fear   ☐ evil

   ☐ love   ☐ goodness

2. Write a story that deals with your chosen theme. You can base the story on a real event, or you can invent a situation.

   Before you begin working, you may want to look back at the paragraphs you wrote for the four Writing on Your Own exercises in this lesson.

3. Write, revise, correct, and rewrite the story until you are sure you have got it just the way you want it.

Unit 6   Conflict

Of Mice and Men
BY JOHN STEINBECK

About the Illustration

How would you describe the relationship between these two men? Point out some details in the drawing to support your response.

Here are some questions to help you think about the chapter:

◆ How do you know that the man on the left is angry?

◆ What do you think the man on the right is doing? Does he look ashamed? How do you know?

◆ How well do these two men know each other? What makes you think so?

Unit 6

Introduction

About the Novel

Of Mice and Men is about George Milton and Lennie Small, two very different men who travel and work together. They are migrant farm laborers and drifters who move from ranch to ranch in the Salinas Valley area in California.

The novel is set in the mid-1930s. These were Depression years when one-third of the workers in the United States were jobless. Thousands of unemployed people traveled to California in search of work harvesting the fruits and vegetables that grew in abundance there. Jobless and homeless people traveled the highways and rode railroad boxcars from one place to another, going wherever they thought they could find work.

It was a lonely life. At night they might "jungle up," which meant camping with other travelers for protection and company. Often they were looked upon as common tramps, hoboes, or "bindle-bums" as some called them then.

Most of these people dreamed that someday there would be something better for them. Though others thought of them as bums, they did not think of themselves that way. They planned somehow to save enough from their pitiful wages to buy little places of their own. "A little place and a couple of acres" is the way George puts it in the story. Unfortunately, it seldom happened that they could ever get that far ahead. They were doomed to spend their lives in endless poverty and loneliness.

George is pretty good at finding work for himself and Lennie. But their lives are complicated by the fact that Lennie is mentally retarded. The two men are exact opposites. George is small, quick, and shrewd. Lennie is huge, powerful, and slow. But Lennie is also childlike and so timid he wouldn't hurt a fly. Even a hint of violence terrifies him. Since he has no memory, he forgets things and never learns from his mistakes. This forgetfulness and his love of petting soft things get him in trouble constantly. And it is George who has to keep getting Lennie out of trouble. When the chapter you will read opens, George and Lennie have just been forced to leave a town called Weed because of some trouble Lennie got into there. George has to take care of Lennie and keep them both in work.

Why, then, does George stay with Lennie? As you read the chapter, this is the most important question to think about.

Author John Steinbeck (1902–1968) may already be familiar to you. He was born and raised in California's Salinas Valley and many of his best stories are set there. He became famous for his realistic novels about the lives of the poor, oppressed Californian farmers and laborers. His California stories and novels include *The Grapes of Wrath, Tortilla Flat, The Pearl, The Leader of the People,* and *Cannery Row.* Steinbeck was awarded the Pulitzer Prize in 1940 and the Nobel Prize in literature in 1962.

About the Lesson

The lesson that follows the reading selection is about conflict. When you hear the word *conflict,* you probably think of a fight or battle of some sort. This is exactly what conflict is. Only most of the time the worst conflicts are not waged with fists or guns.

Many of life's conflicts involve a struggle to get along with other people. For example, there are conflicts with people at school and on the job. These conflicts are rarely violent, but you are still in a fight to get along and get ahead. And there are also constant struggles you wage to get along with yourself. Sometimes when you try to make decisions, you can feel a conflict in yourself. Should you choose one thing or another? Should you act one way or another? And how do you feel after you have made your choice? Feeling self-doubt or guilt is also a kind of conflict in yourself.

Because of all these conflicts, there is a story that can be told about anyone's life. What makes these stories interesting is seeing how each person acts when facing conflicts. In this lesson you will see how conflict is used in fiction to create a story and move it along.

The questions below will help you focus on conflict in the chapter from *Of Mice and Men*. Read the chapter carefully and try to answer these questions as you go along:

◆ There are different kinds of conflict. Sometimes people fight with other people. Sometimes the struggle is within a person. Can you find examples of both kinds of conflict in the chapter?

◆ Facing a conflict usually means doing something about it. You are moved to action by the conflict. How do George's conflicts make him act?

◆ How a person handles conflict tells you a great deal about that person's character. What do you learn about Lennie and George from the way they handle their conflicts?

◆ Conflict makes the plot or story line of a novel move along so that a story is told; it is central to the novel's story. Conflict also ties all the different actions of a story together. How do Lennie's problems (conflicts) make things happen in the story, and how do they move the story along?

Create Conflict for a Story

Generally, there are four kinds of conflict in life as well as in fiction: conflicts with other people, conflicts with oneself, conflicts with society, and conflicts with nature. Try to think of conflicts you can include in your own story by doing the following:

1. Think of an idea for a story. Write a few sentences that tell what the story will be about.

2. Think of at least two kinds of conflict that may occur in your story. Here's an example of a story idea and possible conflicts:

> The story is about a man, his wife, and their children who are traveling west in a covered wagon. They had been slaves in the South but are now free. Against his wife's wishes, he decides to move the family and start a new life in the West.

   Here are a few suggestions for conflicts in the story:

   ◆ **Conflict between two people:** The woman does not want to leave her home in the South.

   ◆ **Conflict with oneself:** The man wonders if he has done the right thing by moving his family so far from what had been their home.

   ◆ **Conflict with society:** A town where the family tries to settle won't allow black settlers to live there.

   ◆ **Conflict with nature:** Winter will begin very soon, so the family must keep moving. If there are any more delays, they won't be able to get through the mountain passes because of the snow.

3. For each conflict you think of for your story, write a few sentences that describe what the conflict is about.

Of Mice and Men

by John Steinbeck

1

A few miles south of Soledad, the Salinas River drops in close to the hillside bank and runs deep and green. The water is warm too, for it has slipped twinkling over the yellow sands in the sunlight before reaching the narrow pool. On one side of the river the golden foothill slopes curve up to the strong and rocky Gabilan mountains, but on the valley side the water is lined with trees—willows fresh and green with every spring, carrying in their lower leaf junctures the debris of the winter's flooding; add sycamores with mottled, white, recumbent limbs and branches that arch over the pool. On the sandy bank under the trees the leaves lie deep and so crisp that a lizard makes a great skittering if he runs among them. Rabbits come out of the brush to sit on the sand in the evening, and the damp flats are covered with the night tracks of 'coons, and with the spread pads of dogs from the ranches, and with the split-wedge tracks of deer that come to drink in the dark.

There is a path through the willows and among the sycamores, a path beaten hard by boys coming down from the ranches to swim in the deep pool, and beaten hard by tramps who come wearily down from the highway in the evening to jungle-up near water. In front of the low horizontal limb of a giant sycamore there is an ash pile made by many fires; the limb is worn smooth by men who have sat on it.

Evening of a hot day started the little wind to moving among the leaves. The shade climbed up the hills toward the top. On the sand banks the rabbits sat as quietly as little gray, sculptured stones. And then from the direction of the state highway came the sound of footsteps on crisp sycamore leaves. The rabbits hurried noiselessly for cover. A stilted heron labored up into the air and pounded down river. For a moment the place was lifeless, and then two men emerged from the path and came into the opening by the green pool.

They had walked in single file down the path, and even in the open one stayed behind the other. Both were dressed in denim trousers and in denim coats with brass buttons. Both wore black, shapeless hats and both carried tight blanket rolls slung over their shoulders. The first man was small and quick, dark of face, with restless eyes and sharp, strong features. Every part of him was defined: small, strong hands, slender arms, a thin and bony nose. Behind him walked his opposite, a huge man, shapeless of face, with large, pale eyes, with wide, sloping shoulders; and he walked heavily, dragging his feet a little, the way a bear drags his paws. His arms did not swing at his sides, but hung loosely.

The first man stopped short in the clearing, and the follower nearly ran over him. He took off his hat and wiped the sweat-band with his forefinger and snapped the moisture off. His huge companion dropped his blankets and flung himself down and drank from the surface of the green pool; drank with long gulps, snorting into the water like a horse. The small man stepped nervously beside him.

"Lennie!" he said sharply. "Lennie, for God' sakes don't drink so much." Lennie continued to snort into the pool. The small man leaned over and shook him by the shoulder. "Lennie. You gonna be sick like you was last night."

Lennie dipped his whole head under, hat and all, and then he sat up on the bank and his hat dripped down on his blue coat and ran down his back. "Tha's good," he said.

"You drink some, George. You take a good big drink." He smiled happily.

George unslung his bindle and dropped it gently on the bank. "I ain't sure it's good water," he said. "Looks kinda scummy."

Lennie dabbled his big paw in the water and wiggled his fingers so the water arose in little splashes; rings widened across the pool to the other side and came back again. Lennie watched them go. "Look, George. Look what I done."

George knelt beside the pool and drank from his hand with quick scoops. "Tastes all right," he admitted. "Don't really seem to be running, though. You never oughta drink water when it ain't running, Lennie," he said hopelessly. "You'd drink out of a gutter if you was thirsty." He threw a scoop of water into his face and rubbed it about with his hand, under his chin and around the back of his neck. Then he replaced his hat, pushed himself back from the river, drew up his knees and embraced them. Lennie, who had been watching, imitated George exactly. He pushed himself back, drew up his knees, embraced them, looked over to George to see whether he had it just right. He pulled his hat down a little more over his eyes, the way George's hat was.

George stared morosely at the water. The rims of his eyes were red with sun glare. He said angrily, "We could just as well of rode clear to the ranch if that bastard bus driver knew what he was talkin' about. 'Jes' a little stretch down the highway,' he says. 'Jes' a little stretch.' God damn near four miles, that's what it was! Didn't wanta stop at the ranch gate, that's what. Too God damn lazy to pull up. Wonder he isn't too damn good to stop in Soledad at all. Kicks us out and says, 'Jes' a little stretch down the road.' I bet it was *more* than four miles. Damn hot day."

Lennie looked timidly over to him. "George?"

"Yeah, what ya want?"

"Where we goin', George?"

The little man jerked down the brim of his hat and

scowled over at Lennie. "So you forgot that awready, did you? I gotta tell you again, do I? Jesus Christ, you're a crazy bastard!"

"I forgot," Lennie said softly. "I tried not to forget. Honest to God I did, George."

"O.K.—O.K. I'll tell ya again. I ain't got nothing to do. Might jus' as well spen' all my time tellin' you things and then you forget 'em, and I tell you again."

"Tried and tried," said Lennie, "but it didn't do no good. I remember about the rabbits, George."

"The hell with the rabbits. That's all you ever can remember is them rabbits. O.K.! Now you listen and this time you got to remember so we don't get in no trouble. You remember settin' in that gutter on Howard Street and watchin' that blackboard?"

Lennie's face broke into a delighted smile. "Why sure, George. I remember that . . . but . . . what'd we do then? I remember some girls come by and you says . . . you say . . ."

"The hell with what I says. You remember about us goin' into Murray and Ready's, and they give us work cards and bus tickets?"

"Oh, sure, George. I remember that now." His hands went quickly into his side coat pockets. He said gently, "George . . . I ain't got mine. I musta lost it." He looked down at the ground in despair.

"You never had none, you crazy bastard. I got both of 'em here. Think I'd let you carry your own work card?"

Lennie grinned with relief. "I . . . I thought I put it in my side pocket." His hand went into the pocket again.

George looked sharply at him. "What'd you take outa that pocket?"

"Ain't a thing in my pocket," Lennie said cleverly.

"I know there ain't. You got it in your hand. What you got in your hand—hidin' it?"

"I ain't got nothin', George. Honest."

"Come on, give it here."

Lennie held his closed hand away from George's direction. "It's on'y a mouse, George."

"A mouse? A live mouse?"

"Uh-uh. Jus' a dead mouse, George. I didn' kill it. Honest! I found it. I found it dead."

"Give it here!" said George.

"Aw, leave me have it, George."

"Give it here!"

Lennie's closed hand slowly obeyed. George took the mouse and threw it across the pool to the other side, among the brush. "What you want of a dead mouse, anyways?"

"I could pet it with my thumb while we walked along," said Lennie.

"Well, you ain't petting no mice while you walk with me. You remember where we're goin' now?"

Lennie looked startled and then in embarrassment hid his face against his knees. "I forgot again."

"Jesus Christ," George said resignedly, "Well—look, we're gonna work on a ranch like the one we come from up north."

"Up north?"

"In Weed."

"Oh, sure. I remember. In Weed."

"That ranch we're goin' to is right down there about a quarter mile. We're gonna go in an' see the boss. Now, look—I'll give him the work tickets, but you ain't gonna say a word. You jus' stand there and don't say nothing. If he finds out what a crazy bastard you are, we won't get no job, but if he sees ya work before he hears ya talk, we're set. Ya got that?"

"Sure, George. Sure I got it."

"O.K. Now when we go in to see the boss, what you gonna do?"

"I . . . I," Lennie thought. His face grew tight with thought. "I . . . ain't gonna say nothin'. Jus' gonna stan' there."

"Good boy. That's swell. You say that over two, three times so you sure won't forget it."

Lennie droned to himself softly, "I ain't gonna say nothin' . . . I ain't gonna say nothin' . . . I ain't gonna say nothin'."

"O.K.," said George. "An' you ain't gonna do no bad things like you done in Weed, neither."

Lennie looked puzzled. "Like I done in Weed?"

"Oh, so ya forgot that too, did ya? Well, I ain't gonna remind ya, fear ya do it again."

A light of understanding broke on Lennie's face. "They run us outa Weed," he exploded triumphantly.

"Run us out, hell," said George disgustedly. "We run. They was lookin' for us, but they didn't catch us."

Lennie giggled happily. "I didn't forget that, you bet."

George lay back on the sand and crossed his hands under his head, and Lennie imitated him, raising his head to see whether he were doing it right. "God, you're a lot of trouble," said George. "I could get along so easy and so nice if I didn't have you on my tail. I could live so easy and maybe have a girl."

For a moment Lennie lay quiet, and then he said hopefully, "We gonna work on a ranch, George."

"Awright. You got that. But we're gonna sleep here because I got a reason."

The day was going fast now. Only the tops of the Gabilan mountains flamed with the light of the sun that had gone from the valley. A water snake slipped along on the pool, its head held up like a little periscope. The reeds jerked slightly in the current. Far off toward the highway a man shouted something, and another man shouted back. The sycamore limbs rustled under a little wind that died immediately.

"George—why ain't we goin' on to the ranch and get some supper? They got supper at the ranch."

George rolled on his side. "No reason at all for you. I like it here. Tomorra we're gonna go to work. I seen thrashin' machines on the way down. That means we'll be bucking grain bags, bustin' a gut. Tonight I'm gonna lay right here and look up. I like it."

Lennie got up on his knees and looked down at George. "Ain't we gonna have no supper?"

"Sure we are, if you gather up some dead willow sticks. I got three cans of beans in my bindle. You get a fire ready. I'll give you a match when you get the sticks together. Then we'll heat the beans and have supper."

Lennie said, "I like beans with ketchup."

"Well, we ain't got no ketchup. You go get wood. An' don't you fool around. It'll be dark before long."

Lennie lumbered to his feet and disappeared in the brush. George lay where he was and whistled softly to himself. There were sounds of splashings down the river in the direction Lennie had taken. George stopped whistling and listened. "Poor bastard," he said softly, and then went on whistling again.

In a moment Lennie came crashing back through the brush. He carried one small willow stick in his hand. George sat up. "Awright," he said brusquely. "Gi'me that mouse!"

But Lennie made an elaborate pantomime of innocence. "What mouse, George? I ain't got no mouse."

George held out his hand. "Come on. Give it to me. You ain't puttin' nothing over."

Lennie hesitated, backed away, looked wildly at the brush line as though he contemplated running for his freedom. George said coldly, "You gonna give me that mouse or do I have to sock you?"

"Give you what, George?"

"You know God damn well what. I want that mouse."

Lennie reluctantly reached into his pocket. His voice broke a little. "I don't know why I can't keep it. It ain't nobody's mouse. I didn't steal it. I found it lyin' right beside the road."

George's hand remained outstretched imperiously. Slowly, like a terrier who doesn't want to bring a ball to its master, Lennie approached, drew back, approached again. George snapped his fingers sharply, and at the sound Lennie laid the mouse in his hand.

"I wasn't doin' nothing bad with it, George. Jus' strokin' it."

George stood up and threw the mouse as far as he could into the darkening brush, and then he stepped to the pool and washed his hands. "You crazy fool. Don't you think I could see your feet was wet where you went acrost the river to get it?" He heard Lennie's whimpering cry and wheeled about. "Blubberin' like a baby! Jesus Christ! A big guy like you." Lennie's lip quivered and tears started in his eyes. "Aw, Lennie!" George put his hand on Lennie's shoulder. "I ain't takin' it away jus' for meanness. That mouse ain't fresh, Lennie; and besides, you've broke it pettin' it. You get another mouse that's fresh and I'll let you keep it a little while."

Lennie sat down on the ground and hung his head dejectedly. "I don't know where there is no other mouse. I remember a lady used to give 'em to me—ever' one she got. But that lady ain't here."

George scoffed. "Lady, huh? Don't even remember who that lady was. That was your own Aunt Clara. An' she stopped givin' 'em to ya. You always killed 'em."

Lennie looked sadly up at him. "They was so little," he said, apologetically. "I'd pet 'em, and pretty soon they bit my fingers and I pinched their heads a little and then they was dead—because they was so little."

"I wish't we'd get the rabbits pretty soon, George. They ain't so little."

"The hell with the rabbits. An' you ain't to be trusted with no live mice. Your Aunt Clara give you a rubber mouse and you wouldn't have nothing to do with it."

"It wasn't no good to pet," said Lennie.

The flame of the sunset lifted from the mountaintops and dusk came into the valley, and a half darkness came in among the willows and the sycamores. A big carp rose to the surface of the pool, gulped air and then sank mysteriously into the dark water again, leaving widening rings on the water. Overhead the leaves whisked again and little puffs of willow cotton blew down and landed on the pool's surface.

"You gonna get that wood?" George demanded. "There's plenty right up against the back of that sycamore. Flood-water wood. Now you get it."

Lennie went behind the tree and brought out a litter of dried leaves and twigs. He threw them in a heap on the old ash pile and went back for more and more. It was almost night now. A dove's wings whistled over the water. George walked to the fire pile and lighted the dry leaves. The flame cracked up among the twigs and fell to work. George undid his bindle and brought out three cans of beans. He stood them about the fire, close in against the blaze, but not quite touching the flame.

"There's enough beans for four men," George said.

Lennie watched him from over the fire. He said patiently, "I like 'em with ketchup."

"Well, we ain't got any," George exploded. "Whatever we ain't got that's what you want. God a'mighty, if I was alone I could live so easy. I could go get a job an' work, an' no trouble. No mess at all, and when the end of the month come I could take my fifty bucks and go into town and get whatever I want. Why, I could stay in a cat house all night. I could eat any place I want, hotel or any place, and order any damn thing I could think of. An' I could do all that every damn month. Get a gallon of whisky, or set in a pool room and play cards or shoot pool." Lennie knelt and looked over the fire at the angry George. And Lennie's face was drawn with terror. "An' whatta I got," George went on furiously. "I got you! You can't keep a job and you lose me ever' job I get. Jus' keep me shovin' all over the country all the time. An' that ain't the worst. You get in trouble. You do bad things and I got to get you out." His voice rose nearly to a shout. "You crazy son-of-a-bitch. You keep me in hot water all the time." He took on the elaborate manner of little girls when they are mimicking one another. "Jus' wanted to feel that girl's dress—jus' wanted to pet it like it was a mouse—Well, how the hell did she know you jus' wanted to feel her dress? She jerks back and you hold on like it was a mouse. She yells and we got to hide in a irrigation ditch all day with guys lookin' for us, and we got to sneak out in the dark and get outta the country. All the time somethin' like that—all the time. I wisht I could put you in a cage with about a million mice an' let you have fun." His anger left him suddenly. He looked across the fire at Lennie's anguished face, and then he looked ashamedly at the flames.

It was quite dark now, but the fire lighted the trunks of the trees and the curving branches overhead. Lennie crawled slowly and cautiously around the fire until he was close to George. He sat back on his heels. George turned the bean cans so that another side faced the fire. He pretended to be unaware of Lennie so close beside him.

"George," very softly. No answer. "George!"

"Whatta you want?"

"I was only foolin', George. I don't want no ketchup. I wouldn't eat no ketchup if it was right here beside me."

"If it was here, you could have some."

"But I wouldn't eat none, George. I'd leave it all for you. You could cover your beans with it and I wouldn't touch none of it."

George still stared morosely at the fire. "When I think of the swell time I could have without you, I go nuts. I never get no peace."

Lennie still knelt. He looked off into the darkness across the river. "George, you want I should go away and leave you alone?"

"Where the hell could you go?"

"Well, I could. I could go off in the hills there. Some place I'd find a cave."

"Yeah? How'd you eat. You ain't got sense enough to find nothing to eat."

"I'd find things, George. I don't need no nice food with ketchup. I'd lay out in the sun and nobody'd hurt me. An' if I foun' a mouse, I could keep it. Nobody'd take it away from me."

George looked quickly and searchingly at him. "I been mean, ain't I?"

"If you don' want me I can go off in the hills an' find a cave. I can go away any time."

"No—look! I was jus' foolin', Lennie. 'Cause I want you to stay with me. Trouble with mice is you always kill 'em." He paused. "Tell you what I'll do, Lennie. First chance I get I'll give you a pup. Maybe you wouldn't kill *it*. That'd be better than mice. And you could pet it harder."

Lennie avoided the bait. He had sensed his advantage. "If you don't want me, you only jus' got to say so, and I'll go off in those hills right there—right up in those hills and live by myself. An' I won't get no mice stole from me."

George said, "I want you to stay with me, Lennie. Jesus Christ, somebody'd shoot you for a coyote if you was by yourself. No, you stay with me. Your Aunt Clara wouldn't like you running off by yourself, even if she is dead."

Lennie spoke craftily, "Tell me—like you done before."

"Tell you what?"

"About the rabbits."

George snapped, "You ain't gonna put nothing over on me."

Lennie pleaded, "Come on, George. Tell me. Please, George. Like you done before."

"You get a kick outta that, don't you? Awright, I'll tell you, and then we'll eat our supper. . . ."

George's voice became deeper. He repeated his words rhythmically as though he had said them many times before. "Guys like us, that work on ranches, are the loneliest guys in the world. They got no family. They don't belong no place. They come to a ranch an' work up a stake and then they go inta town and blow their stake, and the first thing you know they're poundin' their tail on some other ranch. They ain't got nothing to look ahead to."

Lennie was delighted. "That's it—that's it. Now tell how it is with us."

George went on. "With us it ain't like that. We got a future. We got somebody to talk to that gives a damn about us. We don't have to sit in no bar room blowin' our jack jus' because we got no place else to go. If them other guys gets in jail they can rot for all anybody gives a damn. But not us."

Lennie broke in. *"But not us! An' why? Because . . . because I got you to look after me, and you got me to look after you, and that's why."* He laughed delightedly. "Go on now, George!"

"You got it by heart. You can do it yourself."

"No, you. I forget some a' the things. Tell about how it's gonna be."

"O.K. Someday—we're gonna get the jack together and we're gonna have a little house and a couple of acres an' a cow and some pigs and—"

"An' live off the fatta the lan'," Lennie shouted. "An' have *rabbits*. Go on, George! Tell about what we're gonna have in the garden and about the rabbits in the cages and about the rain in the winter and the stove, and how thick the cream is on the milk like you can hardly cut it. Tell about that, George."

"Why'n't you do it yourself? You know all of it."

"No . . . you tell it. It ain't the same if I tell it. Go on . . . George. How I get to tend the rabbits."

"Well," said George, "we'll have a big vegetable patch and a rabbit hutch and chickens. And when it rains in the winter, we'll just say the hell with goin' to work, and we'll build up a fire in the stove and set around it an' listen to the rain comin' down on the roof—Nuts!" He took out his pocket knife. "I ain't got time for no more." He drove his knife through the top of one of the bean cans, sawed out the top and passed the can to Lennie. Then he opened a second can. From his side pocket he brought out two spoons and passed one of them to Lennie.

They sat by the fire and filled their mouths with beans and chewed mightily. A few beans slipped out of the side of Lennie's mouth. George gestured with his spoon. "What you gonna say tomorrow when the boss asks you questions?"

Lennie stopped chewing and swallowed. His face was concentrated. "I . . . I ain't gonna . . . say a word."

"Good boy! That's fine, Lennie! Maybe you're gettin' better. When we get the coupla acres I can let you tend the rabbits all right. 'Specially if you remember as good as that."

Lennie choked with pride. "I can remember," he said.

George motioned with his spoon again. "Look, Lennie. I want you to look around here. You can remember this place, can't you? The ranch is about a quarter mile up that way. Just follow the river?"

"Sure," said Lennie. "I can remember this. Di'n't I remember about not gonna say a word?"

" 'Course you did. Well, look. Lennie—if you jus' happen to get in trouble like you always done before, I want you to come right here an' hide in the brush."

"Hide in the brush," said Lennie slowly.

"Hide in the brush till I come for you. Can you remember that?"

"Sure I can, George. Hide in the brush till you come."

"But you ain't gonna get in no trouble, because if you do, I won't let you tend the rabbits." He threw his empty bean can off into the brush.

"I won't get in no trouble, George. I ain't gonna say a word."

"O.K. Bring your bindle over here by the fire. It's gonna be nice sleepin' here. Lookin' up, and the leaves. Don't build up no more fire. We'll let her die down."

They made their beds on the sand, and as the blaze dropped from the fire the sphere of light grew smaller; the curling branches disappeared and only a faint glimmer showed where the tree trunks were. From the darkness Lennie called, "George—you asleep?"

"No. Whatta you want?"

"Let's have different color rabbits, George."

"Sure we will," George said sleepily. "Red and blue and green rabbits, Lennie. Millions of 'em."

"Furry ones, George, like I seen in the fair in Sacramento."

"Sure, furry ones."

" 'Cause I can jus' as well go away, George, an' live in a cave."

"You can jus' as well go to hell," said George. "Shut up now."

The red light dimmed on the coals. Up the hill from the river a coyote yammered, and a dog answered from the other side of the stream. The sycamore leaves whispered in a little night breeze.

Conflict

Author Katherine Porter once wrote a memorable story called "Rope." It is about a man and his wife who have moved to the country. The man goes to town for groceries. He buys his groceries and comes home. In addition to the groceries, he gets a length of rope he might need "someday," but he forgets to get the coffee his wife wants.

That's no story, you might say. And of course you'd be right. These simple actions need something more to turn them into a story. They need something to capture your interest. In a successful story, that something is conflict. Conflict is a struggle between two or more people, forces, ideas, or feelings. What makes "Rope" so unforgettable is not the action, but the conflict that arises between the man and his wife, who is angry with him for purchasing the rope.

Even if the action in a story is more exciting than a trip to buy groceries, it will not hold your interest for long if it does not involve conflict of some sort. Conflict changes a plain description of actions into a story that has meaning and emotional impact.

For example, in James Dickey's novel *Deliverance* four men take a canoe trip. During the trip one man is killed. The others, after severe hardships, return safely.

You can see that there is a lot of action in the story, but it still doesn't seem very interesting. Yet *Deliverance* is an exciting novel— so exciting that it was made into a movie. It is the conflict in the story, not all the action, that makes it exciting. Once you are exposed to the conflict, you can't put the book down. In Dickey's novel the men are challenged by hardships in nature. They are attacked by other men and must fight back. These outer conflicts lead to inner ones: each man must search his soul because of what happens. Their old ways of living and thinking come into conflict with what they learn on the trip. They have hard choices to make. Without conflicts there would be no story.

This lesson is about conflict and how conflict works to make a story. We will consider four ways in which author John Steinbeck uses conflict:

1 ♦ The author uses different kinds of conflict.

2 ♦ The author uses conflict as a moving, or motivating, force.

3 ♦ The author reveals characters through conflict.

4 ♦ The author uses conflict to produce the plot, or story line, of the novel.

1 ◆ Kinds of Conflict

In general, there are four kinds of conflict: conflict between two people, conflict with oneself, conflict with nature, and conflict with society or a group. The most common conflict is between two people. A fist fight, for example, is certainly conflict between two people. Two people competing for the same job of class president is another example of conflict between people. But there are other kinds of conflict between people that are not quite so obvious. There are quiet conflicts between a child and parent or a student and teacher.

People also find conflict within themselves. A guilty conscience is a form of inner conflict. Struggling to decide what to do in a certain situation is also a personal conflict. Will you go to college or not? Will you follow someone else's advice or your own? Will you break off with a friend? All of these questions that require soul-searching and decision-making are personal, or inner, conflicts.

Conflicts between people and the forces of nature arise too. A trapper lost in a blizzard is in conflict with nature. So is someone who is caught in a flood or a hurricane. And fighting a raging river on a raft is also conflict with nature.

Finally, a person may be in conflict with society. Society can be a group or an institution. A criminal with a grudge against the world would be in conflict with society. Or a conflict with society might involve a homeowner whose house is in the way of a new highway. An animal character faced with the destruction of its forest home is also in conflict with society.

The most important conflicts in a story always involve the main characters, sometimes called the *protagonists*. George and Lennie are the protagonists in *Of Mice and Men*. What kinds of conflict involving George and Lennie do you see in the passage below? (There may be more than one kind of conflict in any situation.)

> . . . George exploded. "Whatever we ain't got, that's what you want. God a'mighty, if I was alone I could live so easy. I could go get a job an' work, an' no trouble.". . . Lennie knelt and looked over the fire at the angry George. And Lennie's face was drawn with terror. "An' whatta I got," George went on furiously. "I got you! You can't keep a job and you lose me ever' job I get. . . . An' that ain't the worst. You get in trouble. You do bad things and I got to

get you out." His voice rose nearly to a shout. . . . "Jus' wanted to feel that girl's dress—jus' wanted to pet it like it was a mouse—Well, how the hell did she know you jus' wanted to feel her dress? . . . She yells and we got to hide in a irrigation ditch all day with guys lookin' for us. . . . I wisht I could put you in a cage with about a million mice an' let you have fun." His anger left him suddenly. He looked across the fire at Lennie's anguished face, and then he looked ashamedly at the flames.

George is fiercely angry. His anger seems directed at Lennie. Lennie is terrified by George's anger. You can clearly see in that passage a conflict between two people.

But there is another kind of conflict here also. George is doing a good bit of soul-searching. He is really asking himself why he stays with Lennie and takes care of him. Then George is suddenly ashamed of his anger. He is ashamed of what he is doing to Lennie. George's personal, or inner conflict, is important throughout the novel.

And there is one other kind of conflict in the story. It seems that Lennie, in a very innocent way, patted a girl's dress. The girl screamed, not understanding that Lennie was harmless. This brought the whole town after both Lennie and George, and they had to flee for their lives. Society then, as now, was a long way from understanding mental retardation. Because people lack understanding, Lennie and George are in direct conflict with society.

1 ◆ Exercise A

Read the following passage and answer the questions about it using what you have learned in this part of the lesson. Use your writing notebook or a separate piece of paper for your answers.

George lay back on the sand and crossed his hands under his head, and Lennie imitated him, raising his head to see whether he were doing it right. "God, you're a lot of trouble," said George. "I could get along so easy and so nice if I didn't have you on my tail."

1. To have conflict, there must be at least two opposing forces or ideas. What are the two opposing ideas in George's inner conflict? Why do you think George has this conflict?

2. The following passage describes a conflict that is similar to George's. It describes an inner conflict that many students feel. How does this conflict affect your life?

> School is a lot of trouble. I could get along so easily if I didn't have to go to school or do all this homework.

Now check your answers using the suggestions in the Answer Key starting on page 451. Review this part of the lesson if you don't understand why an answer was wrong.

1♦Writing on Your Own

Look at the story idea and conflicts you wrote for Create Conflict for a Story on page 227. Now do the following:

1. Choose one of the conflicts you described.

2. Write a scene for your story that shows the conflict in progress. After you have written the scene, tell what kind of conflict is taking place in the story. Here is an example of inner conflict:

> Alice and the children are walking beside the wagon to make the load easier for the oxen to pull. Noah watched as they almost disappeared in the sea of prairie grass and then reappeared again on the next small rise.
> "Families have been lost to the prairie," he thought to himself. "What am I doing to them? Alice never wanted to leave. How could I have thought we could make this trip and survive?"

3. You may want to change and rewrite your paragraph until the events and conflicts are in the correct order.

2 ◆ Conflict as Motivation

Conflict always involves a struggle of some sort, either with forces outside you or tensions inside you. That's why conflicts are usually disturbing or upsetting. Most people don't enjoy arguing or fighting, nor do they like worrying about a decision or coping with their fears. Conflict, then, often becomes a *motive* for action. If you are in conflict, you do something to end the conflict. To put it another way, conflict often gives you the *motivation* to settle the problem. It leads you to action or to a decision.

To imagine conflict causing motivation, think of a pesky fly buzzing about. You are in conflict with this fly: it wants to stay; you want it to go. This conflict will motivate you to take some action to get rid of the fly. In a sense, a story is unfolding, a life-and-death battle between you and the fly that you might title "The SWAT Team."

The relation between conflict and motivation happens in stories just as it does in life. Often, conflicts arise when you, or a character in a story, are pursing a goal. The goal may be small (catching a fly) or big (graduation from school). As you move toward your goal, new conflicts will arise. These new conflicts motivate you to new action, and that's how a story develops. You will see more about this in the section on conflict and plot.

In *Of Mice and Men* there are motivation forces at work that keep George and Lennie together. These forces are the result of certain inner conflicts. The conflicts motivate Lennie and George to act the way they do. What they do creates new conflicts, and so the story goes. You can see that conflict is central to the plot or story line.

The passage below shows the inner conflict that motivates George and Lennie to stick together.

> "Guys like us, that work on ranches, are the loneliest guys in the world. They got no family. They don't belong no place. They come to a ranch an' work up a stake and then they go inta town and blow their stake, and the first thing you know they're poundin' their tail on some other ranch. They ain't got nothing to look ahead to."
>
> Lennie was delighted. "That's it—that's it. Now tell how it is with us."
>
> George went on. "With us it ain't like that. We got a future. We got somebody to talk to that gives a damn about

us. We don't have to sit in no bar room blowin' our jack jus' because we got no place else to go. If them other guys gets in jail they can rot for all anybody gives a damn. But not us."

Lennie broke in. *"But not us! An' why? Because. . . because I got you to look after me, and you got me to look after you, and that's why."* He laughed delightedly.

It is easy to see why Lennie needs George. Lennie is like a child who needs a parent to look after him. But what motivates George to stay with Lennie?

George doesn't want to be a lonely drifter like other ranch workers he sees. "We got a future," he says. It's as if George said, "We have a goal. We have a purpose in life, which is each other."

Keeping their relationship is George's goal. The motivation to work for this goal has come from an inner conflict—George's dread of a lonely and purposeless life is stronger than his anger at all the trouble that Lennie gets them into. As we have seen, this motivation has led to conflicts in the past. It will create new conflicts as the story unfolds.

2 ♦ Exercise B

Read the following passage and answer the questions about it using what you have learned in this part of the lesson. Use your writing notebook or a separate piece of paper for your answers.

[George is answering Lennie's plea to "Tell about how it's gonna be."]

"O.K. Someday—we're gonna get the jack together and we're gonna have a little house and a couple of acres an' a cow and some pigs and—"

"An' live off the fatta the lan'," Lennie shouted. *"An' have rabbits.* Go on George! Tell about what we're gonna have in the garden and about the rabbits in the cages. . . ."

"Well," said George, "we'll have a big vegetable patch and a rabbit hutch and chickens. And when it rains in the winter, we'll just say the hell with goin' to work, and we'll build up a fire in the stove and set around it an' listen to the rain comin' down on the roof—Nuts!" He took out his pocket knife. "I ain't got time for no more."

1. George seems to have a conflict between his dream and what is real at the moment. Why is there a conflict? What causes the conflict?

2. A dream is a motivating force in the lives of George and Lennie. How can a dream be a motivating force in your life? Where might the conflicts arise?

Now check your answers using the suggestions in the Answer Key starting on page 451. Review this part of the lesson if you don't understand why an answer was wrong.

2♦Writing on Your Own

Look at the conflict you created for your story idea in 1♦Writing on Your Own, in part one of the lesson. Now do the following:

1. Write a few sentences that explain how your character's conflicts will be a motivating force for

   ☐ something that will happen later. For example: Suppose the pioneer man regrets his decision to move and must decide if his family should turn back or settle where they are. You can discuss the inner conflict between his dream and the reality of his situation. His decision is an event that will happen later, after his inner conflict is discussed.

   ☐ some other conflict that will occur later on in the story. For example: At this point you would reveal the man's decision. Does his wife agree? What conflict could occur between the two? If they stay, will native American Indians think they are taking their land and attack? If they return home, what kind of life are they returning to? The possibilities discussed here set up the conflicts later in the story.

2. You may want to change and rewrite your paragraph until the events and motivating conflicts are in the correct order.

3 ◆ Conflict and Character

People act differently under pressure from the way they act at other times. A very calm, friendly person may become a monster if given trouble on a job. Other people are unflappable. No matter how difficult a situation, they come through like the Rock of Gibraltar. Take a person, apply pressure, and you will soon see what kind of a character you are dealing with.

Life is filled with conflicts. How a person reacts to conflict is a good measure of that person's character. You can also measure the reactions of fictional characters. In a novel, as in real life, you can learn a lot about a character when you see how the character reacts to the conflicts that arise in the story. What is more, you can see how the character's life is affected by these conflicts and how the course of the story changes as a result. Conflict, character, and story flow along together throughout a book.

The conflict in the passage below is a small one. It is an argument over a dead mouse. But this small conflict tells us a great deal about George and Lennie and their relationship. It also tells us something about Lennie that will be very important later in the novel.

> George sat up. "Awright," he said brusquely. "Gi'me that mouse!"
>
> But Lennie made an elaborate pantomime of innocence. "What mouse, George? I ain't got no mouse."
>
> George held out his hand. "Come on. Give it to me. You ain't puttin' nothing over."
>
> Lennie hesitated, backed away, looked wildly at the brush line as though he contemplated running for his freedom. George said coldly, "You gonna give me that mouse or do I have to sock you?". . .
>
> Lennie reluctantly reached into his pocket. His voice broke a little. "I don't know why I can't keep it. It ain't nobody's mouse. I didn't steal it. I found it lyin' right beside the road."
>
> George's hand remained outstretched imperiously. Slowly, like a terrier who doesn't want to bring a ball to its master, Lennie approached, drew back, approached again. George snapped his fingers sharply, and at the sound Lennie laid the mouse in his hand.

That conflict in itself is not earthshaking. It's more like a conflict between a devoted dog and its master. And that's one important thing we learn about George and Lennie. George is the master and Lennie is the obedient one. Lennie, as big as he is, is frightened of George, or at least in awe of him. This gives us a clue that, though Lennie is a giant, he is quite harmless. He's timid, in fact. He is easily upset by even a hint of violence. This character trait will become extremely important later in the novel.

George seems cold and ill-tempered here. But look at how different he seems in the passage in Exercise C.

3 ♦ Exercise C

Read the following passage and answer the questions about it using what you have learned in this part of the lesson. Use your writing notebook or a separate piece of paper for your answers.

> "I wasn't doin' nothing bad with it, George. Jus' strokin' it."
>
> George stood up and threw the mouse as far as he could into the darkening brush. . . . "You crazy fool. Don't you think I could see your feet was wet where you went acrost the river to get it?" He heard Lennie's whimpering cry and wheeled about. "Blubberin' like a baby! Jesus Christ! A big guy like you." Lennie's lip quivered and tears started in his eyes. "Aw Lennie!" George put his hand on Lennie's shoulder. "I ain't takin' it away jus' for meanness. That mouse ain't fresh, Lennie; and besides, you've broke it pettin' it. You get another mouse that's fresh and I'll let you keep it a little while."

1. What are the sentences that mark the change in George's attitude from anger with Lennie to feelings of sympathy for him? How do those sentences make you feel about George?

2. How is the conflict between George and Lennie like the conflict between a parent and a child?

Now check your answers using the suggestions in the Answer Key starting on page 451. Review this part of the lesson if you don't understand why an answer was wrong.

3◆Writing on Your Own

Reread the writing you have already done for Create Conflict for a Story on page 227 and the last two Writing on Your Own exercises in this lesson. Now do the following:

1. Think about one of the characters you have created who is involved in a conflict.

2. Write a paragraph that tells what kind of person that character is, based on how the character acted during the conflict. For example:

> Noah is a concerned husband and father because he is worried about how his wife and their children will survive the journey west. At the same time he is determined to risk the dangers and start a new life on a farm of his own.

3. Revise and rewrite your paragraph until you are satisfied with your description of the character.

4 ◆ Conflict and Plot

The plot of a novel is made up of all the actions that occur in the story. But an author doesn't throw actions together in a helter-skelter arrangement and expect them to come out as a story or novel you would want to read. All that results from writing down one action after another is a list of events, not a story. To hold your interest, these actions must be arranged according to some order or plan.

Think about the stories and novels you have read, and you will notice that the actions arise from conflicts that have already been carefully described. Because you understand the conflict, you see the reason for the actions that result. If you know there is a certain conflict in a character, you'll be interested in what action is taken to end the conflict. And these actions may lead to new conflicts with other characters, with society, or with nature. These new conflicts can result in still more action. As you can see, conflict and action build on each other to make the story. There is progress in the plot.

Notice how much we can tell about the plot of John Steinbeck's novel from looking at the conflict in the first chapter. Lennie has gotten into trouble in Weed (conflict with society). This explains why he and George have come to look for work on the ranch (action). Because they have to run away, there are arguments about the way Lennie acts (conflict between two people). This conflict leads George to make plans for how to get work when they arrive at the ranch (action).

We suspect that this cycle of conflict and action will continue when they get to the ranch. And that is indeed the case. Conflict and action will continue to build on one another until they reach the highest point of suspense and excitement. This high point is called the *climax* of the plot. The action that solves the final conflict and brings the story to a close is called the *resolution*.

The following passage is from an early episode in the chapter. It tells of two problems (conflicts) and hints at action that may occur later in the novel as a result of these conflicts. George is speaking:

> "That ranch we're goin' to is right down there about a quarter mile. We're gonna go in an' see the boss. Now, look—I'll give him the work tickets, but you ain't gonna say a word. You jus' stand there and don't say nothing. . . . if he sees ya work before he hears ya talk, we're set. Ya got that?"

"Sure, George. Sure I got it."

"O.K. Now when we go in to see the boss, what you gonna do?"

"I . . . I," Lennie thought. His face grew tight with thought. "I . . . ain't gonna say nothin'. Jus' gonna stan' there."

"Good boy. That's swell. You say that over two, three times so you sure won't forget it. . . .

. . . An' you ain't gonna do no bad things like you done in Weed, neither."

The two problems we are told about are that Lennie forgets and that he does "bad things." The trouble in George's life comes from trying to manage Lennie and the problems he creates. There are hints of conflict to come at the ranch. Getting Lennie a job is always a tricky business. George is coaching Lennie to avoid the two things that cause the worst trouble. "Don't say nothing" and "you ain't gonna do no bad things," he tells Lennie.

We suspect that, as usual, Lennie will forget. There will surely be conflict arising from Lennie's doing something bad. These conflicts will, in fact, be exactly what lead the plot to its climax.

4 ◆ Exercise D

Read the following passage and answer the questions about it using what you have learned in this part of the lesson. Use your writing notebook or a separate piece of paper for your answers.

He [Lennie] looked off into the darkness across the river. "George, you want I should go away and leave you alone?"

"Where the hell could you go?"

"Well, I could. I could go off in the hills there. Some place I'd find a cave.". . .

George looked quickly and searchingly at him. "I been mean, ain't I?"

"If you don't want me I can go off in the hills an' find a cave. I can go away any time."

"No—look! I was jus' foolin', Lennie. 'Cause I want you to stay with me. Trouble with mice is you always kill 'em." He paused. "Tell you what I'll do, Lennie. First chance I get I'll give you a pup. Maybe you wouldn't kill *it*. That'd be better than mice. And you could pet it harder."

1. Lennie likes to pet things. How can this lead to serious trouble (conflict) later in the story?

2. You have seen how the conflicts between George and Lennie work themselves out in this chapter. What do you think might happen if Lennie were to get into serious trouble later in the story?

Now check your answers using the suggestions in the Answer Key starting on page 451. Review this part of the lesson if you don't understand why an answer was wrong.

4♦Writing on Your Own

Reread what you wrote for Create Conflict for a Story on page 227 and the last three Writing on Your Own exercises. Now do the following:

1. Write a story plan that shows how one conflict will lead to an action and then to other conflicts and actions as your story moves along. For example:

   a. Noah yearns for a new life in the West.
   b. Alice was reluctant at first to leave the only home she ever knew.
   c. The trip is a dangerous one. Noah thinks about turning back.
   d. Noah worries about his family but wants very much to have his own farm.
   e. The family undergoes hardships including conflicts with native American Indians, with other settlers, and with the harsh weather on the prairie.
   f. The children become ill.
   g. After surviving a harsh winter, Noah and Alice plant their first crop and raise it with great difficulty.
   h. With the help from another family who had already settled in the area, Noah, Alice, and the children manage to survive until harvesttime.

Now go on to Reviewing and Interpreting the Chapter.

Answer these questions without looking back at the selection. Choose the best answer to each question and put an *x* in the box beside it, or write your answer on a separate piece of paper.

Remembering Facts

1. What was Lennie fond of doing?

   ☐ a. He liked to wade in water.

   ☐ b. He liked to pet soft things.

   ☐ c. He was fond of killing animals.

   ☐ d. He enjoyed getting George angry.

2. How would you describe George?

   ☐ a. big and powerful

   ☐ b. heavy and humorous

   ☐ c. small and quick

   ☐ d. skinny and dull

Following the Order of Events

3. Which one of these statements is correct?

   ☐ a. Lennie and George got off the bus and decided to go to the ranch the next day.

   ☐ b. Lennie and George went to the ranch, didn't like it, and decided to camp out.

   ☐ c. Lennie and George were camping out on their way to Weed.

   ☐ d. Having lost their jobs, George and Lennie were on their way to get new job tickets.

4. Lennie and George hid from the townspeople of Weed

☐ a. after arguing with the bus driver.

☐ b. as a result of Lennie killing mice.

☐ c. while trying to get work cards.

☐ d. after Lennie petted a girl's dress.

Understanding Word Choices

5. ". . . and then two men <u>emerged</u> from the path and came into the opening by the green pool." *Emerged* means

☐ a. turned away.

☐ b. ran.

☐ c. walked quickly.

☐ d. came out of.

6. "Lennie <u>lumbered</u> to his feet and disappeared in the brush." *Lumbered* means

☐ a. moved along heavily.

☐ b. barely moved.

☐ c. moved gracefully.

☐ d. got up quickly.

Understanding Important Ideas

7. The story is concerned mostly with showing us about

☐ a. prejudice in a small town.

☐ b. methods of surviving outdoors.

☐ c. labor unions for migrant workers.

☐ d. the strains and bonds in a relationship.

8. The title of the novel, *Of Mice and Men,* is from a line in a poem that says (loosely): "The best laid plans of mice and men often go astray." Which of these other quotations would also make a good title for the novel?

   □ a. "Hear the wagon soldiers shout . . ."

   □ b. "The highwayman came riding . . ."

   □ c. "I have a dream . . ."

   □ d. "Whose woods these are, I think I know . . ."

Understanding Levels of Meaning

9. Why did Lennie always imitate what George did?

   □ a. Lennie was making fun of George.

   □ b. Lennie admired and looked up to George.

   □ c. Lennie couldn't do anything for himself.

   □ d. Lennie was smarter than he seemed.

10. What does George think of Lennie as a ranch worker?

   □ a. He thinks Lennie won't remember how to work.

   □ b. He doesn't expect much from Lennie in the way of work.

   □ c. He is sure Lennie will be fired when the boss sees him work.

   □ d. He knows that Lennie is an excellent worker.

11. Which of the following expressions would you probably use today to describe people like George and Lennie?

    ☐ a. bindle bums

    ☐ b. refugees

    ☐ c. migrant workers

    ☐ d. escapees

12. Which one of the following expressions best describes Lennie's character?

    ☐ a. He was as simple as a child.

    ☐ b. He had a terrible temper.

    ☐ c. He had few human feelings.

    ☐ d. He was stubborn and uncooperative.

13. In this chapter, where are George and Lennie?

    ☐ a. on a ranch

    ☐ b. camped beside a river

    ☐ c. in the California desert

    ☐ d. in a dense forest

14. Many people and animals have come to the spot where George and Lennie spend the night. What attracts animals and travelers to stop there?

    ☐ a. the warmth

    ☐ b. the beauty

    ☐ c. the nearby road

    ☐ d. the water

15. Why did George scold Lennie one minute and
apologize the next?

☐ a. George had an unstable character.

☐ b. George loved Lennie but found caring for
him difficult.

☐ c. George was trying to upset Lennie so that
he would leave.

☐ d. Lennie loved George, but George really did
not love Lennie.

16. Why does Lennie always threaten to go away and
live in a cave?

☐ a. In his simple way he doesn't want to be a
burden to George.

☐ b. He wants to get even with George for the
constant scolding.

☐ c. He is simply tired of doing ranch work.

☐ d. He would rather not be with George.

Now check your answers using the Answer Key starting on page 451. Make no mark for right answers. Correct any wrong answers you may have by putting a check mark (✓) in the box next to the right answer. Count the number of questions you answered correctly and plot the total on the Comprehension Scores graph on page 462.

Next, look at the questions you answered incorrectly. What types of questions were they? Count the number you got wrong of each type and enter the numbers in the spaces below.

Remembering Facts   _____

Following the Order of Events   _____

Understanding Word Choices   _____

Understanding Important Ideas   _____

Understanding Levels of Meaning   _____

Understanding Character   _____

Understanding Setting   _____

Understanding Feelings   _____

Now use these numbers to fill in the Comprehension Skills Profile on page 463.

Discussion Guides

The questions below will help you think about the selection and the lesson you have just read. If you don't discuss these questions in class, try to think about them or discuss them with your classmates. Perhaps you will want to write a few paragraphs in answer to the questions.

Discussing Conflict

1. How would you explain George's inner conflict about staying with Lennie?

2. Lennie also has inner conflicts. What are they? How do they affect the story?

3. Try to predict what conflicts with society George and Lennie may have at the ranch.

Discussing the Chapter

4. The title of the novel comes from "To a Mouse," a poem by Robert Burns:

    The best laid schemes of mice and men
    Gang aft agley.

    Gang aft agley means "go often wrong." Judging from what you have read, how do you think these lines fit the story?

5. What can you find that is lovable or endearing about Lennie?

6. *Of Mice and Men* is often described as a story that touches your heart in some way. How does it affect your feelings?

Discussing the Author's Work

7. John Steinbeck was awarded a Nobel Prize for his work. He writes in plain and simple language about working people, usually poor people. Why do you think he received such a high award for his work?

8. In his later years Steinbeck made his home in New York City. He liked New York, he said, because it is "the world, with every vice and blemish and beauty." Can that same description be applied to the world Steinbeck created for Lennie and George? Explain your answer.

9. John Steinbeck consciously wrote *Of Mice and Men* "like a play."
   Read a page of conversation from the chapter with someone else.
   One person should take the part of Lennie, the other should be
   George. Can you imagine *Of Mice and Men* as a play? In what
   ways?

Writing Exercise

Read <u>all</u> the instructions before you begin writing. If you have any
questions about how to begin the writing assignment, review Using
the Writing Process beginning on page 439, or confer with your
writing coach.

1. In the last Writing on Your Own exercise in this lesson, you made
   a story plan by listing conflicts that will occur at various times in
   your story. If you haven't made your list yet, read the instructions
   for Writing on Your Own in part four and do it now.

2. Write your story using your list of conflicts as a guide.

3. Write, revise, correct, and rewrite your story until you are satisfied
   with it.

Unit 7   Symbolism

A Separate Peace
BY JOHN KNOWLES

About the Illustration

How do you know that this tree has a special importance
in this novel? Point out some details in the drawing to
support your answer.

Here are some questions to help you think about the
chapter:

◆ How would you describe this tree? What effect does it
have on you?

◆ What overall feeling or mood does the scene create?

Unit 7

Introduction

About the Novel

During World War II Gene Forrester was a student at the Devon School. Fifteen years later Gene returns to the school and seeks out two places that have special meaning for him. One place is a marble staircase. The other place is a tree by the river. A bit of innocent horseplay among boys at the tree had begun a chain of events that had led to tragedy. The tragedy had come to its climax at the marble staircase.

After briefly presenting Gene Forrester as a man, *A Separate Peace* flashes back to when he was a boy in school. It is the summer of 1942, and the United States is fighting in World War II. The boys at school who are sixteen and seventeen will soon be old enough to be drafted into service. Many of the teachers have already gone into military service or other war work.

Gene's close friend at school is Phineas, known as Finny. Finny is a very unusual fellow. He is the school's best athlete and he enjoys meeting challenges head-on. His joy is in accomplishing something difficult or dangerous just for the sake of doing it. He is not a braggart or a wise guy. In fact, he would like his friend Gene to have some of his own self-confidence. Finny has a reputation for being fearless, though some think him foolhardy in the chances he takes. Still, he is the envy and wonder of students and teachers alike.

Gene, on the other hand, is more like the rest of us. He has many fears. Challenges upset him. He would rather accept authority than defy it. Finny, his opposite, is always at Gene's side urging him to behave with more self-confidence. At one point in the story it becomes evident that Finny loves Gene like a brother. Gene feels the same way about Finny, but he hasn't the courage to confess even this.

Readers call this a story of friendship and betrayal. In a terrible, unexplained moment Gene jostles his friend from a tree limb. Finny falls, shattering his leg. This leads to an even more tragic series of events, and that is what the book is about.

John Knowles was born in West Virginia in 1926. Like his character Gene Forrester, Knowles was educated at one of New England's best preparatory schools and later at Yale University. *A Separate Peace,* his first and best-known novel, was published in 1960. It won several awards as a novel for adults, but it was quickly adopted by high school students who made it their own. It is still a popular novel in schools, along with *The Catcher in the Rye* and *Lord of the Flies.* If you enjoy reading *A Separate Peace,* you may wish to try another of John Knowles's books with a similar theme: *The Paragon.* This novel is set at Yale in 1953.

About the Lesson

The lesson that follows the reading selection is about symbolism. The novel is about two boys at school and the tragic consequences of an accident that happens to them there. But on another level, the story is about fear and overcoming fear.

Fear is one of our most powerful and most puzzling emotions. It can make people hate, it can paralyze them, it can make them physically and mentally ill. When dealing with a subject as difficult to define as fear, authors often use symbols to help explain complex ideas and feelings. They use a common object to stand for something that can't be seen or grasped so easily.

When one thing stands for another, it is called a symbol. A flag is a symbol that represents a country. A dollar bill is a symbol of value in goods and services. An anchor may symbolize hope, and a cross, a star, or a crescent moon may symbolize faith.

In *A Separate Peace,* John Knowles uses the setting, the actions, and the characters as symbols. Together they help us feel how puzzling, powerful, and emotional fear really is.

The questions below will help you focus on symbolism in the chapter from *A Separate Peace.* Read the chapter carefully and try to answer these questions as you go along:

◆ Gene Forrester returns to Devon School and finds that it seems to have been "preserved." What does he mean by "preserved"? What is the school a symbol of?

◆ What does Finny mean to Gene?

◆ What different ways of looking at life are shown by the behavior of the boys at the river?

◆ What theme is introduced by Gene's description of the tree near the river?

Creating Symbols in a Story

You will learn about three kinds of symbols in the lesson that follows the chapter from *A Separate Peace:* objects may be symbols, characters in the story may be symbols, and actions may be symbols.

1. In your writing notebook or on a separate piece of paper, add four more symbols to each of the three lists: objects, characters, and actions. Each group has been started for you. You may want to exchange ideas with your classmates before you begin your lists.

◆ **Objects as symbols**

An oak tree symbolizes strength.

An eagle symbolizes freedom.

A rose symbolizes love or beauty.

◆ **Characters as symbols**

A school principal symbolizes authority.

A mother symbolizes comfort or understanding.

Scrooge symbolizes greed and meanness.

◆ **Actions as symbols**

A battle symbolizes courage or destruction.

Winning a race symbolizes achievement.

A walk through a cemetery symbolizes a trip through history.

2. Once you have thought of your examples of symbols, add them to each list and explain what you think each symbol stands for.

A Separate Peace

by John Knowles

ONE

I went back to the Devon School not long ago, and found it looking oddly newer than when I was a student there fifteen years before. It seemed more sedate than I remembered it, more perpendicular and strait-laced, with narrower windows and shinier woodwork, as though a coat of varnish had been put over everything for better preservation. But, of course, fifteen years before there had been a war going on. Perhaps the school wasn't as well kept up in those days; perhaps varnish, along with everything else, had gone to war.

I didn't entirely like this glossy new surface, because it made the school look like a museum, and that's exactly what it was to me, and what I did not want it to be. In the deep, tacit way in which feeling becomes stronger than thought, I had always felt that the Devon School came into existence the day I entered it, was vibrantly real while I was a student there, and then blinked out like a candle the day I left.

Now here it was after all, preserved by some considerate hand with varnish and wax. Preserved along with it, like stale air in an unopened room, was the well known fear which had surrounded and filled those days, so much of it that I hadn't even known it was there. Because, unfamiliar with the absence of fear and what that was like, I had not been able to identify its presence.

Looking back now across fifteen years, I could see with

great clarity the fear I had lived in, which must mean that in the interval I had succeeded in a very important under- taking; I must have made my escape from it.

I felt fear's echo, and along with that I felt the unhinged, uncontrollable joy which had been its accompaniment and opposite face, joy which had broken out sometimes in those days like Northern Lights across black sky.

There were a couple of places now which I wanted to see. Both were fearful sites, and that was why I wanted to see them. So after lunch at the Devon Inn I walked back toward the school. It was a raw, nondescript time of year, toward the end of November, the kind of wet, self- pitying November day when every speck of dirt stands out clearly. Devon luckily had very little of such weather— the icy clamp of winter, or the radiant New Hampshire summers, were more characteristic of it—but this day it blew wet, moody gusts all around me.

I walked along Gilman Street, the best street in town. The houses were as handsome and as unusual as I remembered. Clever modernizations of old Colonial manses, extensions in Victorian wood, capacious Greek Revival temples lined the street, as impressive and just as forbidding as ever. I had rarely seen anyone go into one of them, or anyone playing on a lawn, or even an open window. Today with their failing ivy and stripped, moaning trees the houses looked both more elegant and more lifeless than ever.

Like all old, good schools, Devon did not stand isolated behind walls and gates but emerged naturally from the town which had produced it. So there was no sudden moment of encounter as I approached; the houses along Gilman Street began to look more defensive, which meant that I was near the school, and then more exhausted, which meant that I was in it.

It was early afternoon and the grounds and buildings were deserted, since everyone was at sports. There was nothing to distract me as I made my way across a wide yard, called the Far Common, and up to a building as red brick and balanced as the other major buildings, but with a large cupola and a bell and a clock and Latin over the doorway—the First Academy Building.

In through swinging doors I reached a marble foyer, and stopped at the foot of a long white marble flight of stairs. Although they were old stairs, the worn moons in the middle of each step were not very deep. The marble must be unusually hard. That seemed very likely, only too likely, although with all my thought about these stairs this exceptional hardness had not occurred to me. It was surprising that I had overlooked that, that crucial fact.

There was nothing else to notice; they of course were the same stairs I had walked up and down at least once every day of my Devon life. They were the same as ever. And I? Well, I naturally felt older—I began at that point the emotional examination to note how far my convalescence had gone—I was taller, bigger generally in relation to these stairs. I had more money and success and "security" than in the days when specters seemed to go up and down them with me.

I turned away and went back outside. The Far Common was still empty, and I walked alone down the wide gravel paths among those most Republican, bankerish of trees, New England elms, toward the far side of the school.

Devon is sometimes considered the most beautiful school in New England, and even on this dismal afternoon its power was asserted. It is the beauty of small areas of order—a large yard, a group of trees, three similar dormitories, a circle of old houses—living together in contentious harmony. You felt that an argument might begin again any time; in fact it had: out of the Dean's Residence, a pure and authentic Colonial house, there now sprouted an ell with a big bare picture window. Some day the Dean would probably live entirely encased in a house of glass and be happy as a sandpiper. Everything at Devon slowly changed and slowly harmonized with what had gone before. So it was logical to hope that since the buildings and the Deans and the curriculum could achieve this, I could achieve, perhaps unknowingly already had achieved, this growth and harmony myself.

I would know more about that when I had seen the second place I had come to see. So I roamed on past the balanced red brick dormitories with webs of leafless ivy clinging to them, through a ramshackle salient of the town which invaded the school for a hundred yards, past the solid gymnasium, full of students at this hour but silent as a monument on the outside, past the Field House, called The Cage—I remembered now what a mystery references to "The Cage" had been during my first weeks at Devon, I had thought it must be a place of severe punishment—and I reached the huge open sweep of ground known as the Playing Fields.

Devon was both scholarly and very athletic, so the playing fields were vast and, except at such a time of year, constantly in use. Now they reached soggily and emptily away from me, forlorn tennis courts on the left, enormous football and soccer and lacrosse fields in the center, woods on the right, and at the far end a small river detectable from this distance by the few bare trees along its banks. It was such a gray and misty day that I could not see the other side of the river, where there was a small stadium.

I started the long trudge across the fields and had gone some distance before I paid any attention to the soft and muddy ground, which was dooming my city shoes. I didn't stop. Near the center of the fields there were thin lakes of muddy water which I had to make my way around, my unrecognizable shoes making obscene noises as I lifted them out of the mire. With nothing to block it the wind flung wet gusts at me; at any other time I would have felt like a fool slogging through mud and rain, only to look at a tree.

A little fog hung over the river so that as I neared it I felt myself becoming isolated from everything except the river and the few trees beside it. The wind was blowing more steadily here, and I was beginning to feel cold. I never wore a hat, and had forgotten gloves. There were several trees bleakly reaching into the fog. Any one of them might have been the one I was looking for. Unbelievable that there were other trees which looked like it here. It had loomed in my memory as a huge lone spike dominating the riverbank, forbidding as an artillery piece, high as the beanstalk. Yet here was a scattered grove of trees, none of them of any particular grandeur.

Moving through the soaked, coarse grass I began to examine each one closely, and finally identified the tree I was looking for by means of certain small scars rising along its trunk, and by a limb extending over the river, and another thinner limb growing near it. This was the tree, and it seemed to me standing there to resemble those men, the giants of your childhood, whom you encounter years later and find that they are not merely smaller in relation to your growth, but that they are absolutely smaller, shrunken by age. In this double demotion the old giants have become pigmies while you were looking the other way.

The tree was not only stripped by the cold season, it seemed weary from age, enfeebled, dry. I was thankful, very thankful that I had seen it. So the more things remain the same, the more they change after all—*plus c'est la même chose, plus ça change.* Nothing endures, not a tree, not love, not even a death by violence.

Changed, I headed back through the mud. I was drenched; anybody could see it was time to come in out of the rain.

The tree was tremendous, an irate, steely black steeple beside the river. I was damned if I'd climb it. The hell with it. No one but Phineas could think up such a crazy idea.

He of course saw nothing the slightest bit intimidating about it. He wouldn't, or wouldn't admit it if he did. Not Phineas.

"What I like best about this tree," he said in that voice

of his, the equivalent in sound of a hypnotist's eyes, "what I like is that it's such a cinch!" He opened his green eyes wider and gave us his maniac look, and only the smirk on his wide mouth with its droll, slightly protruding upper lip reassured us that he wasn't completely goofy.

"Is that what you like best?" I said sarcastically. I said a lot of things sarcastically that summer; that was my sarcastic summer, 1942.

"Aey-uh," he said. This weird New England affirmative—maybe it is spelled "aie-huh"—always made me laugh, as Finny knew, so I had to laugh, which made me feel less sarcastic and less scared.

There were three others with us—Phineas in those days almost always moved in groups the size of a hockey team—and they stood with me looking with masked apprehension from him to the tree. Its soaring black trunk was set with rough wooden pegs leading up to a substantial limb which extended farther toward the water. Standing on this limb, you could by a prodigious effort jump far enough out into the river for safety. So we had heard. At least the seventeen-year-old bunch could do it; but they had a crucial year's advantage over us. No Upper Middler, which was the name for our class in the Devon School, had ever tried. Naturally Finny was going to be the first to try, and just as naturally he was going to inveigle others, us, into trying it with him.

We were not even Upper Middler exactly. For this was the Summer Session, just established to keep up with the pace of the war. We were in shaky transit that summer from the groveling status of Lower Middlers to the near-respectability of Upper Middlers. The class above, seniors, draft-bait, practically soldiers, rushed ahead of us toward the war. They were caught up in accelerated courses and first-aid programs and a physical hardening regimen, which included jumping from this tree. We were still calmly, numbly reading Virgil and playing tag in the river farther downstream. Until Finny thought of the tree.

We stood looking up at it, four looks of consternation, one of excitement. "Do you want to go first?" Finny asked us, rhetorically. We just looked quietly back at him, and so he began taking off his clothes, stripping down to his underpants. For such an extraordinary athlete—even as a Lower Middler Phineas had been the best athlete in the school—he was not spectacularly built. He was my height—five feet eight and a half inches (I had been claiming five feet nine inches before he became my roommate, but he had said in public with that simple, shocking self-acceptance of his, "No, you're the same height I am, five-eight and a half. We're on the short side"). He weighed a hundred and fifty pounds, a galling ten pounds more than I did, which flowed from his legs to torso around shoulders to arms and full strong neck in an uninterrupted, unemphatic unity of strength.

He began scrambling up the wooden pegs nailed to the side of the tree, his back muscles working like a panther's. The pegs didn't seem strong enough to hold his weight. At last he stepped onto the branch which reached a little farther toward the water. "Is this the one they jump from?" None of us knew. "If I do it, you're all going to do it, aren't you?" We didn't say anything very clearly. "Well," he cried out, "here's my contribution to the war effort!" and he sprang out, fell through the tips of some lower branches, and smashed into the water.

"Great!" he cried, bobbing instantly to the surface again, his wet hair plastered in droll bangs on his forehead. "That's the most fun I've had this week. Who's next?"

I was. This tree flooded me with a sensation of alarm all the way to my tingling fingers. My head began to feel unnaturally light, and the vague rustling sounds from the nearby woods came to me as though muffled and filtered. I must have been entering a mild state of shock. Insulated by this, I took off my clothes and started to climb the pegs. I don't remember saying anything. The branch he had jumped from was slenderer than it looked from the ground and much higher. It was impossible to walk out on it far enough to be well over the river. I would have to spring far out or risk falling into the shallow water next to the bank. "Come on," drawled Finny from below, "stop standing there showing off." I recognized with automatic tenseness that the view was very impressive from here. "When they torpedo the troop-ship," he shouted, "you can't stand around admiring the view. Jump!"

What was I doing up here anyway? Why did I let Finny talk me into stupid things like this? Was he getting some kind of hold over me?

"Jump!"

With the sensation that I was throwing my life away, I jumped into space. Some tips of branches snapped past me and then I crashed into the water. My legs hit the soft mud of the bottom, and immediately I was on the surface being congratulated. I felt fine.

"I think that was better than Finny's," said Elwin— better known as Leper—Lepellier, who was bidding for an ally in the dispute he foresaw.

"All right, pal," Finny spoke in his cordial, penetrating voice, that reverberant instrument in his chest, "don't start awarding prizes until you've passed the course. The tree is waiting."

Leper closed his mouth as though forever. He didn't argue or refuse. He didn't back away. He became inanimate. But the other two, Chet Douglass and Bobby Zane, were vocal enough, complaining shrilly about school regulations, the danger of stomach cramps, physical disabilities they had never mentioned before.

"It's you, pal," Finny said to me at last, "just you and me." He and I started back across the fields, preceding the others like two seigneurs.

We were the best of friends at that moment.

"You were very good," said Finny good-humoredly, "once I shamed you into it."

"You didn't shame anybody into anything."

"Oh, yes I did. I'm good for you that way. You have a tendency to back away from things otherwise."

"I never backed away from anything in my life!" I cried, my indignation at this charge naturally stronger because it was so true. "You're goofy!"

Phineas just walked serenely on, or rather flowed on, rolling forward in his white sneakers with such unthinking unity of movement that "walk" didn't describe it.

I went along beside him across the enormous playing fields toward the gym. Underfoot the healthy green turf was brushed with dew, and ahead of us we could see a faint green haze hanging above the grass, shot through with the twilight sun. Phineas stopped talking for once, so that now I could hear cricket noises and bird cries of dusk, a gymnasium truck gunning along an empty athletic road a quarter of a mile away, a burst of faint, isolated laughter carried to us from the back door of the gym, and then over all, cool and matriarchal, the six o'clock bell from the Academy Building cupola, the calmest, most carrying bell toll in the world, civilized, calm, invincible, and final.

The toll sailed over the expansive tops of all the elms, the great slanting roofs and formidable chimneys of the dormitories, the narrow and brittle old housetops, across the open New Hampshire sky to us coming back from the river. "We'd better hurry or we'll be late for dinner," I said breaking into what Finny called my "West Point stride." Phineas didn't really dislike West Point in particular or authority in general, but just considered authority the necessary evil against which happiness was achieved by reaction, the backboard which returned all the insults he threw at it. My "West Point stride" was intolerable; his right foot flashed into the middle of my fast walk and I went pitching forward into the grass. "Get those hundred and fifty pounds off me!" I shouted, because he was sitting on my back. Finny got up, patted my head genially, and moved on across the field, not deigning to glance around for my counterattack, but relying on his extrasensory ears, his ability to feel in the air someone coming on him from behind. As I sprang at him he side-stepped easily, but I just managed to kick him as I shot past. He caught my leg and there was a brief wrestling match on the turf which he won. "Better hurry," he said, "or they'll put you in the guardhouse." We were walking again, faster; Bobby and Leper and Chet were urging us from ahead for God's sake to hurry up, and then Finny trapped me again in his strongest trap, that is, I suddenly became his collaborator. As we walked rapidly along I abruptly resented the bell and my West Point stride and hurrying and conforming. Finny was right. And there was only one way to show him this. I threw my hip against his, catching him by surprise, and he was instantly down, definitely pleased. This was why he liked me so much. When I jumped on top of him, my knees on his chest, he couldn't ask for anything better. We struggled in some equality for a while, and then when we were sure we were too late for dinner, we broke off.

He and I passed the gym and came on toward the first group of dormitories, which were dark and silent. There were only two hundred of us at Devon in the summer, not enough to fill most of the school. We passed the sprawling Headmaster's house—empty, he was doing something for the government in Washington; past the Chapel—empty again, used only for a short time in the mornings; past the First Academy Building, where there were some dim lights shining from a few of its many windows, Masters at work in their classrooms there; down a short slope into the broad and well clipped Common, on which light fell from the big surrounding Georgian buildings. A dozen boys were loafing there on the grass after dinner, and a kitchen rattle from the wing of one of the buildings accompanied their talk. The sky was darkening steadily, which brought up the lights in the dormitories and the old houses; a loud phonograph a long way off played *Don't Sit Under the Apple Tree*, rejected that and played *They're Either Too Young or Too Old*, grew more ambitious with

The Warsaw Concerto, mellower with *The Nutcracker Suite,* and then stopped.

Finny and I went to our room. Under the yellow study lights we read our Hardy assignments; I was halfway through *Tess of the D'Urbervilles,* he carried on his baffled struggle with *Far from the Madding Crowd,* amused that there should be people named Gabriel Oak and Bathsheba Everdene. Our illegal radio, tuned too low to be intelligible, was broadcasting the news. Outside there was a rustling early summer movement of the wind; the seniors, allowed out later than we were, came fairly quietly back as the bell sounded ten stately times. Boys ambled past our door toward the bathroom, and there was a period of steadily pouring shower water. Then lights began to snap out all over the school. We undressed, and I put on some pajamas, but Phineas, who had heard they were unmilitary, didn't; there was the silence in which it was understood we were saying some prayers, and then that summer school day came to an end.

Symbolism

A well-known author once said, "We live in a world of symbols." To see that he was right, you have only to look at something as common as a dollar. From the front of a dollar, George Washington looks out at you. He is a symbol: the "father" of our country. To the right of Washington is the Treasury seal with its symbols, a scale and a key. On the reverse side is the Great Seal of the United States, an emblem made up of many symbols. The eagle symbolizes power and freedom. The arrows and olive branch it is clutching are symbols of war and peace. The thirteen stars stand for the first thirteen states.

We have symbols for our religions and symbols for our businesses. A group that forms a team always looks for a symbol to represent the team spirit. There are Lions and Bears and Hawks and Spartans and Vikings—all brave and fierce fighters.

People use symbols to express what is difficult to put into words—feelings and ideas. Thus, when you want to express respect for your flag and country, you use an action that is a symbol. You place your hand over your heart. A symbol for education is often shown as a lamp that lights the darkness of ignorance.

You have probably noticed by now that symbols can take three forms. There are symbolic objects—flags, animals, a lamp, a tree. There are symbolic characters—Abe Lincoln, for example, is held up as a symbol of honesty. And there are symbolic actions—saluting, clapping, cheering, or jeering.

There is a Chinese proverb that says, One picture is worth more than ten thousand words. Authors, realizing the proverb is true, use words to create as many pictures as they can to express feelings and ideas in their stories. There may be a forest that stands for fear and darkness. There may be a wizard who symbolizes evil or good. A fearless, persistent older person might symbolize established traditions.

You don't have to be aware of the symbolism in a story to enjoy the story. But you will find most stories more meaningful when you understand and appreciate the symbols an author uses. It's not hard to spot symbolism once you realize it is always there. Simply think of a book as a "world of symbols," just like the world you live in.

In this lesson we will look at four ways an author can develop symbolism:

1 ◆ Objects may be used as symbols.

2 ◆ Characters may be used as symbols.

3 ◆ Actions may be symbolic.

4 ◆ Themes may be presented through symbols.

1 ◆ Objects as Symbols

In literature an author may use almost any object, character, or action as a symbol. Poets especially like symbolic objects. Robert Frost used a fence that must be rebuilt each spring to symbolize a separation between neighbors. William Shakespeare used a bare tree limb in winter to symbolize his feelings about old age. Naturally, fences or tree limbs don't always have these meanings. You may think of something quite different when you see these objects. But a writer can make ordinary objects like fences and trees have larger symbolic meanings because of the way they are described.

John Knowles begins *A Separate Peace* using the Devon School as a symbol. Gene Forrester returns to the campus fifteen years after he finished school there. He describes it as he walks through the campus. Notice how the author makes this description tell more than simply what the buildings look like. He makes the school take on symbolic meaning by the way he describes it.

> I went back to the Devon School not long ago, and found it looking oddly newer than when I was a student there fifteen years before. It seemed more sedate than I remembered it, more perpendicular and strait-laced, with narrower windows and shinier woodwork, as though a coat of varnish had been put over everything for better preservation. . . .
>
> I didn't entirely like this glossy new surface, because it made the school look like a museum, and that's exactly what it was to me, and what I did not want it to be.

Clearly, that passage is not a simple description of the way the Devon School looks. You couldn't draw a picture of the campus after reading it. Instead, you are given a sense of what the school means in Gene's mind. It is a symbol of everything that is stiff and proper and unchanging. The author creates this symbolic meaning by using words like "strait-laced" and "sedate" and "perpendicular" in his description.

But the school has another symbolic meaning for Gene. When he returns to Devon, he is struck by memories of his youth. He compares the school to a museum. It is as if all his memories are stored and displayed there waiting for him to return. In Gene's mind, and in the mind of the reader, the school becomes a symbol of Gene's past life. And there's yet another meaning connected with this symbol, as you will see in Exercise A.

1 ◆ Exercise A

Read the following passage and answer the questions about it using what you have learned in this part of the lesson. Use your writing notebook or a separate piece of paper for your answers.

> Now here it was after all, preserved by some considerate hand with varnish and wax. Preserved along with it, like stale air in an unopened room, was the well known fear which had surrounded and filled those days, so much of it that I hadn't even known it was there. Because, unfamiliar with the absence of fear and what that was like, I had not been able to identify its presence.
>
> Looking back now across fifteen years, I could see with great clarity the fear I had lived in, which must mean that in the interval I had succeeded in a very important undertaking; I must have made my escape from it.

1. Gene Forrester has symbolically left something behind in the school building that is "preserved." What has been symbolically "preserved" in the building for Gene?

2. Think of your kindergarten or first-grade classroom as a symbol of your childhood. If you were to look at that classroom today, what feelings would be "preserved" there for you? fear? joy? uncertainty?

Now check your answers using the suggestions in the Answer Key starting on page 451. Review this part of the lesson if you don't understand why your answer was wrong.

1 ◆ Writing on Your Own

Look at the list of object symbols you wrote for Creating Symbols in a Story on page 271. Choose a symbol from that list that you think you might like to use in a story. Now do the following:

1. Think of a story idea in which you might be able to use this symbol. Tell in a few sentences what you think the story will be about. Here are a few suggestions:

   ☐ If you chose a steep mountain to symbolize a goal you want to reach, you will want to include that symbol in your story. Explain what the mountain means to you. The steepness of the mountain may represent the struggle, uncertainty, and fear you feel toward reaching your goal. You want to reach the top, but it might be difficult to get there. Build your story idea around your goal and your struggle to achieve it.

   ☐ Perhaps you chose a rainbow to symbolize peace or a dream fulfilled. What is at the end of the rainbow? harmony? peace? happiness?

2. Now write a paragraph for your story that uses that object as a symbol. It can be a paragraph that might be used in any part of your story—the beginning, the middle, or the end.

3. Rewrite your paragraph until you are satisfied with the symbolism of the object.

2 ♦ Characters as Symbols

Symbolic characters are everywhere, not just in books. There are probably people in your own life who have some symbolic meaning. For example, think of someone you admire. Doesn't that person symbolize success of some sort to you? When you think of ideas like courage or cowardice, don't people you know come to mind? To put it another way, you probably associate some of the people you know with larger ideas. As a result, they have a symbolic meaning for you.

A character in a book becomes symbolic in much the same way. An author will associate certain qualities with a character. Then that character comes to have a symbolic meaning in the story. Finny becomes a symbolic character in *A Separate Peace*. Notice how the qualities associated with Finny give him symbolic meaning to Gene and to you, as the reader.

> The tree was tremendous, an irate, steely black steeple beside the river. I was damned if I'd climb it. The hell with it. No one but Phineas could think up such a crazy idea.
>
> He of course saw nothing the slightest bit intimidating about it. He wouldn't, or wouldn't admit it if he did. Not Phineas.
>
> "What I like best about this tree," he said in that voice of his, the equivalent in sound of a hypnotist's eyes, "what I like is that it's such a cinch!"
>
> . . . .
>
> . . . even as a Lower Middler Phineas had been the best athlete in the school. . . . He weighed a hundred and fifty pounds . . . which flowed from his legs to torso around shoulders to arms and full strong neck in an uninterrupted, unemphatic unity of strength.
>
> He began scrambling up the wooden pegs nailed to the side of the tree, his back muscles working like a panther's.

To Gene and to us, Finny is clearly a symbol of confidence, strength, and courage. He dares to do anything, and he is good at everything he tries. He is well-liked and admired. He is, in short, everything Gene would like to be, but isn't.

Gene becomes symbolic as a contrast to Finny. Gene is associated with fear and with an effort to overcome fear. The author reminds us of these qualities in Gene as often as he reminds us of the opposite qualities in Finny. Notice the way Gene is presented in the passage below.

> This tree flooded me with a sensation of alarm all the way to my tingling fingers. My head began to feel unnaturally light, and the vague rustling sounds from the nearby woods came to me as though muffled and filtered. I must have been entering a mild state of shock. . . .
>
> What was I doing up here anyway? Why did I let Finny talk me into stupid things like this? Was he getting some kind of hold over me?
>
> "Jump!"
>
> With the sensation that I was throwing my life away, I jumped into space. . . . My legs hit the soft mud of the bottom, and immediately I was on the surface being congratulated. I felt fine.

Gene is frightened at the thought of following Finny's jump from the tree. He thinks he has entered "a mild state of shock." And yet, in this scene and others, Gene manages to overcome his fear and follow Finny's lead. Through the use of these repeated associations with larger ideas like fear and courage, the author makes characters symbolic.

2 ◆ Exercise B

Read the following passage and answer the questions about it using what you have learned in this part of the lesson. Use your writing notebook or a separate piece of paper for your answers.

> "I think that [Gene's jump] was better than Finny's," said Elwin—better known as Leper—Lepellier, who was bidding for an ally in the dispute he foresaw.
>
> "All right, pal," Finny spoke in his cordial, penetrating voice . . . "don't start awarding prizes until you've passed the course. The tree is waiting."
>
> Leper closed his mouth as though forever. He didn't argue or refuse. He didn't back away. He became inanimate. But the other two, Chet Douglass and Bobby Zane, were vocal

enough, complaining shrilly about school regulations, the danger of stomach cramps, physical disabilities they had never mentioned before.

"It's you, pal," Finny said to me at last, "just you and me." He and I started back across the fields, preceding the others like two seigneurs.

1. "It's you, pal," Finny said to me at last, "just you and me." The author has linked two characters symbolically. What is the meaning of the two symbols that are linked by Gene and Finny?

2. What do Leper, Chet, and Bobby represent as character symbols?

Now check your answers using the suggestions in the Answer Key starting on page 451. Review this part of the lesson if you don't understand why your answer was wrong.

2♦Writing on Your Own

Look at the list of character symbols you wrote for Creating Symbols in a Story on page 271. Choose a character symbol from the list that you think you might like to use in a story. Now do the following:

1. Reread the story idea you created for 1♦Writing on Your Own.

2. Write a paragraph for your story that uses this character as a symbol. Remember, your character doesn't have to be a person. Here are a few suggestions:

   □ Perhaps a dragon sits on top of the mountain. You have to reach the top of the mountain (your goal), but you must also overcome the dragon (your fear).

   □ If you chose a rainbow to symbolize fulfilling a dream, think about who might stand in your way and who might help you. Is there a Scrooge-like character who will try to stop you? Is there a friendly character who symbolizes hope and will help you?

3. Rewrite your paragraph until you are satisfied with your character and symbol.

3 ◆ Actions as Symbols

The only way you can know what people are like is by looking at the way they act. In the same way, you can only know what characters in a novel are like by looking at what they do and say. Authors choose the actions they include in a story very carefully. The meaning an action has is one of the reasons for including it. In other words, an action can represent an idea. When it does, it is called a symbolic action.

Not all actions in a story are symbolic. An author may include an action just to move the story along or to provide a bit of humor. Actions become symbolic only when they are associated with some larger meaning or idea in the story. For example, the actions at the tree reveal something about courage, fear, and the effort to overcome fear. Because those actions represent, or stand for, something else, they are called symbolic actions. It is when actions are used to deal with ideas that they become symbols. Finny is fearless and jumps quickly and easily. Gene is fearful, but controls his fear and finally dares to jump. Each action symbolizes a way of looking at life.

The next passages are about actions that are also symbolic. This time, however, the larger idea the author is writing about is authority.

> "We'd better hurry or we'll be late for dinner," I said, breaking into what Finny called my "West Point stride." Phineas didn't really dislike West Point in particular or authority in general, but just considered authority the necessary evil against which happiness was achieved by reaction, the backboard which returned all the insults he threw at it. My "West Point stride" was intolerable; his right foot flashed into the middle of my fast walk and I went pitching forward into the grass.

Finny doesn't trip Gene because he wants to hurt him. He trips Gene because he wants to make a point. Finny's action has a symbolic meaning. But how do we know that? And how do we know exactly what the action symbolizes? We have to look closely at the way the author describes what happens.

A school rule says that the boys must go to dinner at a certain time. The dinner bell has rung and Gene starts to hurry. Gene is clearly worried about breaking the rule. The author emphasizes the way Gene is conforming to the rules by mentioning his "West Point stride." He is suggesting that Gene is following rules as if he were in the army.

Finny, by contrast, sees rules and authority as a "necessary evil." He feels he must rebel against them. When Finny trips Gene, his action becomes a symbol of that rebellion against authority. Finny will not hurry to be on time for dinner. Gene gets caught up in this mood, and his actions take on a different symbolic meaning in Exercise C.

3 ◆ Exercise C

Read the following passage and answer the questions about it using what you have learned in this part of the lesson. Use your writing notebook or a separate piece of paper for your answers.

> "Better hurry," he [Finny] said, "or they'll put you in the guardhouse." We were walking again, faster; Bobby and Leper and Chet were urging us from ahead for God's sake to hurry up, and then Finny trapped me again in his strongest trap, that is, I suddenly became his collaborator. As we walked rapidly along I abruptly resented the bell and my West Point stride and hurrying and conforming. Finny was right. And there was only one way to show him this. I threw my hip against his, catching him by surprise, and he was instantly down, definitely pleased. This was why he liked me so much. When I jumped on top of him, my knees on his chest, he couldn't ask for anything better. We struggled in some equality for a while, and then when we were sure we were too late for dinner, we broke off.

1. The two character symbols come together in that passage. They briefly represent the same things—courage and defiance of authority. There are several sentences and phrases in the passage that tell you about courage and defiance of authority. Write down at least two of them.

2. What does the author mean when he has Gene say, ". . . then Finny trapped me again in his strongest trap, that is, I suddenly became his collaborator"?

Now check your answers using the suggestions in the Answer Key starting on page 451. Review this part of the lesson if you don't understand why your answer was wrong.

3♦Writing on Your Own

Look at the list of action symbols you wrote for Creating Symbols in a Story on page 271. Choose an action symbol from the list that you think you might like to use in your story. Now do the following:

1. Reread the story idea you created for 1♦Writing on Your Own.

2. Write a paragraph for your story that uses this action as a symbol. Here are a few suggestions:

☐ Perhaps you realize that you must *climb* the mountain to achieve your goal. By climbing the mountain (action), you will face your fear and uncertainty and overcome them.

☐ Perhaps you decide you must find the end of the rainbow to find out if your dream really can be fulfilled there. Your journey and what you learn on the way becomes the symbolic action.

Your paragraph can be used in any part of the story—the beginning, the middle, or the end.

3. You may want to change and rewrite your paragraph several times until you are satisfied with the action.

4 ◆ Symbols and Themes

A theme is a larger idea that an author wants to explore or express in a book. On one level, *A Separate Peace* is a story about two boys at school. On a thematic level, it is about fear, and about how people handle that troubling emotion.

You've seen that symbols are connected with larger ideas too. For example, you've seen how a character, Finny, can become a symbol of courage and confidence. It's not surprising, then, that authors often use symbols to help them develop their themes. Both symbols and themes are connected with the ideas that a book expresses.

John Knowles introduces the theme of fear in *A Separate Peace* through the use of a symbolic object. The tree that Finny and Gene jump from as boys plays a major role in Chapter 1, which you have just read. The tree is a symbol of the fear that Gene experienced as a youth. In creating this symbol, John Knowles is announcing his theme to us.

> There were several trees bleakly reaching into the fog. Anyone of them might have been the one I was looking for. Unbelievable that there were other trees which looked like it here. It had loomed in my memory as a huge lone spike dominating the riverbank, forbidding as an artillery piece, high as a beanstalk.

Once we understand what this tree means to Gene, we understand more clearly what other scenes mean. By showing us how people respond to this symbolic tree, John Knowles is developing his theme about fear. Some people, like Finny, seem to welcome the challenge of it. Others, like Leper, Chet, and Bobby, back away and make excuses. And people like Gene are almost overwhelmed by it, but learn to overcome their fear.

By showing how Gene's attitude toward this tree changes, John Knowles can tell us more of his idea about fear. When Gene returns to Devon as an adult, the tree seems different to him: "Yet here was a scattered grove of trees, none of them of any particular grandeur." The tree doesn't seem frightening to Gene any more. Knowles is developing his theme through this change in the symbolic object. Fear can be paralyzing, but it can also be overcome. We can grow out of it, as Gene has done. Notice how Gene responds to the tree in the passage in Exercise D. What is John Knowles telling us about his theme of fear?

4 ♦ Exercise D

Read the following passage and answer the questions about it using what you have learned in this part of the lesson. Use your writing notebook or a separate piece of paper for your answers.

> This was the tree, and it seemed to me standing there to resemble those men, the giants of your childhood, whom you encounter years later and find that they are not merely smaller in relation to your growth, but that they are absolutely smaller, shrunken by age. . . .
> The tree was not only stripped by the cold season, it seemed weary from age, enfeebled, dry. I was thankful, very thankful that I had seen it. . . . Nothing endures, not a tree, not love, not even a death by violence.

1. Gene faces a fearful symbol from his childhood and feels thankful. Why do you think he feels thankful?

2. What people are the "giants" of Gene's childhood? What people or what sort of things represent the giants of your childhood?

Now check your answers using the suggestions in the Answer Key starting on page 451. Review this part of the lesson if you don't understand why an answer was wrong.

4 ♦ Writing on Your Own

Reread the story idea or ideas you wrote about in the first three Writing on Your Own exercises in this lesson. Now do the following:

1. Write two or three sentences that tell the major idea, or theme, you would like to bring out in your story.

   ☐ The mountain may represent the themes of challenge and the importance of self-confidence and overcoming fear.

   ☐ The rainbow may represent the themes of learning more about yourself and what you are really looking for in life.

2. Make a short list of symbols that might help express your idea in a story. You can use the list of symbols you thought of earlier in the lesson or think of new ones.

3. Write a paragraph that uses one of the symbols to illustrate your theme.

4. You may want to change and rewrite your paragraph several times until you are satisfied with your theme.

Now go on to Reviewing and Interpreting the Chapter.

Reviewing and Interpreting the Chapter

Answer these questions without looking back at the selection. Choose the best answer to each question and put an x in the box beside it, or write your answer on a separate piece of paper.

Remembering
Facts

1. Where was the Devon School?

   ☐ a. South Carolina

   ☐ b. Maryland

   ☐ c. New Hampshire

   ☐ d. New York

2. Why was it dangerous to jump from the tree?

   ☐ a. The water was too deep.

   ☐ b. It was difficult to jump from the limb to deep water.

   ☐ c. The tree was too big to climb.

   ☐ d. There was a treacherous river current.

Following the
Order of Events

3. When did Gene return to look at the tree?

   ☐ a. right after wrestling Finny

   ☐ b. during World War II

   ☐ c. the day after he missed dinner

   ☐ d. on his return to Devon as an adult

4. How old do you think Gene is when the chapter opens?

☐ a. not more than sixteen

☐ b. fifty or older

☐ c. about forty

☐ d. in his thirties

Understanding Word Choices

5. "In through swinging doors I reached a marble foyer . . ." A *foyer* is a(n)

☐ a. statue.

☐ b. pool with a fountain.

☐ c. coat room.

☐ d. entrance hall.

6. Finny had a "cordial, penetrating voice." This means his voice was

☐ a. friendly and impressive.

☐ b. knotty and rough.

☐ c. raspy and harsh.

☐ d. fierce and commanding.

Understanding Important Ideas

7. When Gene Forrester came back to school, he wanted to see two "fearful" sites: a tree and a marble staircase. Why?

☐ a. He wondered if they would still seem fearful.

☐ b. They had provided unforgettable thrills.

☐ c. He had extra time before his visit.

☐ d. It was an old school tradition.

8. Why were there so many references in the chapter to military ideas and practices?

☐ a. Devon was a military school.

☐ b. The boys liked to play soldier.

☐ c. The United States had entered World War II.

☐ d. Discipline at the school was very strict.

Understanding Levels of Meaning

9. Finny said, "What I like about this tree . . . is that it's such a cinch!" What did he really like about the tree?

☐ a. The great view over the water from the branch.

☐ b. The challenge it presented.

☐ c. The memories it held for him.

☐ d. The feeling of security it gave him.

10. Why did Gene tend to follow Finny's lead?

☐ a. Gene had no mind of his own.

☐ b. It was fashionable to copy an older boy.

☐ c. Finny had the best judgment of all the boys.

☐ d. Gene probably wanted to be more like Finny.

Understanding Character

11. What was the difference between Gene as a boy and Gene as a man?

☐ a. Gene as a man was more reckless than he was as a boy.

☐ b. There really was no difference and no change.

☐ c. Gene as a man had overcome many of his fears.

☐ d. Gene as a man liked authority; the boy did not.

12. Which one of the following did Finny like to challenge the most?

□ a. Gene

□ b. authority

□ c. the tree

□ d. Devon traditions

13. How did the Devon campus look to Gene Forrester when he returned?

□ a. beautiful but fearful

□ b. old but beautiful

□ c. large but friendly

□ d. old and dismal

14. How are the settings different in the two parts of the chapter?

□ a. spring versus winter

□ b. pleasant versus fearsome

□ c. cold and snowy versus cold and rainy

□ d. cold and wet versus warm and pleasant

15. What is the dominant feeling that is discussed in the chapter?

□ a. wistful remembering

□ b. fear

□ c. courage

□ d. doubt

16. How did Finny feel when Gene knocked him down and jumped on him?

□ a. He was definitely pleased.

□ b. He was unpleasantly surprised.

□ c. He was angry.

□ d. He felt stupid.

Now check your answers using the Answer Key starting on page 451. Make no mark for right answers. Correct any wrong answers you may have by putting a check mark (✓) in the box next to the right answer. Count the number of questions you answered correctly and plot the total on the Comprehension Scores graph on page 462.

Next, look at the questions you answered incorrectly. What types of questions were they? Count the number you got wrong of each type and enter the numbers in the spaces below.

Remembering Facts   _____

Following the Order of Events   _____

Understanding Word Choices   _____

Understanding Important Ideas   _____

Understanding Levels of Meaning   _____

Understanding Character   _____

Understanding Setting   _____

Understanding Feelings   _____

Now use these numbers to fill in the Comprehension Skills Profile on page 463.

Discussion Guides

The questions below will help you think about the selection and the lesson you have just read. If you don't discuss these questions in class, try to think about them or discuss them with your classmates. Perhaps you will want to write a few paragraphs in answer to the questions.

Discussing Symbolism

1. At the end of the novel Gene says about World War II: "My war ended before I ever put on a uniform; I was on active duty all my time at school; I killed my enemy there." What do you suppose was Gene's "war" at school?

2. The Devon School represents everything in society that is prim, proper, well organized, and civilized. How does the author make this point?

3. World War II becomes an important symbol as the story goes along. How does it seem important in this chapter?

Discussing the Chapter

4. What is your opinion of Finny? of Gene?

5. When afraid, some people run away. Others fight or strike out at what they are afraid of. Leper did nothing. Why can Leper's reaction be the worst way to face fear?

6. What were you afraid of ten years ago that you are not afraid of now? Why did you change? Why did Gene change?

Discussing the Author's Work

7. The chapter starts with five pages of description, no conversation and very little action. Still, the author manages to hold your attention. How?

8. The tone and mood of the story change when the story changes from 1958 to 1942. How do they change and *why* do they change?

9. *A Separate Peace* has been called "a piercingly accurate recollection of life in a boy's preparatory school." In what ways do you find it "piercingly accurate"?

Writing Exercise

Read all the instructions before you begin writing. If you have any questions about how to begin the writing assignment, review Using the Writing Process beginning on page 439, or confer with your writing coach.

1. Write a short story that has as its themes fear and overcoming fear, as in *A Separate Peace*. Reread the paragraphs you wrote for the four Writing on Your Own exercises for ideas on how to add symbolism to a story.

2. In your story use your school and your friends in place of the Devon School. Or you can make up an imaginary school if you prefer.

3. Use your school and things around it as object symbols: the neighborhood, the school building, classrooms, the gym, the school grounds, the cafeteria, and so on as symbols of your fears.

4. Use character symbols who might cause you fear or help you to overcome it: friends, people you were once afraid of, teachers and principals who have helped you or perhaps made you afraid.

5. Tell about something that happened (an action symbol) in which you faced your fear and overcame it: trying out for a sport or making a presentation to the class.

6. Write, revise, correct, and rewrite your story until you are satisfied with the symbols, characters, action, and theme.

Unit 8   Autobiography and
Biography

Anne Frank: The Diary of a Young Girl

BY ANNE FRANK

About the Illustration

How do you know that something frightening and sad is happening to these people? Point out some details in the drawing to support your answer.

Here are some questions to help you think about the chapter:

◆ How would you describe the expressions on the girls' faces?

◆ Why do you think the people in this picture might be worried?

Unit 8

Introduction

About the Novel

During World War II, Nazi soldiers broke into an apartment in Amsterdam, Holland, where two Jewish families were in hiding. The soldiers' job was to remove everyone who was Jewish from Holland. The Jews were to be sent to forced labor camps and gas chambers in Germany and Eastern Europe.

Another part of the soldiers' job was to loot or destroy any evidence of their evil work. They were to leave behind no record for the rest of the world to see. During the search, one sergeant in charge found a briefcase. "Are there any jewels?" he asked. "No," said Otto Frank, now under arrest with his family and friends, "there are only papers."

The sergeant dumped the papers on the floor in disgust. He put some silverware and a candlestick in the briefcase and left with the prisoners.

With this act the sergeant had botched his job. Among the papers he had dumped on the floor was a document that would one day reveal to the world the truth about the Nazi horror. It was a diary written by Anne Frank, a young Jewish girl, during her two years in hiding.

Anne Frank received her diary in 1942 as a gift for her thirteenth birthday. A month later, she, her father, mother, and older sister Margot were forced to go into hiding to avoid arrest by the Nazis. Another family, the Van Daans, went into hiding with them. This second family consisted of Mr. and Mrs. Van Daan and their son, Peter, two years older than Anne. A dentist, Mr. Dussel, joined them later.

So they were eight in all. Their hiding place was a group of rooms behind the office where Otto Frank had worked as a manager. Business friends who still worked there kept their secret. They also kept the fugitives supplied with food and other necessities.

Anne's diary is not a record of the horrors she endured at the hands of the Nazis. It is a simple record of her life in hiding. Anne tells of ordinary daily events and of news on the radio. She records her thoughts and feelings. It is this personal record that makes her diary an autobiography.

Anne's writing showed great promise. Had she lived, there is little doubt that she would have become a great writer. Instead, not yet sixteen, she died alone in the Belsen concentration camp in Germany, barely two months before the end of the war in Europe.

Of the eight people who went into hiding, only Otto Frank survived. Mrs. Frank, Anne's mother, died mentally ill as a result of her experience at the Auschwitz camp. Mr. Frank watched Mr. Van Daan taken off to be gassed. Mr. Dussel died in another camp, and Peter Van Daan was taken away, never to be heard from again. Mrs. Van Daan and Margot died at Belsen shortly before Anne.

When Otto Frank returned to Amsterdam after the War, the friends who had helped him in hiding gave him the papers they had found dumped on the floor. Among them was Anne's diary.

After some years the diary was published and Anne belonged to the world. Her diary has become one of the most widely read autobiographies of our time. It was made into a prize-winning play in 1956, a movie in 1959, and was adapted for television in 1967.

The house where Anne lived in hiding for two years is now kept as a memorial to her. Located on the Prinsengracht Canal in Amsterdam, Holland, Anne's memorial is visited by thousands of people each year. There are also other memorials in her honor located in Germany, Israel, the United States, and other countries around the world. But her diary remains her greatest living memorial.

It is probably worthwhile to note that there are no memorials to Adolf Hitler, Anne's great tormentor. While *Anne Frank: The Diary of a Young Girl* is still very much alive, Hitler's autobiography, *Mein Kampf* (My Struggle), remains a dusty curiosity of hate on library shelves.

About the Lesson

The lesson that follows the reading selection is about biography and autobiography. *Biography* is the story of one person's life. *Autobiography* is also such a story, but it is written by the person whose life is described.

A biography looks at a person against the background of his or her environment. It tries to give a feeling for the time and place that person lived in. A biography examines the whole person. It is not the purpose of a biography to praise or make a hero out of the person. A good biography includes the bad and the good, the failures and the successes, the good judgments and the bad ones. And, above all, it tries to describe the innermost feelings of the person.

A diary or journal is not strictly an autobiography. Diaries are usually a day-to-day record of events and thoughts. They do not examine a person's entire life and times the way biography and autobiography do. They are generally written for the benefit of the diarist and no one else.

Anne Frank used a technique, however, that turned her diary into a true autobiography. She addressed her writing to "Kitty," an imaginary friend, and thus gave herself an audience of one. As a result, she was not writing just for herself. For Kitty, she examined her own character and described those around her. She discussed the times and looked at her life in relation to those times. You will soon see that what she wrote is considerably more than a record of events.

The questions below will help you focus on some characteristics of autobiography in *Anne Frank: The Diary of a Young Girl*. Read the selections carefully and try to answer these questions as you go along:

◆ What effect do time and place have on Anne's life? What was it like to be Jewish in Holland in 1942?

◆ We see Anne's character as she speaks of what she needs, wants, or longs for in life. What are some of her desires, and what do they show about her?

◆ What do you learn about Anne and Peter from stories of their friendship?

◆ What facts of history do you learn about from your reading? How do historical events affect Anne?

Keeping a Journal

1. Think about your own life. You probably have many stories each day to tell to your family and friends. Writing about these events can be easier than writing about something not so familiar to you.

2. Record a journal entry for today in your writing notebook. In the course of a day, many things happen. Since it will be impossible to write about everything that happened to you, include only those events that seem significant to you.

   ☐ Perhaps you missed the bus and had to run to school so that you wouldn't be late.

   ☐ Maybe you encountered some trouble along the way: a stray dog, a lost child, a sudden storm.

   ☐ How did you explain to your teacher, the principal, and your mom why you were late: "I helped a lost dog find his home"?

3. Your journal entry can be only a few paragraphs, or a few pages if you like. You'll notice that writing about the events of your life is much easier than writing about anything else.

Anne Frank:
The Diary of a Young Girl

by Anne Frank

Saturday, 20 June, 1942

I haven't written for a few days, because I wanted first of all to think about my diary. It's an odd idea for someone like me to keep a diary; not only because I have never done so before, but because it seems to me that neither I—nor for that matter anyone else—will be interested in the unbosomings of a thirteen-year-old schoolgirl. Still, what does that matter? I want to write, but more than that, I want to bring out all kinds of things that lie buried deep in my heart.

There is a saying that "paper is more patient than man"; it came back to me on one of my slightly melancholy days, while I sat chin in hand, feeling too bored and limp even to make up my mind whether to go out or stay at home. Yes, there is no doubt that paper is patient and as I don't intend to show this cardboard-covered notebook, bearing the proud name of "diary," to anyone, unless I find a real friend, boy or girl, probably nobody cares. And now I come to the root of the matter, the reason for my starting a diary: it is that I have no such real friend.

Let me put it more clearly, since no one will believe that a girl of thirteen feels herself quite alone in the world, nor is it so. I have darling parents and a sister of sixteen. I know about thirty people whom one might call friends— I have strings of boy friends, anxious to catch a glimpse of me and who, failing that, peep at me through mirrors in class. I have relations, aunts and uncles, who are darlings too, a good home, no—I don't seem to lack anything. But it's the same with all my friends, just fun and joking, nothing more. I can never bring myself to talk of anything outside the common round. We don't seem to be able to get any closer, that is the root of the trouble. Perhaps I lack confidence, but anyway, there it is, a stubborn fact and I don't seem to be able to do anything about it.

Hence, this diary. In order to enhance in my mind's eye the picture of the friend for whom I have waited so long, I don't want to set down a series of bald facts in a diary like most people do, but I want this diary itself to be my friend, and I shall call my friend Kitty. No one will grasp what I'm talking about if I begin my letters to Kitty just out of the blue, so albeit unwillingly, I will start by sketching in brief the story of my life.

My father was thirty-six when he married my mother, who was then twenty-five. My sister Margot was born in 1926 in Frankfort-on-Main, I followed on June 12, 1929, and, as we are Jewish, we emigrated to Holland in 1933, where my father was appointed Managing Director of Travies N.V. This firm is in close relationship with the firm of Kolen & Co. in the same building, of which my father is a partner.

The rest of our family, however, felt the full impact of Hitler's anti-Jewish laws, so life was filled with anxiety. In 1938 after the pogroms, my two uncles (my mother's brothers) escaped to the U.S.A. My old grandmother came to us, she was then seventy-three. After May 1940 good times rapidly fled: first the war, then the capitulation, followed by the arrival of the Germans, which is when the sufferings of us Jews really began. Anti-Jewish decrees followed each other in quick succession. Jews must wear a yellow star,[1] Jews must hand in their bicycles, Jews are

---

[1] To distinguish them from others, all Jews were forced by the Germans to wear, prominently displayed, a yellow six-pointed star.

banned from trains and are forbidden to drive. Jews are only allowed to do their shopping between three and five o'clock and then only in shops which bear the placard "Jewish shop." Jews must be indoors by eight o'clock and cannot even sit in their own gardens after that hour. Jews are forbidden to visit theaters, cinemas, and other places of entertainment. Jews may not take part in public sports. Swimming baths, tennis courts, hockey fields, and other sports grounds are all prohibited to them. Jews may not visit Christians. Jews must go to Jewish schools, and many more restrictions of a similar kind.

So we could not do this and were forbidden to do that. But life went on in spite of it all. Jopie used to say to me, "You're scared to do anything, because it may be forbidden." Our freedom was strictly limited. Yet things were still bearable.

Granny died in January 1942; no one will ever know how much she is present in my thoughts and how much I love her still.

In 1934 I went to school at the Montessori Kindergarten and continued there. It was at the end of the school year, I was in form 6B, when I had to say good-by to Mrs. K. We both wept, it was very sad. In 1941 I went, with my sister Margot, to the Jewish Secondary School, she into the fourth form and I into the first.

So far everything is all right with the four of us and here I come to the present day.

. . . .

Wednesday, 8 July, 1942

Dear Kitty,

Years seem to have passed between Sunday and now. So much has happened, it is just as if the whole world had turned upside down. But I am still alive, Kitty, and that is the main thing, Daddy says.

Yes, I'm still alive, indeed, but don't ask where or how.

You wouldn't understand a word, so I will begin by telling you what happened on Sunday afternoon.

At three o'clock (Harry had just gone, but was coming back later) someone rang the front doorbell. I was lying lazily reading a book on the veranda in the sunshine, so I didn't hear it. A bit later, Margot appeared at the kitchen door looking very excited. "The S.S. have sent a call-up notice for Daddy," she whispered. "Mummy has gone to see Mr. Van Daan already." (Van Daan is a friend who works with Daddy in the business.) It was a great shock to me, a call-up; everyone knows what that means. I picture concentration camps and lonely cells—should we allow him to be doomed to this? "Of course he won't go," declared Margot, while we waited together. "Mummy has gone to the Van Daans to discuss whether we should move into our hiding place tomorrow. The Van Daans are going with us, so we shall be seven in all." Silence. We couldn't talk any more, thinking about Daddy, who, little knowing what was going on, was visiting some old people in the Joodse Invalide; waiting for Mummy, the heat and suspense, all made us very overawed and silent.

Suddenly the bell rang again. "That is Harry," I said. "Don't open the door." Margot held me back, but it was not necessary as we heard Mummy and Mr. Van Daan downstairs, talking to Harry, then they came in and closed the door behind them. Each time the bell went, Margot or I had to creep softly down to see if it was Daddy, not opening the door to anyone else.

Margot and I were sent out of the room. Van Daan wanted to talk to Mummy alone. When we were alone together in our bedroom, Margot told me that the call-up was not for Daddy, but for her. I was more frightened than ever and began to cry. Margot is sixteen; would they really take girls of that age away alone? But thank goodness she won't go, Mummy said so herself; that must be what Daddy meant when he talked about us going into hiding.

Into hiding—where would we go, in a town or the country,

in a house or a cottage, when, how, where. . . ?

These were questions I was not allowed to ask, but I couldn't get them out of my mind. Margot and I began to pack some of our most vital belongings into a school satchel. The first thing I put in was this diary, then hair curlers, handkerchiefs, schoolbooks, a comb, old letters; I put in the craziest things with the idea that we were going into hiding. But I'm not sorry, memories mean more to me than dresses.

At five o'clock Daddy finally arrived, and we phoned Mr. Koophuis to ask if he could come around in the evening. Van Daan went and fetched Miep. Miep has been in the business with Daddy since 1933 and has become a close friend, likewise her brand-new husband, Henk. Miep came and took some shoes, dresses, coats, underwear, and stockings away in her bag, promising to return in the evening. Then silence fell on the house; not one of us felt like eating anything, it was still hot and everything was very strange. We let our large upstairs room to a certain Mr. Goudsmit, a divorced man in his thirties, who appeared to have nothing to do on this particular evening; we simply could not get rid of him without being rude; he hung about until ten o'clock. At eleven o'clock Miep and Henk Van Santen arrived. Once again, shoes, stockings, books, and underclothes disappeared into Miep's bag and Henk's deep pockets, and at eleven-thirty they too disappeared. I was dog-tired and although I knew that it would be my last night in my own bed, I fell asleep immediately and didn't wake up until Mummy called me at five-thirty the next morning. Luckily it was not so hot as Sunday; warm rain fell steadily all day. We put on heaps of clothes as if we were going to the North Pole, the sole reason being to take clothes with us. No Jew in our situation would have dreamed of going out with a suitcase full of clothing. I had on two vests, three pairs of pants, a dress, on top of that a skirt, jacket, summer coat, two pairs of stockings, lace-up shoes, woolly cap, scarf, and still more; I was nearly stifled before we started, but no one inquired about that.

Margot filled her satchel with schoolbooks, fetched her bicycle, and rode off behind Miep into the unknown, as far as I was concerned. You see I still didn't know where our secret hiding place was to be. At seven-thirty the door closed behind us. Moortje, my little cat, was the only creature to whom I said farewell. She would have a good home with the neighbors. This was all written in a letter addressed to Mr. Goudsmit.

There was one pound of meat in the kitchen for the cat, breakfast things lying on the table, stripped beds, all giving the impression that we had left helter-skelter. But we didn't care about impressions, we only wanted to get away, only escape and arrive safely, nothing else. Continued tomorrow.

Yours, Anne

Thursday, 9 July, 1942

Dear Kitty,

So we walked in the pouring rain, Daddy, Mummy, and I, each with a school satchel and shopping bag filled to the brim with all kinds of things thrown together anyhow.

We got sympathetic looks from people on their way to work. You could see by their faces how sorry they were they couldn't offer us a lift; the gaudy yellow star spoke for itself.

Only when we were on the road did Mummy and Daddy begin to tell me bits and pieces about the plan. For months as many of our goods and chattels and necessities of life as possible had been sent away and they were sufficiently ready for us to have gone into hiding of our own accord on July 16. The plan had had to be speeded up ten days because of the call-up, so our quarters would not be so well organized, but we had to make the best of it. The hiding place itself would be in the building where Daddy has his office. It will be hard for outsiders to understand, but I shall explain that later on. Daddy didn't have many people working for him: Mr. Kraler, Koophuis, Miep, and Elli Vossen, a twenty-three-year-old typist who all knew of our arrival. Mr. Vossen, Elli's father, and two boys worked in the warehouse; they had not been told.

I will describe the building: there is a large warehouse on the ground floor which is used as a store. The front door to the house is next to the warehouse door, and inside the front door is a second doorway which leads to a staircase. . . .

The right-hand door leads to our "Secret Annexe." No one would ever guess that there would be so many rooms hidden behind that plain gray door. There's a little step in front of the door and then you are inside. . . .

If you go up the next flight of stairs and open the door, you are simply amazed that there could be such a big light room in such an old house by the canal. There is a gas stove in this room (thanks to the fact that it was used as a laboratory) and a sink. This is now the kitchen for the Van Daan couple, besides being general living room, dining room, and scullery.

A tiny little corridor room will become Peter Van Daan's apartment. Then, just as on lower landing, there is a large attic. So there you are, I've introduced you to the whole of our beautiful "Secret Annexe."

Yours, Anne

. . . .

Friday, 21 August, 1942

Dear Kitty,

The entrance to our hiding place has now been properly concealed. Mr. Kraler thought it would be better to put a cupboard in front of our door (because a lot of houses are being searched for hidden bicycles), but of course it had to be a movable cupboard that can open like a door.

Mr. Vossen made the whole thing. We had already let him into the secret and he can't do enough to help. If we want to go downstairs, we have to first bend down and then jump, because the step has gone. The first three days we were all going about with masses of lumps on our foreheads, because we all knocked ourselves against the low doorway. Now we have nailed a cloth filled with wood wool against the top of the door. Let's see if that helps!

I'm not working much at present; I'm giving myself holidays until September. Then Daddy is going to give me lessons; it's shocking how much I've forgotten already. There is little change in our life here. Mr. Van Daan and I usually manage to upset each other, it's just the opposite with Margot whom he likes very much. Mummy sometimes treats me just like a baby, which I can't bear. Otherwise things are going better. I still don't like Peter any more, he is so boring; he flops lazily on his bed half the time, does a bit of carpentry, and then goes back for another snooze. What a fool!

It is lovely weather and in spite of everything we make the most we can of it by lying on a camp bed in the attic, where the sun shines through an open window.

Yours, Anne

· ·

Friday, 24 December, 1943

Dear Kitty,

I have previously written about how much we are affected by atmospheres here, and I think in my own case this trouble is getting much worse lately.

"Himmelhoch jauchzend und zum Tode betrübt"[1] certainly fits here. I am *"Himmelhoch jauchzend"* if I only

[1] A famous line from Goëthe: "On top of the world, or in the depths of despair."

think how lucky we are here compared with other Jewish children, and *"zum Tode betrübt"* comes over me when, as happened today, for example, Mrs. Koophuis comes and tells us about her daughter Corry's hockey club, canoe trips, theatrical performances, and friends. I don't think I'm jealous of Corry, but I couldn't help feeling a great longing to have lots of fun myself for once, and to laugh until my tummy ached. Especially at this time of the year with all the holidays for Christmas and the New Year, and we are stuck here like outcasts. Still, I really ought not to write this, because it seems ungrateful and I've certainly been exaggerating. But still, whatever you think of me, I can't keep everything to myself, so I'll remind you of my opening words—"Paper is patient."

When someone comes in from outside, with the wind in their clothes and the cold on their faces, then I could bury my head in the blankets to stop myself thinking: "When will we be granted the privilege of smelling fresh air?" And because I must not bury my head in the blankets, but the reverse—I must keep my head high and be brave, the thoughts will come, not once, but oh, countless times. Believe me, if you have been shut up for a year and a half, it can get too much for you some days. In spite of all justice and thankfulness, you can't crush you feelings. Cycling, dancing, whistling, looking out into the world, feeling young, to know that I'm free—that's what I long for; still, I musn't show it, because I sometimes think if all eight of us began to pity ourselves, or went about with discontented faces, where would it lead us? I sometimes ask myself, "Would anyone, either Jew or non-Jew, understand this about me, that I am simply a young girl badly in need of some rollicking fun?" I don't know, and I couldn't talk about it to anyone, because then I know I should cry. Crying can bring such relief. . . .

Yours, Anne

. . . .

Sunday, 13 February, 1944

Dear Kitty,

Since Saturday a lot has changed for me. It came about like this. I longed—and am still longing—but . . . now something has happened, which has made it a little, just a little, less.

To my great joy—I will be quite honest about it—already this morning I noticed that Peter kept looking at me all the time. Not in the ordinary way, I don't know how, I just can't explain.

I used to think that Peter was in love with Margot, but yesterday I suddenly had the feeling that it is not so. I made a special effort not to look at him too much, because whenever I did, he kept on looking too and then—yes, then—it gave me a lovely feeling inside, but which I mustn't feel too often.

I desperately want to be alone. Daddy had noticed that I'm not quite my usual self, but I really can't tell him everything. "Leave me in peace, leave me alone," that's what I'd like to keep crying out all the time. Who knows, the day may come when I'm left alone more than I would wish!

Yours, Anne

Monday, 14 February, 1944

Dear Kitty,

On Sunday evening everyone except Pim and me was sitting beside the wireless in order to listen to the "Immortal Music of the German Masters." Dussel fiddled with the knobs continually. This annoyed Peter, and the others too. After restraining himself for half an hour, Peter asked somewhat irritably if the twisting and turning might stop. Dussel answered in his most hoity-toity manner, "I'm getting it all right." Peter became angry, was rude, Mr. Van Daan took his side, and Dussel had to give in. That was all.

The reason in itself was very unimportant, but Peter seems to have taken it very much to heart. In any case, when I was rummaging about in the bookcase in the attic, he came up to me and began telling me the whole story. I didn't know anything about it, but Peter soon saw that he had found an attentive ear and got fairly into his stride.

"Yes, and you see," he said. "I don't easily say anything, because I know beforehand that I'll only become tongue-tied. I begin to stutter, blush, and twist around what I want to say, until I have to break off because I simply can't find the words. That's what happened yesterday, I wanted to say something quite different, but once I had started, I got in a hopeless muddle and that's frightful. I used to have a bad habit; I wish I still had it now. If I was angry with anyone, rather than argue it out I would get to work on him with my fists. I quite realize that this method doesn't get me anywhere; and that is why I admire you. You are never at a loss for a word, you say exactly what you want to say to people and are never the least bit shy."

"I can tell you, you're making a big mistake," I answered. "I usually say things quite differently from the way I meant to say them, and then I talk too much and far too long, and that's just as bad."

I couldn't help laughing to myself over this last sentence. However, I wanted to let him go on talking about himself, so I kept my amusement to myself, went and sat on a cushion on the floor, put my arms around my bent knees, and looked at him attentively.

I am very glad that there is someone else in the house who can get into the same fits of rage as I get into. I could see it did Peter good to pull Dussel to pieces to his heart's content, without fear of my telling tales. And as for me, I was very pleased, because I sensed a real feeling of fellowship, such as I can only remember having had with my girl friends.

Yours, Anne

Dear Kitty,

It's Margot's birthday. Peter came at half past twelve to look at the presents and stayed talking much longer than was strictly necessary—a thing he'd have never done otherwise. In the afternoon I went to get some coffee and, after that, potatoes, because I wanted to spoil Margot for just that one day in the year. I went through Peter's room; he took all his papers off the stairs at once and I asked whether I should close the trap door to the attic. "Yes," he replied, "knock when you come back, then I'll open it for you."

I thanked him, went upstairs, and searched at least ten minutes in the large barrel for the smallest potatoes. Then my back began to ache and I got cold. Naturally I didn't knock, but opened the trap door myself, but still he came to meet me most obligingly, and took the pan from me.

"I've looked for a long time, these are the smallest I could find," I said.

"Did you look in the big barrel?"

"Yes, I've been over them all."

By this time I was standing at the bottom of the stairs and he looked searchingly in the pan which he was still holding. "Oh, but these are first-rate," he said, and added when I took the pan from him, "I congratulate you!" At the same time he gave me such a gentle warm look which made a tender glow within me. I could really see that he wanted to please me, and because he couldn't make a long complimentary speech he spoke with his eyes. I understood him, oh, so well, and was very grateful. It gives me pleasure even now when I recall those words and that look he gave me.

When I went downstairs, Mummy said that I must get some more potatoes, this time for supper. I willingly offered to go upstairs again.

When I came into Peter's room, I apologized at having to disturb him again. When I was already on the stairs he got up, and went and stood between the door and the wall, firmly took hold of my arm, and wanted to hold me back by force.

"I'll go," he said. I replied that it really wasn't necessary and that I didn't have to get particularly small ones this time. Then he was convinced and let my arm go. On the way down, he came and opened the trap door and took the pan again. When I reached the door, I asked, "What are you doing?" "French," he replied. I asked if I might glance through the exercises, washed my hands, and went and sat on the divan opposite him.

We soon began talking, after I'd explained some of the French to him. He told me that he wanted to go to the Dutch East Indies and live on a plantation later on. He talked about his home life, about the black market, and then he said that he felt so useless. I told him that he certainly had a very strong inferiority complex. He talked about the Jews. He would have found it much easier if he'd been a Christian and if he could be one after the war. I asked if he wanted to be baptized, but that wasn't the case either. Who was to know whether he was a Jew when the war was over? he said.

This gave me rather a pang; it seems such a pity that there's always just a tinge of dishonesty about him. For the rest we chatted very pleasantly about Daddy, and about judging people's characters and all kinds of things, I can't remember exactly what now.

It was half past four by the time I left.

In the evening he said something else that I thought was nice. We were talking about a picture of a film star that I'd given him once, which has now been hanging in his room for at least a year and a half. He liked it very much and I offered to give him a few more sometime. "No," he replied, "I'd rather leave it like this. I look at these every day and they have grown to be my friends."

Now I understand more why he always hugs Mouschi. He needs some affection, too, of course.

I'd forgotten something else that he talked about. He said, "I don't know what fear is, except when I think of my own shortcomings. But I'm getting over that too."

Peter has a terrible inferiority complex. For instance, he always thinks that he is so stupid and we are so clever. If I help him with French he thanks me a thousand times. One day I shall turn around and say: "Oh, shut up, you're much better at English and geography!"

Yours, Anne

Friday, 18 February, 1944

Dear Kitty,

Whenever I go upstairs now I keep on hoping that I shall see "him." Because my life now has an object, and I have something to look forward to, everything has become more pleasant.

At least the object of my feelings is always there, and I needn't be afraid of rivals, except Margot. Don't think I'm in love, because I'm not, but I do have the feeling all the time that something fine can grow up between us, something that gives confidence and friendship. If I get half a chance, I go up to him now. It's not like it used to be when he didn't know how to begin. It's just the opposite—he's still talking when I'm half out of the room.

Mummy doesn't like it much, and always says I'll be a nuisance and that I must leave him in peace. Honestly, doesn't she realize that I've got some intuition? She looks at me so queerly every time I go into Peter's little room. If I come downstairs from there, she asks me where I've been. I simply can't bear it, and think it's horrible.

Yours, Anne

· ·

Friday, 21 July, 1944

Dear Kitty,

Now I am getting really hopeful, now things are going well at last. Yes, really, they're going well! Super news! An attempt has been made on Hitler's life and not even by Jewish communists or English capitalists this time, but by a proud German general, and what's more, he's a count, and still quite young. The Führer's life was saved by Divine Providence and, unfortunately, he managed to get off with just a few scratches and burns. A few officers and generals who were with him have been killed and wounded. The chief culprit was shot.

Anyway, it certainly shows that there are lots of officers and generals who are sick of the war and would like to see Hitler descend into a bottomless pit. When they've disposed of Hitler, their aim is to establish a military dictator, who will make peace with the Allies, then they intend to rearm and start another war in about twenty years' time. Perhaps the Divine Power tarried on purpose in getting him out of the way, because it would be much easier and more advantageous to the Allies if the impeccable Germans kill each other off; it'll make less work for the Russians and the English and they'll be able to begin rebuilding their own towns all the sooner.

But still, we're not that far yet, and I don't want to anticipate the glorious events too soon. Still, you mush have noticed, this is all sober reality and that I'm in quite a matter-of-fact mood today; for once, I'm not jabbering about high ideals. And what's more, Hitler has even been so kind as to announce to his faithful, devoted people that from now on everyone in the armed forces must obey the Gestapo, and that any soldier who knows that one of his superiors was involved in this low, cowardly attempt upon his life may shoot the same on the spot, without court-martial.

What a perfect shambles it's going to be. Little Johnnie's feet begin hurting him during a long march, he's snapped at by his boss, the officer, Johnnie grabs his rifle and cries out: "You wanted to murder the Führer, so there's your reward." One bang and the proud chief who dared to tick off little Johnnie has passed into eternal life (or is it eternal death?). In the end, whenever an officer finds himself up against a soldier, or having to take the lead, he'll be wetting his pants from anxiety, because the soldiers will dare to say more than they do. Do you gather a bit what I mean, or have I been skipping too much from one subject to another? I can't help it; the prospect that I may be sitting on school benches next October makes me feel far too cheerful to be logical! Oh, dearie me, hadn't I just told you that I didn't want to be too hopeful? Forgive me, they haven't given me the name "little bundle of contradictions" all for nothing!

Yours, Anne

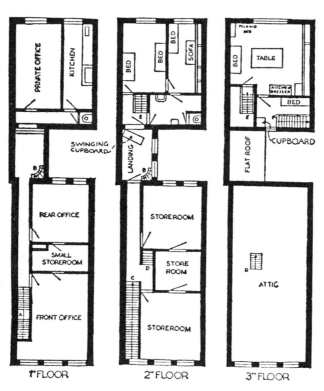

Autobiography and Biography

Bio- is a prefix that means "life," as you probably know from studying biology, the science of life. The suffix *-graph* means "something written." Combining the two creates *biography,* "writing about life." And since *auto-* means "self," *autobiography* is "writing about one's own life."

Biography is a very old form of writing. In fact, it is one of the oldest forms. Long before novels appeared, stone carvings told of the lives of real kings and heroes. Later, early books continued these stories and added to them the lives of saints and martyrs. Much of the Bible is considered a biography.

These old biographies, however, were not at all like those written today. Stories of kings and heroes were usually exaggerated. Their purpose was to praise the king or make the hero seem larger than life. Often they were written to teach a lesson about the rewards for being loyal and heroic, and the punishments for being evil and cowardly.

In contrast, modern biography looks at all sides of a person. It also examines the times in which the person lived. It exposes the bad along with the good. Even in autobiography the writer will confess to troubles and problems in an effort to present an honest and realistic picture.

A well-told story of a person's life is always interesting. It is like peeking through someone's window or living with the subject through some very personal moments. You share the person's most private thoughts and feelings. You really come to know what it must have been like to live in a different time and place under different conditions.

There are many values in autobiography that make it so popular. In the lesson we will talk about four of those values:

1 ♦ Autobiographies give a view of setting, of life in a certain time and place.

2 ♦ Autobiographies give a view of the character of the writer.

3 ♦ Autobiographies tell anecdotes, small interesting stories from life.

4 ♦ Autobiographies give a sense of history beyond the simple facts.

1 ♦ Autobiography and Setting

Setting is as important in an autobiography as it is in fiction. When reading an autobiography, you must know where and when the events occurred. But besides the facts of time and place, you must also understand the total environment.

The total environment consists of everything that is happening at a certain place at a certain time. It includes the way the place looks and the different ways the people behave. It also includes a more general feeling of what life was like at that time. The environment of Dallas, Texas, in 1880 would be quite different from the environment of Dallas today. The environment of New York's relaxed Greenwich Village is different from the hustle and bustle of its Upper East Side neighborhoods.

The total environment should come through to you as vividly in autobiography as it does in fiction. In autobiography, after all, you are reading about real people, real places, and real experiences. If the writer is honest, you can actually feel for yourself what it would have been like to be alive in that place at that time.

Notice how you begin to get a feeling for Anne's world in the following passage. Try to sense the environment—the air of the times—as it was for Anne Frank on June 20, 1942.

> My father was thirty-six when he married my mother, who was then twenty-five. My sister Margot was born in 1926 in Frankfort-on-Main, I followed on June 12, 1929, and, as we are Jewish, we emigrated to Holland in 1933, where my father was appointed Managing Director of Travies N.V. . . .
>
> The rest of our family, however, felt the full impact of Hitler's anti-Jewish laws, so life was filled with anxiety. . . . After May 1940 good times rapidly fled: first the war, then the capitulation, followed by the arrival of the Germans, which is when the sufferings of us Jews really began. Anti-Jewish decrees followed each other in quick succession. Jews must wear a yellow star, Jews must hand in their bicycles, Jews are banned from trains and are forbidden to drive. . . . Jews must be indoors by eight o'clock and cannot even sit in their own gardens after that hour. . . .

So we could not do this and were forbidden to do that. But life went on in spite of it all. . . . Our freedom was strictly limited. Yet things were still bearable.

What is going on outside the home is extremely important to the Frank family. The Nazis have arrived. They have put into effect the frightening "anti-Jewish decrees" that the Frank family fled from in Germany. "But," Anne says, "life went on in spite of it all." She finds her life "still bearable." She gives us details about her family and creates for us the feeling of a closely knit family that provides comfort in a time of horrible political turmoil. Anne's words create a vivid picture of her environment.

1 ◆ Exercise A

Read the following passage and answer the questions about it using what you have learned in this part of the lesson. Use your writing notebook or a separate piece of paper for your answers.

> We put on heaps of clothes as if we were going to the North Pole, the sole reason being to take clothes with us. No Jew in our situation would have dreamed of going out with a suitcase full of clothing. I had on two vests, three pairs of pants, a dress, on top of that a skirt, jacket, summer coat, two pairs of stockings, lace-up shoes, woolly cap, scarf, and still more; I was nearly stifled before we started, but no one inquired about that. . . .
> So we walked in the pouring rain, Daddy, Mummy, and I, each with a school satchel and shopping bag filled to the brim with all kinds of things thrown together anyhow.
> We got sympathetic looks from people on their way to work. You could see by their faces how sorry they were they couldn't offer us a lift; the gaudy yellow star spoke for itself.

1. The Franks feel very self-conscious in this setting. Do you agree or disagree with this statement? Use examples from the passage to explain your reasoning.

2. The people passing by are an important part of the setting here. What do they add to the scene?

Now check your answers using the suggestions in the Answer Key starting on page 451. Review this part of the lesson if you don't understand why an answer was wrong.

1♦Writing on Your Own

Look at the journal entry you have written for Keeping a Journal on page 312. Now do the following:

1. Choose one the events you wrote about in your journal. Think about the setting of that event. Were you indoors or outdoors? Were there other people around or were you alone? Was the sun out or was it pitch black?

2. Write a paragraph describing the setting. Be sure to include details such as time, place, weather, scenery, sounds, and smells. If your event concerns a current historical event, be sure to include details about that event and how it affects you and others around you.

3. You may want to change and rewrite your paragraph several times until you have a realistic, descriptive setting.

2 ◆ Autobiography and Character

The main purpose of a biography is to help readers know and understand a particular person. In modern biography, the author looks at every side of the person's character to understand fully that person. In an honest autobiography, the writer tries to do the same thing. In fact, sometimes a person looks at himself or herself more carefully than at others.

It is not often that you get the chance to know a person as well as you get to know the author of an autobiography. In an autobiography you learn of a character's ideals and goals. You see how those ideals and goals are pursued. You learn about the person's accomplishments and failures. And you come to know the person's most secret needs and wishes.

Here Anne Frank exposes one of her deepest feelings to readers.

> When someone comes in from outside, with the wind in their clothes and the cold on their faces, then I could bury my head in the blankets to stop myself thinking: "When will we be granted the privilege of smelling fresh air?" . . . Believe me, if you have been shut up for a year and a half, it can get too much for you some days. In spite of all justice and thankfulness, you can't crush your feelings. Cycling, dancing, whistling, looking out into the world, feeling young, to know that I'm free—that's what I long for. . . . I sometimes ask myself, "Would anyone, either Jew or non-Jew, understand this about me, that I am simply a young girl badly in need of some rollicking fun?" I don't know, and I couldn't talk about it to anyone, because then I know I should cry.

You have probably never known a young, active girl who has been cooped up in an apartment with seven other people for a year and a half. After reading this, however, you know one. You know what Anne thinks, how she feels, and what she longs for. In fact, this is one of the most moving passages in her book. Anne emerges as a thoughtful, sensitive girl. She can express her feelings far better than most people. Readers are privileged to be able to share those feelings with her.

2 ✦ Exercise B

Read the following passage and answer the questions about it using what you have learned in this part of the lesson. Use your writing notebook or a separate piece of paper for your answers.

> . . . *"zum Tode betrübt"* [the depths of despair] comes over me when, as happened today, for example, Mrs. Koophuis comes and tells us about her daughter Corry's hockey club, canoe trips, theatrical performances, and friends. I don't think I'm jealous of Corry, but I couldn't help feeling a great longing to have lots of fun myself for once, and to laugh until my tummy ached. Especially at this time of year with all the holidays for Christmas and the New Year, and we are stuck here like outcasts. Still, I really ought not to write this, because it seems ungrateful. . . . But still, whatever you think of me, I can't keep everything to myself, so I'll remind you of my opening words—"Paper is patient."

1. Anne reveals many of her feelings in this passage. (Example: the depths of despair) List some of her other feelings. Do you blame her for feeling left out?

2. At the beginning of the diary, Anne said, "Paper is more patient than man." She says it again here. What does she mean?

Now check your answers using the suggestions in the Answer Key starting on page 451. Review this part of the lesson if you don't understand why an answer was wrong.

2 ✦ Writing on Your Own

Look at the journal entry you have written for Keeping a Journal on page 312. Now do the following:

1. Keeping a journal can be fun because it gives you a chance to really examine yourself. You not only report the events of your life, but also record your thoughts, feelings, triumphs, and failures.

2. Write a paragraph in which you examine your thoughts and feelings. Give a complete picture of yourself.

   ☐ Why did you risk the anger of your teacher or parents for a stray dog?

   ☐ How are you affected by a particular current event?

   ☐ What kind of a mood were you in today: happy, sad, questioning, thoughtful?

3. You may want to rewrite your paragraph several times until you are happy with your own character description.

3 ◆ Autobiography and Anecdote

An anecdote is a brief story that tells of an interesting, amusing, or biographical event. It's the kind of story you hear in everyday conversation. An anecdote from a friend might begin, "Wait till I tell you what happened. . . ." And a story follows of some great or little adventure your friend had. Or someone in your family might say, "That reminds me of the time. . . ." And you might be in for a story you've heard a dozen times before. But if you're lucky, it will be a story that is new and interesting.

Because an autobiography is about a person's life, it is filled with anecdotes. That is why well-written autobiographies are so interesting and easy to read. Reading an autobiography is like listening to family gossip. One of the problems of writing an autobiography, however, is deciding which anecdotes to include. Since there are many stories in everyone's life, choosing the important anecdotes is not always easy. Each anecdote must have a purpose for being included in an autobiography. The main purpose of an anecdote is to help readers understand the subject of the autobiography and his or her environment.

Consider this anecdote from Anne's diary. She tells you in her first sentence why she considers this anecdote important: "Since Saturday a lot has changed for me."

> Since Saturday a lot has changed for me. It came about like this. . . .
>
> To my great joy—I will be quite honest about it—already this morning I noticed that Peter kept looking at me all the time. Not in the ordinary way, I don't know how, I just can't explain.
>
> I used to think that Peter was in love with Margot, but yesterday I suddenly had the feeling that it is not so. I made a special effort not to look at him too much, because whenever I did, he kept on looking too and then—yes, then—it gave me a lovely feeling inside, but which I mustn't feel too often.

What Anne seems to be saying is that she is afraid she is falling in love with Peter. She's not sure if she wants to, or even if it's right. It gives her a feeling, she says, "which I mustn't feel too often."

The small anecdote is interesting for two reasons. It sheds more light on Anne, and it is the kind of experience everyone can relate to. Surely you have had this same feeling at one time or another. And, like Anne, you weren't quite sure at the moment what to do about it.

3 ◆ Exercise C

Read the following passage and answer the questions about it using what you have learned in this part of the lesson. Use your writing notebook or a separate piece of paper for your answers.

> In the evening he [Peter] said something else that I thought was nice. We were talking about a picture of a film star that I'd given him once, which has now been hanging in his room for at least a year and a half. He liked it very much and I offered to give him a few more sometime. "No," he replied. "I'd rather leave it like this. I look at these every day and they have grown to be my friends."
>
> Now I understand more why he always hugs Mouschi. He needs some affection, too, of course.

1. Why do you think Anne chose to write about this particular anecdote?

2. Anne has learned something in her conversation with Peter. What does this anecdote teach Anne about Peter?

Now check your answers using the suggestions in the Answer Key starting on page 451. Review this part of the lesson if you don't understand why an answer was wrong.

3 ◆ Writing on Your Own

Look at the journal entry you have written for Keeping a Journal on page 312. Now do the following:

1. Choose another event from your journal entry that is interesting or amusing. It could be as simple as eating someone else's lunch by mistake. Or it could involve being mistaken for someone else and winding up with a day in detention.

2. Write a brief paragraph reporting the facts of your incident. Include details that you think are funny or interesting and that others can appreciate. Make your story as interesting to others as possible. Have you learned a lesson as a result of this incident? Can others learn from your experience?

3. You may want to rewrite your paragraph several times until your story sounds just as it happened.

4 ♦ Autobiography and the Sense of History

Reading about history can sometimes be dull. But if you are able to imagine vividly the times and people you are reading about, history can be very exciting. If history is presented in an interesting way, it is no longer a boring series of events from a dead past. Another way to look at history, though, is to see that it is about people with thoughts and feelings much like your own. Being able to see the past in this way is called having a sense of history. It means you have a feeling for the way events actually affected the people who lived through them.

It is true, unfortunately, that few history texts give the feeling of what it was like to be alive at a different time. They usually look at very large pictures: wars, laws, political activities, public events, and trends. There is little room for the most interesting part of history—getting to know the people. Autobiography, however, does allow you to get to know how real people lived at a particular time. You learn how these people felt about what was happening around them. You get a sense of the moment because you live through it in your reading.

Here Anne comments on an historic event of her time—the attempted assassination of Adolf Hitler in 1944.

> Now I am getting really hopeful, now things are going well at last. Yes, really, they're going well! Super news! An attempt has been made on Hitler's life and not even by Jewish communists or English capitalists this time, but by a proud German general, and what's more, he's a count, and still quite young. The Führer's life was saved by Divine Providence and, unfortunately, he managed to get off with just a few scratches and burns. A few officers and generals who were with him have been killed and wounded. The chief culprit was shot.
>
> Anyway, it certainly shows that there are lots of officers and generals who are sick of the war and would like to see Hitler descend into a bottomless pit.

These two small paragraphs have taught you as much as a chapter from a history text. Hitler liked to blame all of Germany's problems on Jewish communists or English capitalists. The young people, he claimed, were his greatest supporters. But in this passage, Anne is overjoyed at evidence of how wrong Hitler's ideas have been. She has learned, from a newspaper story or a radio broadcast, of a plot to kill Hitler. Not only was the plot cooked up by his own officers, but it was a young man who tried to kill him. Quite naturally, Anne wishes Hitler in a "bottomless pit." Now it seems to her that some of his own people feel the same way. There are no dry facts here. Instead, the facts about the plot are made lively by Anne's intense feelings.

4 ◆ Exercise D

Read the following passage and answer the questions about it using what you have learned in this part of the lesson. Use your writing notebook or a separate piece of paper for your answers.

> [Anne is summing up her feelings about the news of the attempt on Hitler's life.]
>   Do you gather a bit what I mean, or have I been skipping too much from one subject to another? I can't help it; the prospect that I may be sitting on school benches next October makes me feel far too cheerful to be logical! Oh, dearie me, hadn't I just told you that I didn't want to be too hopeful? Forgive me. . . .

1. What are the two feelings that Anne has at this moment in history?

2. What does Anne see as a prospect for next October?

Now check your answers using the suggestions in the Answer Key starting on page 451. Review this part of the lesson if you don't understand why an answer was wrong.

4 ◆ Writing on Your Own

Look at the journal entry you have written for Keeping a Journal on page 312. Now do the following:

1. If you did not write about a current historical event in your journal entry, jot down your feelings about one now.

2. Write a paragraph describing how the historical event has influenced your life. Maybe you are *not* affected by the event. Maybe your life-style has changed as a result of the event. Below is an example of a significant event that may have affected many people in the past.

   ☐ In 1969 an American astronaut walked on the moon. Do you think this event had an effect on most Americans? Would it have affected your life at all?

   ☐ Think of a major event in history that is happening now. Is it affecting your life? Your parents' lives?

3. You may want to rewrite your paragraph several times until you capture a true feeling for the historical event.

Now go on to Reviewing and Interpreting the Chapter.

Reviewing and Interpreting the Chapter

Answer these questions without looking back at the selection. Choose the best answer to each question and put an *x* in the box beside it, or write your answer on a separate piece of paper.

Remembering
Facts

1. How was the entrance to the secret annex hidden?

   ☐ a. with a trap door

   ☐ b. by a curtain

   ☐ c. by a cupboard

   ☐ d. with a false stairway

2. Who tried to kill Hitler?

   ☐ a. a German general

   ☐ b. a Jewish communist

   ☐ c. an English capitalist

   ☐ d. a German soldier

Following the
Order of Events

3. Which one of the following is a correct statement?

   ☐ a. The Franks went into hiding after the German officer's attempt to kill Hitler.

   ☐ b. The Franks moved to Holland shortly after their marriage.

   ☐ c. The Franks lived in Frankfort-on-Main before they moved to Holland.

   ☐ d. The Franks went into hiding before Margot was called up.

4. When did hard times begin for the Jews in Holland?

   ☐ a. just after the beginning of the war

   ☐ b. just after the Franks went into hiding

   ☐ c. just before Peter came to the annex

   ☐ d. just before Anne was born

5. Anne says that on her <u>melancholy</u> days she sits with her chin in her hand. *Melancholy* means

   ☐ a. joy.

   ☐ b. patience.

   ☐ c. sadness.

   ☐ d. thoughtfulness.

6. After <u>restraining</u> himself for half an hour, Peter told Mr. Dussel to stop turning the radio dial. What did Peter do for half an hour?

   ☐ a. He held back.

   ☐ b. He moved quickly.

   ☐ c. He argued.

   ☐ d. He complained.

7. What common need brought Peter and Anne together?

   ☐ a. a need to hear news from the outside

   ☐ b. a need to escape from harsh parents

   ☐ c. a need to share secrets in their diaries

   ☐ d. a need to tell their thoughts to someone

8. The Franks went into hiding when the Nazis sent a call-up notice for Margot. What did the call-up notice mean?

☐ a. Margot would have been sent to a concentration camp.

☐ b. Margot was called for military service against her will.

☐ c. Margot had violated some of the new decrees.

☐ d. Margot was probably a member of a resistance movement.

Understanding Levels of Meaning

9. Anne quotes an old saying: "On top of the world or in the depths of despair." What does she mean by that statement?

☐ a. Life is not worth living.

☐ b. I wish I were free again.

☐ c. The world is a crazy place to live.

☐ d. Life is extreme: either very good or really terrible.

10. Why was Anne so excited about the attempt on Hitler's life?

☐ a. It seemed a good way to get even with him.

☐ b. It meant she would be able to marry Peter.

☐ c. She felt the war would soon be over.

☐ d. It meant there had been a revolution in Germany.

11. Probably the most important reason that Anne
wrote to Kitty was that she was

☐ a. always happy.

☐ b. often lonely.

☐ c. afraid of people.

☐ d. angry with the world.

12. Anne believes Peter has "a terrible inferiority
complex." She feels this way because Peter

☐ a. refuses to learn new things.

☐ b. feels everyone is smarter than he is.

☐ c. keeps to himself.

☐ d. is in love with Margot.

13. Anne writes "we are stuck here [in the Secret
Annexe] like outcasts." Choose the word that best
describes Anne's feelings about her surroundings.

☐ a. serious

☐ b. relieved

☐ c. confined

☐ d. satisfied

14. Anne writes, "When someone comes in from
outside, with the wind in their clothes and the
cold on their faces. . ." she wonders, ". . . When
will we be granted the privilege of smelling fresh
air?" Which word best describes Anne's feelings?

☐ a. resentment

☐ b. anger

☐ c. rebellion

☐ d. longing

15. What does Anne wish for most of all?

    ☐ a. to be a successful writer

    ☐ b. to be free

    ☐ c. Peter's love

    ☐ d. to be like Margot

16. In what way does Anne's diary provide comfort for her?

    ☐ a. Anne can tell her diary everything.

    ☐ b. It gives her the chance to improve her writing.

    ☐ c. She is able to pass the time writing.

    ☐ d. No one else is willing to listen to Anne.

Now check your answers using the Answer Key starting on page 451. Make no mark for right answers. <u>Correct</u> any wrong answers you may have by putting a check mark (✓) in the box next to the right answer. Count the number of questions you answered correctly and plot the total on the Comprehension Scores graph on page 462.

Next, look at the questions you answered incorrectly. What types of questions were they? Count the number you got wrong of each type and enter the numbers in the spaces below.

Remembering Facts   _____

Following the Order of Events   _____

Understanding Word Choices   _____

Understanding Important Ideas   _____

Understanding Levels of Meaning   _____

Understanding Character   _____

Understanding Setting   _____

Understanding Feelings   _____

Now use these numbers to fill in the Comprehension Skills Profile on page 463.

Discussion Guides

The questions below will help you think about the selection and the lesson you have just read. If you don't discuss these questions in class, try to think about them or discuss them with your classmates. Perhaps you will want to write a few paragraphs in answer to the questions.

Discussing Autobiography

1. An autobiography is supposed to explore human problems and values. How do the selections from Anne's diary do this?

2. It was pointed out in the lesson that history books look at large pictures. Autobiographies often look at very small pictures. The small picture here is Anne Frank in hiding in Amsterdam, Holland, between 1942 and 1944. After reading about Anne Frank, what questions would you like to ask about the larger picture? Some larger pictures would be Europe, 1933–1945; World War II; the Netherlands in World War II.

3. *I Know Why the Caged Bird Sings* (Unit 2) is also an autobiography. Compare Anne Frank's diary with Maya Angelou's autobiography. How is it the same? How is it different?

Discussing the Selection

4. There are memorials to Anne Frank in many places around the world. Her book has been published in thirty-three languages and in virtually every country. The play and movie about her experience are done over and over again. What, in your opinion, makes her such a well-known heroine?

5. What in these selections from Anne's diary makes you feel sad about her life? What gives you a good feeling?

6. Anne Frank has been called a symbol. How is she a symbol?

Discussing the Author's Work

7. Anne wrote in the Dutch language. What you have read is a translation. Are there ways you can tell that it wasn't written in English? Does it sound different from the way an American or English girl would write?

8. Most diaries are not written as if they were letters to an imaginary friend. How do you think writing to "Kitty" affected Anne's work?

9. Anne began writing her diary when she was thirteen. She was almost fifteen when she wrote the later entries. How are the first entries different from the later entries? How would you account for the differences?

Writing Exercise

Read <u>all</u> the instructions before you begin writing. If you have any questions about how to begin the writing assignment, review Using the Writing Process, beginning on page 439, or confer with your writing coach.

1. Write a journal entry about a recent day in your past. It could be yesterday or last Friday. Make sure the day you choose includes some interesting events.

2. Make sure to include the following details in your journal entry:

   ◆ **Describe the setting.** Make sure you include the time and place in your description. What day is it? Where does each event occur? Is there any event of historical importance in the daily news? Are you affected by this event?

   ◆ **Describe yourself.** You do not need to describe what you look like. What is important is that you describe the kind of person you are. Include your thoughts, feelings, and emotions.

   ◆ **Relate an anecdote.** Include a brief, but interesting, event that happened to you on this day.

3. You may want to write, revise, correct, and rewrite your entry until you have included all the important elements of autobiography.

Unit 9 Fantasy

The Hobbit
BY J.R.R. TOLKIEN

About the Illustration

How would you describe the world where this scene takes place? Point out some details in the drawing to support your response.

Here are some questions to help you think about the chapter:

◆ How do you know that this scene couldn't be happening in the real world? What details make it seem like a fantasy world?

◆ What details in this picture make it seem realistic? What things in the drawing might you see in your everyday experience?

Unit 9

Introduction

About the Novel

Hobbits are little people about half our size. They tend to be fat in the stomach, which is not surprising since they eat six meals a day. They dress in brightly colored clothes but wear no shoes on their furry, thick-soled feet. They live in a land called the Shire, which might be anywhere. They're a peaceful people who would prefer to let the rest of the world pass them by. They like nothing better than to have a neighbor in for tea—or to be invited out to tea.

But there's more to a hobbit than meets the eye. They are fiercely loyal to their friends. They are clever and quick-witted. They will fight to the death if they have to.

Bilbo Baggins would rather not have to. He's 50 years old (that's younger than it sounds; hobbits live to be about 120 years old) and perfectly content with his life, which revolves around the preparation of meals. An adventure is the last thing Bilbo wants.

But adventure comes knocking on his door in the form of thirteen dwarves. They are looking for a fourteenth member (thirteen is an unlucky number) to help them reclaim their ancestors' gold. It is presently guarded by a dragon, which sleeps on it. The dwarves are looking for a "burglar"—an expert treasure hunter, if you wish—to make up their party. Bilbo, as one dwarf notes, looks more like a grocer than a burglar. But Gandalf the wizard thinks differently: "There is a lot more in him than you guess, and a deal more than he has any idea of himself."

So Bilbo sets out on a quest for gold. Along the way, he meets many dangers (and misses a great many meals). And he wins a game of riddles with a slimy, pale creature called Gollum. The prize is a gold ring that makes its wearer invisible.

The ring has other powers, too, though Bilbo doesn't realize it. The ring plays a small part in *The Hobbit*. But the ring is the focus of the author's great trilogy, *The Lord of the Rings*, which you will want to read after *The Hobbit*.

The Hobbit and its sequel, *The Lord of the Rings,* were written by an Englishman, J.R.R. Tolkien (1892–1973). When asked about how he created hobbits, Tolkien said, "I am in fact a hobbit in all but size. I like gardens, trees, and unmechanized farmlands; I smoke a pipe, and like good plain food . . . I am fond of mushrooms, have a very simple sense of humor; I go to bed late and get up late. I do not travel much."

The Hobbit tells of an entire fantasy world with a history and culture all its own. The appeal of the stories is enormous. Their many fans have created a "hobbit market" of calendars, games, T-shirts, and the like. The world of the hobbits can seem very real and very appealing. It is probably one of the best and most ambitious example of what fantasy is.

About the Lesson

The lesson that follows the reading selection is about fantasy. A fantasy is a story in which an author "breaks free" from the real world. It will, therefore, take place in an unreal world—a fairyland, an unknown planet, a time in the future, a city beneath the sea. In a fantasy there are unreal characters too. In *The Hobbit* we meet hobbits, dwarves, elves, dragons, a wizard, and many other strange creatures. In other fantasies there may be talking rabbits or lovable robots.

Everyone grows up with fantasy. And no one ever grows too old to enjoy this story form. Fairy tales are fantasies. Most of Walt Disney's stories are set in fantasy lands with fantastic characters. Millions enjoy the living fantasies of Disneyland and Disney World year after year. Science fiction, folktales, and myths are all examples of fantasy.

Fantasy as a story form has certain basic characteristics. We will discuss some of them in this lesson.

The questions below will help you focus on some characteristics of fantasy in the chapter from *The Hobbit*. Read the chapter and try to answer these questions as you go along:

◆ The author describes a fantasy world where hobbits live, but there are still familiar things in this world. What are they?

◆ Everyone knows that hobbits and dwarves are unreal creatures. How does the author make them seem real and believable within the fantasy world?

◆ Magic is part of fantasy. How are readers told early in the chapter that there will be magic in the story?

◆ How is Bilbo Baggins like you and other people you know? Who or what in the real world is like Smaug the dragon?

Create Your Own Fantasy Story

The first step you need to take in creating your own fantasy story is to choose an idea. Next you need a setting and characters. Discuss ideas with your classmates, or try the following suggestions. Use your writing notebook or a separate piece of paper to list your ideas.

1. Make a list of what your story will be about. Will your characters have to go on a quest? Will they have to escape from an evil force? For example, you might write about an elf who must go on a quest to find and bring back a golden orb. Only the person with the golden orb will be able to save the village.

2. Your story will take place in a fantasy, or unreal, world. Make a list of settings in which your story could take place. Here are a few ideas to help you get started:

   ◆ **Place**
   fairyland—a place of magical charm
   underground—tunnels or caves
   another planet—perhaps another galaxy
   under water—an undiscovered colony of "beings"

   ◆ **Time**
   Will your story take place far in the future or in the past?

3. Now you're ready to think of ideas for your characters. What will they look like? What will they wear? Make a list of possible characters for your story.

   ◆ **Character**
   elves
   dwarves
   talking animals
   dragons
   robots
   mythological creatures

The Hobbit

by J.R.R. Tolkien

Chapter 1
An Unexpected Party

In a hole in the ground there lived a hobbit. Not a nasty, dirty, wet hole, filled with the ends of worms and an oozy smell, nor yet a dry, bare, sandy hole with nothing in it to sit down on or to eat: it was a hobbit-hole, and that means comfort.

It had a perfectly round door like a porthole, painted green, with a shiny yellow brass knob in the exact middle. The door opened on to a tube-shaped hall like a tunnel: a very comfortable tunnel without smoke, with panelled walls, and floors tiled and carpeted, provided with polished chairs, and lots and lots of pegs for hats and coats—the hobbit was fond of visitors. The tunnel wound on and on, going fairly but not quite straight into the side of the hill—The Hill, as all the people for many miles round called it—and many little round doors opened out of it, first on one side and then on another. No going upstairs for the hobbit: bedrooms, bathrooms, cellars, pantries (lots of these), wardrobes (he had whole rooms devoted to clothes), kitchens, dining-rooms, all were on the same floor, and indeed on the same passage. The best rooms were all on the left-hand side (going in), for these were the only ones to have windows, deep-set round windows looking over his garden and meadows beyond, sloping down to the river.

This hobbit was a very well-to-do hobbit, and his name

was Baggins. The Bagginses had lived in the neighbourhood of The Hill for time out of mind, and people considered them very respectable, not only because most of them were rich, but also because they never had any adventures or did anything unexpected: you could tell what a Baggins would say on any question without the bother of asking him. This is a story of how a Baggins had an adventure, and found himself doing and saying things altogether unexpected. He may have lost the neighbours' respect, but he gained—well, you will see whether he gained anything in the end.

The mother of our particular hobbit—what is a hobbit? I suppose hobbits need some description nowadays, since they have become rare and shy of the Big People, as they call us. They are (or were) a little people, about half our height, and smaller than the bearded Dwarves. Hobbits have no beards. There is little or no magic about them, except the ordinary everyday sort which helps them to disappear quietly and quickly when large stupid folk like you and me come blundering along, making a noise like elephants which they can hear a mile off. They are inclined to be fat in the stomach; they dress in bright colours (chiefly green and yellow); wear no shoes, because their feet grow natural leathery soles and thick warm brown hair like the stuff on their heads (which is curly); have long clever brown fingers, good-natured faces, and laugh deep fruity laughs (especially after dinner, which they have twice a day when they can get it). Now you know enough to go on with. As I was saying, the mother of this hobbit—of Bilbo Baggins, that is—was the fabulous Belladonna Took, one of the three remarkable daughters of the Old Took, head of the hobbits who lived across The Water, the small river that ran at the foot of The Hill. It was often said (in other families) that long ago one of the Took ancestors must have taken a fairy wife. That was, of course, absurd, but certainly there was still something not entirely hobbit-like about them, and once in a while members of the Took-clan would go and have adventures. They discreetly disappeared, and the family hushed it up; but the fact remained that the Tooks were not as respectable as the Bagginses, though they were undoubtedly richer.

Not that Belladonna Took ever had any adventures after she became Mrs. Bungo Baggins. Bungo, that was Bilbo's father, built the most luxurious hobbit-hole for her (and partly with her money) that was to be found either under The Hill or over The Hill or across The Water, and there they remained to the end of their days. Still it is probable that Bilbo, her only son, although he looked and behaved exactly like a second edition of his solid and comfortable father, got something a bit queer in his makeup from the Took side, something that only waited for a chance to come out. The chance never arrived, until Bilbo Baggins was grown up, being about fifty years old or so, and living in the beautiful hobbit-hole built by his father, which I have just described for you, until he had in fact apparently settled down immovably.

By some curious chance one morning long ago in the quiet of the world, when there was less noise and more green, and the hobbits were still numerous and prosperous, and Bilbo Baggins was standing at his door after breakfast smoking an enormous long wooden pipe that reached nearly down to his woolly toes (neatly brushed)— Gandalf came by. Gandalf! If you had heard only a quarter of what I have heard about him, and I have only heard very little of all there is to hear, you would be prepared for any sort of remarkable tale. Tales and adventures sprouted up all over the place wherever he went, in the most extraordinary fashion. He had not been down that way under The Hill for ages and ages, not since his friend the Old Took died, in fact, and the hobbits had almost forgotten what he looked like. He had been away over The Hill and across The Water on business of his own since they were all small hobbit-boys and hobbit-girls.

All that the unsuspecting Bilbo saw that morning was an old man with a staff. He had a tall pointed blue hat, a long grey cloak, a silver scarf over which a white beard hung down below his waist, and immense black boots.

"Good morning!" said Bilbo, and he meant it. The sun was shining, and the grass was very green. But Gandalf looked at him from under long bushy eyebrows that stuck out further than the brim of his shady hat.

"What do you mean?" he said. "Do you wish me a good morning, or mean that it is a good morning whether I want it or not; or that you feel good this morning; or that it is a morning to be good on?"

"All of them at once," said Bilbo. "And a very fine morning for a pipe of tobacco out of doors, into the bargain. If you have a pipe about you, sit down and have a fill of mine! There's no hurry, we have all the day before us!" Then Bilbo sat down on a seat by his door, crossed his legs, and blew out a beautiful grey ring of smoke that sailed up into the air without breaking and floated away over The Hill.

"Very pretty!" said Gandalf. "But I have no time to blow smoke-rings this morning. I am looking for someone to share in an adventure that I am arranging, and it's very difficult to find anyone."

"I should think so—in these parts! We are plain quiet folk and have no use for adventures. Nasty disturbing uncomfortable things! Make you late for dinner! I can't think what anybody sees in them," said our Mr. Baggins, and stuck one thumb behind his braces, and blew out another even bigger smoke-ring. Then he took out his morning letters, and began to read, pretending to take no more notice of the old man. He had decided that he was not quite his sort, and wanted him to go away. But the old man did not move. He stood leaning on his stick and gazing at the hobbit without saying anything, till Bilbo got quite uncomfortable and even a little cross.

"Good morning!" he said at last. "We don't want any adventures here, thank you! You might try over The Hill or across The Water." By this he meant that the conversation was at an end.

"What a lot of things you do use *Good morning* for!" said Gandalf. "Now you mean that you want to get rid of me, and that it won't be good till I move off."

"Not at all, not at all, my dear sir! Let me see, I don't think I know your name?"

"Yes, yes, my dear sir—and I do know your name, Mr. Bilbo Baggins. And you do know my name, though you don't remember that I belong to it. I am Gandalf, and Gandalf means me! To think that I should have lived to be good-morninged by Belladonna Took's son, as if I was selling buttons at the door!"

"Gandalf, Gandalf! Good gracious me! Not the wandering wizard that gave Old Took a pair of magic diamond studs that fastened themselves and never came undone till ordered? Not the fellow who used to tell such wonderful tales at parties, about dragons and goblins and giants and the rescue of princesses and the unexpected luck of widows' sons? Not the man that used to make such particularly excellent fireworks! I remember those! Old Took used to have them on Midsummer's Eve. Splendid! They used to go up like great lilies and snapdragons and laburnums of fire and hang in the twilight all evening!" You will notice already that Mr. Baggins was not quite so prosy as he liked to believe, also that he was very fond of flowers. "Dear me!" he went on. "Not the Gandalf who was responsible for so many quiet lads and lasses going off into the Blue for mad adventures. Anything from climbing trees to visiting Elves—or sailing in ships, sailing to other shores! Bless me, life used to be quite inter—I mean, you used to upset things badly in these parts once upon a time. I beg your pardon, but I had no idea you were still in business."

"Where else should I be?" said the wizard. "All the same I am pleased to find you remember something about me. You seem to remember my fireworks kindly, at any rate, and that is not without hope. Indeed for your old grand-father Took's sake, and for the sake of poor Belladonna, I will give you what you asked for."

"I beg your pardon, I haven't asked for anything!"

"Yes, you have! Twice now. My pardon. I give it you. In fact I will go so far as to send you on this adventure. Very amusing for me, very good for you—and profitable too, very likely, if you ever get over it."

"Sorry! I don't want any adventures, thank you. Not today. Good morning! But please come to tea—any time you like! Why not tomorrow? Come tomorrow! Good-bye!" With that the hobbit turned and scuttled inside his round green door, and shut it as quickly as he dared, not to seem rude. Wizards after all are wizards.

"What on earth did I ask him to tea for!" he said to himself, as he went to the pantry. He had only just had breakfast, but he thought a cake or two and a drink of something would do him good after his fright.

Gandalf in the meantime was still standing outside the door, and laughing long but quietly. After a while he stepped up, and with the spike of his staff scratched a queer sign on the hobbit's beautiful green front-door. Then he strode away, just about the time when Bilbo was finishing his second cake and beginning to think that he had escaped adventures very well.

The next day he had almost forgotten about Gandalf. He did not remember things very well, unless he put them down on his Engagement Tablet: like this: *Gandalf Tea Wednesday*. Yesterday he had been too flustered to do anything of the kind.

Just before tea-time there came a tremendous ring on the front-door bell, and then he remembered! He rushed and put on the kettle, and put out another cup and saucer, and an extra cake or two, and ran to the door.

"I am so sorry to keep you waiting!" he was going to say, when he saw that it was not Gandalf at all. It was a dwarf with a blue beard tucked into a golden belt, and very bright eyes under his dark-green hood. As soon as the door was opened, he pushed inside, just as if he had been expected.

He hung his hooded cloak on the nearest peg, and "Dwalin at your service!" he said with a low bow.

"Bilbo Baggins at yours!" said the hobbit, too surprised to ask any questions for the moment. When the silence that followed had become uncomfortable, he added: "I am just about to take tea; pray come and have some with me." A little stiff perhaps, but he meant it kindly. And what would you do, if an uninvited dwarf came and hung his things up in your hall without a word of explanation?

They had not been at table long, in fact they had hardly reached the third cake, when there came another even louder ring at the bell.

"Excuse me!" said the hobbit, and off he went to the door.

"So you have got here at last!" was what he was going to say to Gandalf this time. But it was not Gandalf. Instead there was a very old-looking dwarf on the step with a white beard and a scarlet hood; and he too hopped inside as soon as the door was open, just as if he had been invited.

"I see they have begun to arrive already," he said when he caught sight of Dwalin's green hood hanging up. He hung his red one next to it, and "Balin at your service!" he said with his hand on his breast.

"Thank you!" said Bilbo with a gasp. It was not the correct thing to say, but *they have begun to arrive* had flustered him badly. He liked visitors, but he liked to know them before they arrived, and he preferred to ask them himself. He had a horrible thought that the cakes might run short, and then he—as the host: he knew his duty and stuck to it however painful—he might have to go without.

"Come along in, and have some tea!" he managed to say after taking a deep breath.

"A little beer would suit me better, if it is all the same to you, my good sir," said Balin with the white beard. "But I don't mind some cake—seed-cake, if you have any."

"Lots!" Bilbo found himself answering, to his own surprise; and he found himself scuttling off, too, to the cellar to fill a pint beer-mug, and to the pantry to fetch two beautiful round seed-cakes which he had baked that afternoon for his after-supper morsel.

When he got back Balin and Dwalin were talking at the table like old friends (as a matter of fact they were brothers). Bilbo plumped down the beer and the cake in front of them, when loud came a ring at the bell again, and then another ring.

"Gandalf for certain this time," he thought as he puffed along the passage. But it was not. It was two more dwarves, both with blue hoods, silver belts, and yellow beards; and each of them carried a bag of tools and a spade. In they hopped, as soon as the door began to open—Bilbo was hardly surprised at all.

"What can I do for you, my dwarves?" he said.

"Kili at your service!" said the one. "And Fili!" added the other; and they both swept off their blue hoods and bowed.

"At yours and your family's!" replied Bilbo, remembering his manners this time.

"Dwalin and Balin here already, I see," said Kili. "Let us join the throng!"

"Throng!" thought Mr. Baggins. "I don't like the sound of that. I really must sit down for a minute and collect my wits, and have a drink." He had only just had a sip—in the corner, while the four dwarves sat around the table, and talked about mines and gold and troubles with the goblins, and the depredations of dragons, and lots of other things which he did not understand, and did not want to, for they sounded much too adventurous—when, *ding-dong-a-ling-dang,* his bell rang again, as if some naughty little hobbit-boy was trying to pull the handle off.

"Someone at the door!" he said, blinking.

"Some four, I should say by the sound," said Fili. "Besides, we saw them coming along behind us in the distance."

The poor little hobbit sat down in the hall and put his head in his hands, and wondered what had happened, and what was going to happen, and whether they would all stay to supper. Then the bell rang again louder than ever, and he had to run to the door. It was not four after all, it was FIVE. Another dwarf had come along while he was wondering in the hall. He had hardly turned the knob, before they were all inside, bowing and saying "at your service" one after another. Dori, Nori, Ori, Oin, and Gloin were their names; and very soon two purple hoods, a grey hood, a brown hood, and a white hood were hanging on the pegs, and off they marched with their broad hands stuck in their gold and silver belts to join the others. Already it had almost become a throng. Some called for ale, and some for porter, and one for coffee, and all of them for cakes; so the hobbit was kept very busy for a while.

A big jug of coffee had just been set in the hearth, the seed-cakes were gone, and the dwarves were starting on a round of buttered scones, when there came—a loud knock. Not a ring, but a hard rat-tat on the hobbit's beautiful green door. Somebody was banging with a stick!

Bilbo rushed along the passage, very angry, and altogether bewildered and bewuthered—this was the most awkward Wednesday he ever remembered. He pulled open the door with a jerk, and they all fell in, one on top of the other. More dwarves, four more! And there was Gandalf behind, leaning on his staff and laughing. He had made quite a dent on the beautiful door; he had also, by the way, knocked out the secret mark that he had put there the morning before.

"Carefully! Carefully!" he said. "It is not like you, Bilbo, to keep friends waiting on the mat, and then open the door like a pop-gun! Let me introduce Bifur, Bofur, Bombur, and especially Thorin!"

"At your service!" said Bifur, Bofur, and Bombur standing in a row. Then they hung up two yellow hoods and a pale green one; and also a sky-blue one with a long silver tassel. This last belong to Thorin, an enormously important dwarf, in fact no other than the great Thorin Oakenshield himself, who was not at all pleased at falling flat on Bilbo's mat with Bifur, Bofur, and Bombur on top of him. For one thing Bombur was immensely fat and heavy. Thorin indeed was very haughty, and said nothing about *service;* but poor Mr. Baggins said he was sorry so many times, that at last he grunted "pray don't mention it," and stopped frowning.

"Now we are all here!" said Gandalf, looking at the row of thirteen hoods—the best detachable party hoods—and his own hat hanging on the pegs. "Quite a merry gathering! I hope there is something left for the late-comers to eat and drink! What's that? Tea! No thank you! A little red wine, I think, for me."

"And for me," said Thorin.

"And raspberry jam and apple-tart," said Bifur.

"And mince-pies and cheese," said Bofur.

"And pork-pie and salad," said Bombur.

"And more cakes—and ale—and coffee, if you don't mind," called the other dwarves through the door.

"Put on a few eggs, there's a good fellow!" Gandalf called after him, as the hobbit stumped off to the pantries. "And just bring out the cold chicken and pickles!"

"Seems to know as much about the inside of my larders as I do myself!" thought Mr. Baggins, who was feeling positively flummoxed, and was beginning to wonder whether a most wretched adventure had not come right into his house. By the time he had got all the bottles and dishes and knives and forks and glasses and plates and spoons and things piled up on big trays, he was getting very hot, and red in the face, and annoyed.

"Confusticate and bebother these dwarves!" he said aloud. "Why don't they come and lend a hand?" Lo and behold! there stood Balin and Dwalin at the door of the kitchen, and Fili and Kili behind them, and before he could say *knife* they had whisked the trays and a couple of small tables into the parlour and set out everything afresh.

Gandalf sat at the head of the party with the thirteen dwarves all round: and Bilbo sat on a stool at the fireside, nibbling at a biscuit (his appetite was quite taken away), and trying to look as if this was all perfectly ordinary and not in the least an adventure. The dwarves ate and ate, and talked and talked, and time got on. At last they pushed their chairs back, and Bilbo made a move to collect the plates and glasses.

"I suppose you will all stay to supper?" he said in his politest unpressing tones.

"Of course!" said Thorin. "And after. We shan't get through the business till late, and we must have some music first. Now to clear up!"

. . . .

That evening the dwarves sing a song of "long forgotten gold . . . in dungeons deep and caverns old." The gold and other treasure had belonged to their ancestors. It is treasure their ancestors died for when Smaug the dragon attacked. Only a few dwarves escaped to tell the story. One of those who escaped the dragon was Thorin's grandfather, who left a map and a key. Armed with the map and key, the thirteen dwarves hope to reclaim their treasure. That's where Bilbo comes in. Gandalf has told the dwarves that Bilbo is a "burglar." That is to say, he is an expert treasure hunter. Or at least he "will be when the time comes," Gandalf insists.

Bilbo has never thought of himself as either a burglar or a treasure hunter. At first, the very idea of a dangerous mission sends him into a fit and a faint. But then the Tookish side of his nature takes hold of him. His ancestor Bullroarer

Took had been a great fighter. And besides, Bilbo overhears the dwarves doubting his courage and ability. "He looks more like a grocer than a burglar!" they say.

That does it. "You think I am no good," says the injured Bilbo. "I will show you. Tell me what you want done and I will try it." And as Gandalf has known he would all along, Bilbo agrees to join the dwarves in their adventure.

"First I should like to know a bit more about things," said he, feeling all confused and a bit shaky inside, but so far still Tookishly determined to go on with things. "I mean about the gold and the dragon, and all that, and how it got there, and who it belongs to, and so on and further."

"Bless me!" said Thorin, "haven't you got a map? and didn't you hear our song? and haven't we been talking about all this for hours?"

"All the same, I should like it all plain and clear," said he obstinately, putting on his business manner (usually reserved for people who tried to borrow money off him), and doing his best to appear wise and prudent and professional and live up to Gandalf's recommendation. "Also I should like to know about risks, out-of-pocket expenses, time required and remuneration, and so forth"—by which he meant: "What am I going to get out of it? and am I going to come back alive?"

"O very well," said Thorin. "Long ago in my grandfather Thror's time our family was driven out of the far North, and came back with all their wealth and their tools to this Mountain on the map. It had been discovered by my far ancestor, Thrain the Old, but now they mined and they tunnelled and they made huger halls and greater workshops—and in addition I believe they found a good deal of gold and a great many jewels too. Anyway they grew immensely rich and famous, and my grandfather was King under the Mountain again and treated with great reverence by the mortal men, who lived to the South, and were gradually spreading up the Running River as far as the valley overshadowed by the Mountain. They built the merry town of Dale there in those days. Kings used to send for our smiths, and reward even the least skillful most richly. Fathers would beg us to take their sons as apprentices, and pay us handsomely, especially in food-supplies, which we never bothered to grow or find for ourselves. Altogether those were good days for us, and the poorest of us had money to spend and to lend, and leisure to make beautiful things just for the fun of it, not to speak of the most marvelous and magical toys, the like of which is not to be found in the world now-a-days. So my grand-father's halls became full of armour and jewels and carvings and cups, and the toy market of Dale was the wonder of the North.

"Undoubtedly that was what brought the dragon. Dragons steal gold and jewels, you know, from men and elves and dwarves, wherever they can find them; and they guard their plunder as long as they live (which is prac-tically forever, unless they are killed), and never enjoy a brass ring of it. Indeed they hardly know a good bit of work from a bad, though they usually have a good notion of the current market value; and they can't make a thing for themselves, not even mend a little loose scale of their armour. There were lots of dragons in the North in those days, and gold was probably getting scarce up there, with the dwarves flying south or getting killed, and all the general waste and destruction that dragons make going from bad to worse. There was a most specially greedy, strong and wicked worm called Smaug. One day he flew up into the air and came south. The first we heard of it was a noise like a hurricane coming from the North, and the pine-trees on the Mountain creaking and cracking in the wind. Some of the dwarves who happened to be outside (I was one luckily—a fine adventurous lad in those days, always wandering about, and it saved my life that day)—

well, from a good way off we saw the dragon settle on our mountain in a spout of flame. Then he came down the slopes and when he reached the woods they all went up in fire. By that time all the bells were ringing in Dale and the warriors were arming. The dwarves rushed out of their great gate; but there was the dragon waiting for them. None escaped that way. The river rushed up in steam and a fog fell on Dale, and in the fog the dragon came on them and destroyed most of the warriors—the usual unhappy story, it was only too common in those days. Then he went back and crept in through the Front Gate and routed out all the halls, and lanes, and tunnels, alleys, cellars, mansions and passages. After that there were no dwarves left alive inside, and he took all their wealth for himself. Probably, for that is the dragons' way, he has piled it all up in a great heap far inside, and sleeps on it for a bed. Later he used to crawl out of the great gate and come by night to Dale, and carry away people, especially maidens, to eat, until Dale was ruined, and all the people dead or gone. What goes on there now I don't know for certain, but I don't suppose anyone lives nearer to the Mountain than the far edge of the Long Lake now-a-days.

"The few of us that were well outside sat and wept in hiding, and cursed Smaug; and there we were unexpectedly joined by my father and my grandfather with singed beards. They looked very grim but they said very little. When I asked how they had got away, they told me to hold my tongue, and said that one day in the proper time I should know. After that we went away, and we have had to earn our livings as best we could up and down the lands, often enough sinking as low as blacksmith-work or even coal-mining. But we have never forgotten our stolen treasure. And even now, when I will allow we have a good bit laid by and are not so badly off"—here Thorin stroked the gold chain round his neck—"we still mean to get it back, and to bring our curses home to Smaug—if we can.

"I have often wondered about my father's and my grandfather's escape. I see now they must have had a private Side-door which only they knew about. But apparently they made a map, and I should like to know how Gandalf got hold of it, and why it did not come down to me, the rightful heir."

"I did not 'get hold of it,' I was given it," said the wizard. "Your grandfather Thror was killed, you remember, in the mines of Moria by Azog and Goblin—"

"Curse his name, yes," said Thorin.

"And Thrain your father went away on the twenty-first of April, a hundred years ago last Thursday, and has never been seen by you since—"

"True, true," said Thorin.

"Well, your father gave me this to give to you; and if I have chosen my own time and way of handing it over, you can hardly blame me, considering the trouble I had to find you. Your father could not remember his own name when he gave me the paper, and he never told me yours; so on the whole I think I ought to be praised and thanked. Here it is," said he handing the map to Thorin.

"I don't understand," said Thorin, and Bilbo felt he would have liked to say the same. The explanation did not seem to explain.

"Your grandfather," said the wizard slowly and grimly, "gave the map to his son for safety before he went to the mines of Moria. Your father went away to try his luck with the map after your grandfather was killed; and lots of adventures of a most unpleasant sort he had, but he never got near the Mountain. How he got there I don't know, but I found him a prisoner in the dungeons of the Necromancer."

"Whatever were you doing there?" asked Thorin with a shudder, and all the dwarves shivered.

"Never you mind. I was finding things out, as usual; and a nasty dangerous business it was. Even I, Gandalf, only just escaped. I tried to save your father, but it was too late. He was witless and wandering, and had forgotten almost everything except the map and the key."

"We have long ago paid the goblins of Moria," said Thorin; "we must give a thought to the Necromancer."

"Don't be absurd! He is an enemy quite beyond the powers of all the dwarves put together, if they could all be collected again from the four corners of the world. The one thing your father wished was for his son to read the map and use the key. The dragon and the Mountain are more than big enough tasks for you!"

"Hear, hear!" said Bilbo, and accidentally said it aloud.

"Hear what?" they all said turning suddenly towards him, and he was so flustered that he answered "Hear what I have got to say!"

"What's that?" they asked.

"Well, I should say that you ought to go East and have a look round. After all there is the Side-door, and dragons must sleep sometimes, I suppose. If you sit on the door-step long enough, I daresay you will think of something. And well, don't you know, I think we have talked long enough for one night, if you see what I mean. What about bed, and an early start, and all that? I will give you a good breakfast before you go."

"Before *we* go, I suppose you mean," said Thorin. "Aren't you the burglar? And isn't sitting on the door-step your job, not to speak of getting inside the door? But I agree about bed and breakfast. I like eggs with my ham, when starting on a journey: fried not poached, and mind you don't break 'em."

After all the others had ordered their breakfasts without so much as a please (which annoyed Bilbo very much), they all got up. The hobbit had to find room for them all, and filled all his spare-rooms and made beds on chairs and sofas, before he got them all stowed and went to his own little bed very tired and not altogether happy. One thing he did make his mind up about was not to bother to get up very early and cook everybody else's wretched breakfast. The Tookishness was wearing off, and he was not now quite so sure that he was going on any journey in the morning.

As he lay in bed he could hear Thorin still humming to himself in the best bedroom next to him:

Far over the misty mountains cold
To dungeons deep and caverns old
We must away, ere break of day,
To find our long-forgotten gold.

Bilbo went to sleep with that in this ears, and it gave him very uncomfortable dreams. It was long after the break of day, when he woke up.

Fantasy

"Ridiculous," you might say to yourself as you begin reading a fantasy. "Utterly fantastic." And so it is, in a way. A fantasy does not pretend to be real. In fact, it is aimed at being just the opposite. It may be full of characters who, though they may act like people, aren't people at all. It could be placed in a setting that is out of this world. It is like a daydream or a fairy tale where things happen that couldn't possibly occur outside the book.

Yet fantasy has a way of taking hold of your mind. What seems at first to be silly turns out to be interesting. As you read on, the fantasy grows on you little by little. You begin to take it seriously. You become involved with the fantastic characters and their problems. If the fantasy is well written, the fantasy world becomes as real to you as your own world. In the end you find yourself wanting to believe that the fantasy world in the story really exists—somewhere—if only you could find it.

People of all ages enjoy fanstasy. There is no Wonderland down a rabbit hole like the one that Alice found. Still, people have been talking about the fantasy world in *Alice's Adventures in Wonderland* for more than a hundred years. And people so want to believe in the fantasy world of Walt Disney characters that they flock to Disneyland and Disney World by the millions year after year to see those characters come alive.

You are not likely to stumble upon the Shire where Bilbo Baggins lives. But that doesn't make the place any less real while you are reading the book or while you are thinking about it. A good fantasy persuades you to forget for a moment what is real and what is not. You stop worrying whether or not something is possible or impossible. Anything is possible within the world of the story. You just settle back and enjoy it.

J.R.R. Tolkien is one of the great masters of fantasy. His famous novel *The Hobbit* contains all the elements of a fantasy world. In this lesson we will look at four elements most fantasies have in common:

1 ◆ They take place in an unreal world.

2 ♦ They present incredible or unreal characters.

3 ♦ They involve magic and the impossible.

4 ♦ They reflect, or mirror, some important aspect of our own world.

1 ◆ The Unreal World of Fantasy

If there are going to be strange creatures or strange characters in a story, they cannot be placed in the everyday world. You know your backyard too well to ever believe there could be dragons there. You would never be comfortable with the idea of a small man with furry feet in your local supermarket.

But imagine the setting is another planet. Or perhaps it is your hometown, but far in the future—or far in the past. Or suppose it is just "sometime" and "somewhere," and you are left to imagine when and where it might be.

You could believe in little green men, for example, if they lived on Mars. Or you could say, yes, there might have been dragons—somewhere at sometime. In cases like those, you believe in strange creatures and strange places for the sake of the story. You believe because you want to.

In *The Hobbit,* J.R.R. Tolkien created an entire fantasy world so that his story would be believable. He made the creation of that world his first priority. Before you meet any of the characters or find out what they are up to, you are introduced to their world.

> In a hole in the ground there lived a hobbit. Not a nasty, dirty, wet hole, filled with the ends of worms and an oozy smell, nor yet a dry, bare, sandy hole with nothing in it to sit down on or to eat: it was a hobbit-hole, and that means comfort.
>
> It had a perfectly round door like a porthole, painted green, with a shiny yellow brass knob in the exact middle. The door opened on to a tube-shaped hall like a tunnel: a very comfortable tunnel without smoke, with panelled walls, and floors tiled and carpeted, provided with polished chairs, and lots and lots of pegs for hats and coats—the hobbit was fond of visitors.

From reading the very first sentence, you can tell you are entering a fantasy world. Something strange, a hobbit, lives in a hole in the ground. But this is no ordinary animal's hole. Notice how the author takes great pains to furnish this hole with familiar things. It is tiled and panelled just as your home might be. It has furniture and coat pegs because the hobbit likes visitors. He seems a likable middle-class gentleman in a neat home. But you are still a little puzzled. What, after all, is a hobbit, and what is he doing in a hole in the ground?

The author's desire to help you imagine his fantasy world is very important. He has helped you over your first disbelief by setting a scene that is not completely foreign to you. You believe in the fantasy world because the author makes it easy and fun to imagine. You want to see what goes on in this strange place.

1 ◆ Exercise A

Read the following passage and answer the questions about it using what you have learned in this part of the lesson. Use your writing notebook or a separate piece of paper for your answers.

> [Thorin is telling the story of lost gold.]
> "Long ago in my grandfather Thror's time our family was driven out of the far North, and came back with all their wealth and their tools to this Mountain on the map. It had been discovered by my far ancestor, Thrain the Old, but now they mined and they tunnelled and they made huger halls and greater workshops—and in addition I believe they found a good deal of gold and a great many jewels too. Anyway they grew immensely rich and famous, and my grandfather was King under the Mountain again and treated with great reverence by the mortal men, who lived to the South. . . ."

1. The author provides details about the time and the place where this fantastic kingdom was. But these details leave much to your imagination. The time, for example, was "long ago." But when, exactly? What other vague details can you find about the kingdom's location? What ideas in the passage make the fantasy world seem real?

2. How do you know that the world described in the passage is a fantasy?

Now check your answers using the suggestions in the Answer Key starting on page 451. Review this part of the lesson if you don't understand why an answer was wrong.

1♦Writing on Your Own

Look at the lists you have written for Create Your Own Fantasy Story on page 355 that tell about setting and characters for your story. Now do the following:

1. Select an idea from your list that tells where the story is set. Write a paragraph or two describing where and when it takes place.

2. To help your readers believe your fantastic setting, include details that will be familiar to them. For example, if your story takes place long ago and your elf character lives in a hole in a tree, describe the interior of the home.

   □ What does it look like inside? Are there tiny hooked rugs in the living room? Are there paintings on the wall? Are there windows and curtains? What about furniture? Is it cold or cozy?

   □ If your story takes place long ago, add details that describe the time. For example, perhaps the elves must hunt everyday with bow and arrows. (There are no modern conveniences.)

3. Rewrite your paragraph until you are satisfied with the mix of fantastic setting and familiar objects.

2 ◆ The Unreal Characters of Fantasy

Most of the characters in a fantasy are unreal. There are frequently ordinary humans about, but they are rarely as interesting as the fantasy characters. Alice in her famous Wonderland is a human character, but she is not nearly as much fun as the talking rabbits, the Cheshire Cat, and the playing cards. R2-D2 and Darth Vader of *Star Wars* are much more popular than the ordinary human Luke Skywalker. We are more interested in ET and his problems than we are in the humans around him. Most of us are fascinated with the alien characters in *Star Trek*. There are mortals in *The Hobbit*, but they also play minor roles.

But in fantasy even unusual or unreal characters are given some human traits to make them seem believable to you. The White Rabbit of *Alice's Adventures in Wonderland* is always late. The Queen of Hearts is a jealous old woman. R2-D2 is a lovable, clever little fellow. And thousands cheered when ET "phoned home."

See how carefully Tolkien describes his hobbits.

> They are (or were) a little people, about half our height. . . .
> There is little or no magic about them, except the ordinary everyday sort which helps them to disappear quietly and quickly when large stupid folk like you and me come blundering along. . . . They are inclined to be fat in the stomach; they dress in bright colours . . . wear no shoes, because their feet grow natural leathery soles and thick warm brown hair like the stuff on their heads (which is curly); have long clever brown fingers, good-natured faces, and laugh deep fruity laughs (especially after dinner, which they have twice a day when they can get it).

Now you can easily imagine a hobbit even though one has never existed. Hobbits are paunchy because they eat too much. They have long, nimble fingers. And they have a distinctive sort of personality. They are good-natured and have a pleasant laugh. Perhaps you have an Uncle Julius who could be a hobbit—if he had leathery, hair-covered feet, that is. The author has described characters you can believe in, ones with a variety of human traits.

Notice one other way that the author tricks you into believing in the possibility of hobbits. For a moment, he places you in the world of his story. He says that hobbits have only the "ordinary everyday sort" of magic that lets them disappear when people come along. Briefly, you almost believe that there is an "ordinary everyday sort" of magic, and that the only reason you've never seen a hobbit is that they disappear—not because they don't exist.

Readers want to believe in a fantasy world and its fantasy characters. But the author still has to work hard to make these seem believable to you. Little by little, Tolkien brings your world and the fantasy world closer together.

2 ◆ Exercise B

Read the following passage and answer the questions about it using what you have learned in this part of the lesson. Use your writing notebook or a separate piece of paper for your answers.

> Just before tea-time there came a tremendous ring on the front-door bell. . . .
>
> . . . It was a dwarf with a blue beard tucked into a golden belt, and very bright eyes under his dark-green hood. As soon as the door was opened, he pushed inside, just as if he had been expected.
>
> He hung his hooded cloak on the nearest peg, and "Dwalin at your service!" he said with a low bow.
>
> "Bilbo Baggins at yours!" said the hobbit, too surprised to ask any questions for the moment. When the silence that followed had become uncomfortable, he added: "I am just about to take tea; pray come and have some with me." A little stiff perhaps, but he meant it kindly. And what would you do, if an uninvited dwarf came and hung his things up in your hall without a word of explanation?

1. The author uses a trick in this passage. In the last sentence he talks directly to you. How does that sentence pull you into the story and make the event seem real?

2. Dwalin is a fantasy character. Yet he seems human. What is it about Dwalin that makes him seem human?

Now check your answers using the suggestions in the Answer Key starting on page 451. Review this part of the lesson if you don't understand why an answer was wrong.

2♦Writing on Your Own

Look at the list you have written for Create Your Own Fantasy Story on page 355 that tells about settings and characters for your story. Now do the following:

1. Select a character from your list of ideas. In a paragraph describe that character in more detail.

   □ For example, the elf might be small and wiry and wear a green tunic and yellow shoes. Describe how tall the elf is and what he or she looks like.

2. To make your fantasy character believable to your readers, add a few human traits in another paragraph.

   □ Perhaps your elf is ill-tempered and prefers to spend most of his time in his home in the tree. Or perhaps your elf boasts too often or is courageous or loves to cook. Is your character good-natured, nervous, hard-working? Give your character traits you find in people.

3. You may want to change and rewrite your paragraphs several times until you are satisfied with your character.

3 ◆ Fantasy, Magic, and the Impossible

The world we live in behaves in a predictable way. Objects fall down, not up. People grow older, not younger. The wind blows and the sun shines. We are used to these things, and their occurrence does not surprise us.

By contrast, strange things may happen in a fantasy world. There may be strange creatures. People may have strange powers. Almost anything can happen. But before readers will accept something strange, they must be prepared for it. The author must establish rules that support the characters and fantasy world. And once the author sets the rules, they cannot be changed in the middle of the story.

Readers love magic in stories. But the author first has to set this up as a "rule" of the book. You have already noticed Tolkien's observation of the hobbits' "ordinary everyday" magical powers. Just this casual mention is enough to tell you that magic is part of this story.

Later in the story a magic ring will play a very important part. When it does, you are not at all disbelieving because passages like this early in the story tell you about other pieces of magic jewelry.

> "Gandalf, Gandalf! Good gracious me! Not the wandering wizard that gave Old Took a pair of magic diamond studs that fastened themselves and never came undone till ordered? . . . Not the man that used to make such particularly excellent fireworks! I remember those! Old Took used to have them on Midsummer's Eve. Splendid! They used to go up like great lilies and snapdragons and laburnums of fire and hang in the twilight all evening!" . . . "Dear me!" he went on. "Not the Gandalf who was responsible for so many quiet lads and lasses going off into the Blue for mad adventures. . . ."

In this excited conversation with Gandalf, many "rules" for this fantasy are laid down. You see that wizards are part of this world. Later, when a sorcerer is mentioned, you will be ready to accept that too. The wizard, you are told, can make fireworks. When he does that later in the book, you will accept it as natural in this world. And if there are magic cuff links, why not a magic ring? These are the rules of the game that you are playing with the author. And it's the author's job to let you know what they are.

3 ♦ Exercise C

Read the following passage and answer the questions about it using what you have learned in this part of the lesson. Use your writing notebook or a separate piece of paper for your answers.

> ". . . Dragons steal gold and jewels, you know, from men and elves and dwarves, wherever they can find them; and they guard their plunder as long as they live (which is practically forever, unless they are killed). . . . There was a most specially greedy, strong and wicked worm named Smaug. One day he flew up into the air and came south. The first we heard of it was a noise like a hurricane coming from the North. . . . we saw the dragon settle on our mountain in a spout of flame. Then he came down the slopes and when he reached the woods they all went up in fire. . . ."

1. There is a fierce battle with the dragon later in the novel. The dragon will fight like an airborne flamethrower. How does the author prepare you for this battle that will come later in the story? Use words from the passage to support your answer.

2. In this passage the author foreshadows, or hints, at what might come next in the story. What event that might happen later in the novel are you prepared for?

Now check your answers using the suggestions in the Answer Key starting on page 451. Review this part of the lesson if you don't understand why an answer was wrong.

3 ♦ Writing on Your Own

Look at the list you have written for Create Your Own Fantasy Story on page 355 that tells about settings and characters for your story. Now do the following:

1. Choose two characters from your list. You may want to use the character you created in the last Writing on Your Own exercise. In your conversation have the two characters discuss some event that has occurred in the past.

□ For example, the elves are discussing rumors they have heard about the horrible "Cave of Troubles." No elf has ever been inside the cave, and no elf ever wants to go. He or she would need special magic, which most elves no longer have. You want to foreshadow, or hint at, the problems to come.

2. Try to make your conversation casual.

□ For example, your readers do not know that the elf will have to enter the "Cave of Troubles" to find the golden orb. Yet they are prepared for the strange things that can happen there.

3. Rewrite your conversation until you are satisfied with how it hints at events to come and prepares your readers for strange events that will follow.

4 ♦ The Distorted Mirror of Fantasy

So far you have seen how fantasy is different from other kinds of stories. The setting is unreal, the characters are strange, and the action is impossible or magical. But one more quality separates excellent fantasies, those that last many generations, from those that are not so enduring. The best fantasies speak to you about your own life. Even though they are set in fantasy worlds, they tell you about the world we all inhabit. To put it another way, our own world is mirrored or reflected in the fantasy world. This is what author Lewis Carroll had in mind when, in naming the sequel to *Alice's Adventures in Wonderland,* he chose the title *Through the Looking Glass.*

Fantasy does not, however, mirror our world in the usual way. The fantasy world and the real world do not seem exactly alike. Rather, like a mirror in a fun house, fantasy reflects a distorted image of our world. But when you look twice in the strange looking glass of fantasy, you see a situation that could occur in real life. At first *The Hobbit* seems nothing more than a fantastic entertainment. But look again. The author is using his fantasy world to say something about real life.

An injustice has been done. An evil and greedy individual has seized wealth that is not his. He doesn't use the wealth for any good purpose. He just sits on it and enjoys the greedy pleasure of having it. What is worse, he destroys the country around him. No doubt you can name a few greedy and evil people in the real world who do much the same thing.

A group bands together to try to recover the treasure the dragon has stolen. Reluctant Bilbo Baggins is not convinced he wants to be part of this group. He is very much self-satisfied and content to let the evil of the world alone as long as it doesn't bother him. He won't do anything that makes him late for dinner. But along comes a wizard who shakes Bilbo from his indifference. Bilbo decides to join the crusade against the evil in the world.

Knowing what you do about the dwarves and their problem with the dragon, can you see that Bilbo's indifference is really a reflection of similar attitudes in our world?

> Then Bilbo sat down on a seat by his door, crossed his legs, and blew out a beautiful grey ring of smoke that sailed up into the air without breaking and floated away over The Hill.

"Very pretty!" said Gandalf. "But I have no time to blow smoke-rings this morning. I am looking for someone to share in an adventure that I am arranging, and it's very difficult to find anyone."

"I should think so—in these parts! We are plain quiet folk and have no use for adventures. Nasty disturbing uncomfortable things! Make you late for dinner! I can't think what anybody sees in them," said our Mr. Baggins, and stuck one thumb behind his braces [suspenders], and blew out another even bigger smoke-ring.

Bilbo is complacent and self-satisfied. He enjoys his comfortable home and his easy life a great deal—perhaps too much. He has no use for "nasty disturbing uncomfortable things," especially if they "make you late for dinner." You probably laughed at Bilbo here. He seems stuffy.

For all Bilbo knows, there may be great evil in the world. But he is content to let someone else tend to such matters. He doesn't even want to hear about problems. And, says this mirror in the fantasy world, that's just the way most of you out there are. You would rather blow smoke rings (or sit home and watch TV) than get out and do something good in the world. The wizards of the world have a very difficult time finding anyone willing to share in an adventure.

4 ◆ Exercise D

Read the following passage and answer the questions about it using what you have learned in this part of the lesson. Use your writing notebook or a separate piece of paper for your answers.

"All the same, I should like it all plain and clear," said he [Bilbo] obstinately, putting on his business manner (usually reserved for people who tried to borrow money off him), and doing his best to appear wise and prudent and professional and live up to Gandalf's recommendation. "Also I should like to know about risks, out-of-pocket expenses, time required and remuneration, and so forth"— by which he meant: "What am I going to get out of it? and am I going to come back alive?"

1. When we think selfishly about doing work for a good cause, we may privately ask ourselves selfish questions. What is the selfish question that Bilbo asks? How does Bilbo's attitude mirror our world?

2. When we have mixed feelings about doing something, we often behave just as Bilbo does. Explain how Bilbo acts. Describe a situation you've been in where you've had mixed feelings.

Now check your answers using the suggestions in the Answer Key starting on page 451. Review this part of the lesson if you don't understand why an answer was wrong.

4 ◆ Writing on Your Own

Look at the list you have written for Create Your Own Fantasy Story on page 355 that tells about setting and characters for your story. Now do the following:

1. Select a character from your list or use the characters you have developed in the first three Writing on Your Own exercises in this lesson.

2. Write a paragraph or two that describes how the characters and events in your story mirror people and events in your fantasy world.

   □ Make one of the events in the story similar to an event in the real world. Perhaps your characters can no longer grow food in their area because the climate has changed or there is a war.

   □ Make the attitudes of the characters similar to the attitudes of people. Is your character brave? Or is your character unconcerned about what is happening in his or her world? Will your character change the selfish outlook of the village and inspire them to do what is right?

3. Rewrite your paragraph until events and attitudes in our world and in the fantasy world mirror each other.

Now go on to Reviewing and Interpreting the Chapter.

Answer these questions without looking back at the selection. Choose the best answer to each question and put an *x* in the box beside it, or write your answer on a separate piece of paper.

Remembering Facts

1. Who was the leader of the group of dwarves?
   - ☐ a. Dwalin
   - ☐ b. Balin
   - ☐ c. Thorin
   - ☐ d. Bombur

2. What did the dwarves do for a living?
   - ☐ a. They were millers and bakers.
   - ☐ b. They were smiths and miners.
   - ☐ c. They were wizards and magicians.
   - ☐ d. They were traders and shopkeepers.

Following the Order of Events

3. When did the dwarves begin to arrive at Bilbo's home?
   - ☐ a. six days after Gandalf's visit
   - ☐ b. just before tea-time on Wednesday
   - ☐ c. during breakfast on Tuesday
   - ☐ d. right after Gandalf's visit

4. When did Gandalf get possession of the map?

   ☐ a. after Thrain had been captured by the
          Necromancer

   ☐ b. during Smaug's raid on the mountain

   ☐ c. after he spoke with Bilbo the first time

   ☐ d. before Thor went to the mines of Moria

Understanding
Word Choices
5. When Gandalf left, Bilbo Baggins was too
   flustered to make a note on his Engagement
   Tablet. *Flustered* means that Bilbo was

   ☐ a. happy and excited.

   ☐ b. quite frightened by what had happened.

   ☐ c. in a state of nervous confusion.

   ☐ d. anxiously awaiting coming events.

6. The King under the Mountain was "treated with
   great reverence by the mortal men." That means
   that they treated the king with

   ☐ a. fear and suspicion.

   ☐ b. respect.

   ☐ c. hostility.

   ☐ d. good cheer and affection.

7. Both the dwarves and the dragons were wealthy. What was the difference in their attitudes toward wealth?

 ☐ a. The dragons were thrifty; the dwarves spent freely.

 ☐ b. The dragons earned their wealth; the dwarves inherited theirs.

 ☐ c. The dwarves kept trying to increase their wealth; the dragons were careless about theirs.

 ☐ d. The dwarves used their wealth; the dragons hoarded theirs.

8. Which of the following titles hints at what the story is about?

 ☐ a. *A Tale of a Lonesome Dragon*

 ☐ b. *The Fourteen Wizards*

 ☐ c. *The Reluctant Adventurer*

 ☐ d. *A Hobbit in Search of a Battle*

9. The author says hobbits disappear quietly and quickly when large, stupid folk like you and me come along. When he says that, the author is explaining why

 ☐ a. hobbits hate humans.

 ☐ b. we will never see a hobbit.

 ☐ c. Gandalf will have a hard time finding a hobbit.

 ☐ d. hobbits never make much noise.

10. Gandalf scratched a sign on the hobbit's door. What was it for?

☐ a. It was a good luck symbol.

☐ b. It had something to do with magic.

☐ c. It was to remind Gandalf where Bilbo Baggins lived.

☐ d. It was probably a signal for the dwarves.

Understanding Character

11. To what kind of person in our society could you compare Gandalf?

☐ a. A social leader who makes things happen.

☐ b. A troublemaker who should know better.

☐ c. A soldier of fortune who goes looking for wars.

☐ d. An old busybody who won't leave others alone.

12. What adjectives best describe Bilbo Baggins?

☐ a. unconcerned and casual

☐ b. alert and sharp

☐ c. desperate and unhappy

☐ d. cautious and nervous

Understanding Setting

13. The hobbit's home is described as a hole in the ground, but with "panelled walls, and floors tiled and carpeted." Why does the author add familiar details to the setting?

☐ a. He wants to create an unbelievable setting.

☐ b. The details are not important to the story.

☐ c. The familiar details make the setting seem
real.

☐ d. The familiar details do not add to the
setting.

14. The author's description of Bilbo's home gives you
a feeling that it is

☐ a. damp and musty.

☐ b. clean, warm, and comfortable.

☐ c. cold and sparse.

☐ d. hot, humid, and uncomfortable.

Understanding
Feelings

15. Gandalf recommends Bilbo for the adventure
because Gandalf

☐ a. realizes that Bilbo isn't important.

☐ b. thinks that Bilbo deserves to be frightened.

☐ c. believes that Bilbo will be right for the job.

☐ d. distrusts Bilbo.

16. Bilbo finally agrees to go with the other dwarves,
but he has mixed feelings of

☐ a. pride and fear.

☐ b. pity and pride.

☐ c. weakness and confusion.

☐ d. courage and strength.

Now check your answers using the Answer Key starting on page 451. Make no mark for right answers. <u>Correct</u> any wrong answers you may have by putting a check mark (✓) in the box next to the right answer. Count the number of questions you answered correctly and plot the total on the Comprehension Scores graph on page 462.

Next, look at the questions you answered incorrectly. What types of questions were they? Count the number you got wrong of each type and enter the numbers in the spaces below.

Remembering Facts   _____

Following the Order of Events   _____

Understanding Word Choices   _____

Understanding Important Ideas   _____

Understanding Levels of Meaning   _____

Understanding Character   _____

Understanding Setting   _____

Understanding Feelings   _____

Now use these numbers to fill in the Comprehension Skills Profile on page 463.

Discussion Guides

The questions below will help you think about the selection and the lesson you have just read. If you don't discuss these questions in class, try to think about them or discuss them with your classmates. Perhaps you will want to write a few paragraphs in answer to the questions.

Discussing Fantasy

1. Review the names of the characters in the story. How do these names add to the sense of fantasy? Why didn't Tolkien call some of them Bob, David, or Michael?

2. A story has to happen at a particular time and place. How does the author seem to tell you the time and place without really giving any details? (Reread the beginning of the chapter to find examples.)

3. Things in fantasy are often a mixture of what is real and what is unreal. What is real and what is unreal about the hobbit's house, Gandalf's clothing, the dwarves, and Smaug and the mountain where he lives?

Discussing the Chapter

4. Who can you name from real life who is like Gandalf? Give reasons for your ideas.

5. Who or what in real society might be like Smaug? (What familiar word sounds the same as Smaug?)

6. In what ways do you consider yourself like Bilbo Baggins? How are you different from him?

Discussing the Author's Work

7. This is an adventure story, but Tolkien has mixed in humor as well. What did you find humorous in the chapter?

8. The dwarves could all have arrived together at one time. What did the author accomplish by having them come in small groups of two and three?

9. If you had to pick somewhere in the world where the story takes place, you would have to say England. J.R.R. Tolkien was English. What in the story makes it sound more English than American?

Writing Exercise

Read all the instructions before you begin writing. If you have any questions about how to begin the writing assignment, review Using the Writing Process beginning on page 439, or confer with your writing coach.

1. At the beginning of this unit you were asked to make a list of story ideas, settings, and characters for your own fantasy story. If you haven't done that yet, read the instructions for Create Your Own Fantasy Story on page 355, and make your list now.

2. Write a rough draft of a fantasy story based on the list you made. Try to include all the elements of fantasy that you have learned in this lesson:

   ◆ **Unreal world:** Make your setting a fantasy world, but be sure to add a few familiar details that will help make the story believable for your readers.

   ◆ **Unreal characters:** Your character may be a robot, an elf, or a talking animal. Even though your character is not real, it is important to give that character a few human traits. Is he or she bossy, good-hearted, nervous, calm?

   ◆ **Magic and the impossible:** Hint at events that might occur later in the story by discussing them now. If your character will eventually use magic or has some special, unbelievable power, try to work that fact into the story now by casually mentioning it. When the event happens in the story, your readers will be more willing to believe it.

   ◆ **Reflect the real world:** To make the events and characters in your fantasy world seem believable, you must convince your readers that the fantasy world is similar to ours. Your characters might fight for good over evil, or they might have attitudes that your readers can recognize in themselves.

3. If you have written the paragraphs in the four Writing on Your Own exercises in this lesson, you may use them to help you write your rough draft:

☐ Make an outline of which parts of the story come first, second, third, and fourth.

☐ Rewrite your story. If you are having trouble with your idea, you may want to look at other fantasy stories.

☐ Reread your story once again. Make changes and corrections. You may want a friend, teacher, or your writing coach to make suggestions at this point.

☐ Write your story in its final form. Some authors write a final draft two or three times until they are satisfied with the story.

Unit 10   The Historical Novel

The True Confessions of Charlotte Doyle
BY AVI

About the Illustration

How do you know that this scene takes place in the past?
Use details from the illustration to support your response.

Here are some questions to help you think about the
chapter:

◆ How is this ship different from ships you see today?

◆ What can you tell about the characters from their
clothing?

◆ How do you know that this girl lived long ago?

Unit 10

Introduction

About the Novel

The year is 1832, and thirteen-year-old Charlotte Doyle is looking forward to a long, relaxing sea voyage from England to the United States. The daughter of a wealthy New England merchant, Charlotte is leaving boarding school in England to join her family in Rhode Island.

When Charlotte first boards the *Seahawk,* she behaves like a typical upper-class girl in the early 1800s. She has definite ideas about what it means to be a lady or a gentleman. She thinks that certain kinds of people are better than others. And she would never dream of working with her hands or spoiling her beautiful clothes.

But the sea voyage isn't the pleasant, relaxing trip that Charlotte expects. She gets involved in the growing tensions between the ship's captain and the crew. At first she automatically sides with the captain because he is a gentleman who reminds her of her father. But when she sees his cruel behavior to the crew members, she begins to fear and distrust him.

Charlotte is forced to make a difficult choice between the captain and the crew. But her choice doesn't solve her problems. To make things even worse, she is accused of murdering a crew member. And after she is found guilty, she must do everything she can to stay alive.

The chapters you will read show you what it was like to be on a ship in the early 1800s. In this selection, you watch Charlotte change from a prim, ladylike girl to an active, determined crew member. And you see how she challenges some of the values that most people took for granted in 1832.

The selection includes some unusual words to describe the *Seahawk,* a brig that was typical of the kinds of ships that crossed the Atlantic Ocean in the early 1800s. The drawings below identify the parts of a brig and its mainmast. You may want to refer to these drawings as you read.

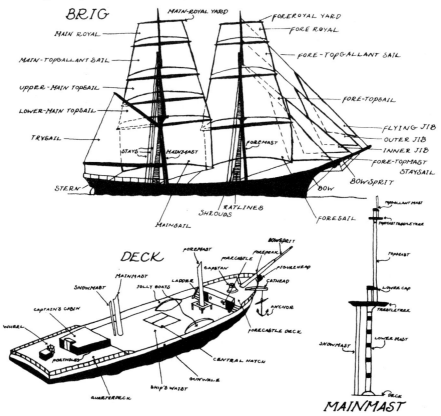

The author of *The True Confessions of Charlotte Doyle* publishes books under the name Avi, but his full name is Avi Wortis. He was born in New York City in 1937, where he grew up in a very artistic family. His grandmother and his parents were writers, and his uncles were painters and composers. From the beginning, Avi's family encouraged him to be creative.

Even as a child, Avi knew he wanted to be a writer. But he was a terrible speller, and his teachers constantly complained about his work. That discouragement didn't bother him. He remembers, "I wasn't even paying attention to it. I liked what I wrote."

For several years Avi worked as a librarian, but he never gave up his dreams of writing. He published his first children's book in 1970, a book based on stories he told to his young sons. He soon realized, however, that his real interest was in writing novels for young adults. Over the years he has won many awards for his work. But he once said that readers are "the greatest gift a writer can receive."

Many of Avi's most popular books are based on historical events. If you are interested in reading other historical novels, you might look for *Captain Grey, The Fighting Ground,* or *Something Upstairs: A Tale of Ghosts.*

About the Lesson

The lesson that follows the reading selection is about the historical novel. Historical novels are part history and part fiction. Authors choose an actual historical event or situation and then build a fictional story around that real incident. Sometimes all the characters are fictional. Sometimes authors include both imagined characters and real historical figures. But no matter how the author chooses to build the novel, he or she pays attention to details and ideas that help readers picture a particular period in history.

The following questions will help you focus on the ideas and details that make *The True Confessions of Charlotte Doyle* an interesting and believable historical novel. Read the selection carefully and try to answer these questions as you go along:

◆ How does Charlotte's way of speaking and writing remind you that she is a character from the past?

◆ Why does the author include so many details about the *Seahawk*?

◆ How is Charlotte different from most girls who lived in 1832? Why are those differences important to the story?

◆ How is Charlotte similar to a modern teenager? Why does Avi want you to notice that similarity?

Writing about a Historical Event

If you write a story around a historical event, you have to think about making your story seem realistic. Use your writing notebook or a separate piece of paper and try the following suggestions:

1. Choose one of the following historical events or think of an event of your own.

   ☐ A native American Indian watching Columbus arrive in the New World in 1492

   ☐ A slave during the early 1800s who is trying to escape to freedom

   ☐ A friend of the Wright brothers who is helping them experiment with airplanes in the early 1900s

2. What details come to mind when you picture this event? Where is it taking place? What clothes is the character wearing? What kinds of experiences has the character had?

   Make a list of details that tell about the historical event. If you need to, you can use an encyclopedia to help you learn more about a particular period in history.

3. Rewrite your list and try to add as many details as possible. You may want to rewrite your list several times until you are satisfied with the order.

The True Confessions of Charlotte Doyle

by Avi

AN IMPORTANT WARNING

Not every thirteen-year-old girl is accused of murder, brought to trial, and found guilty. But I was just such a girl, and my story is worth relating even if it did happen years ago. Be warned, however, this is no *Story of a Bad Boy,* no *What Katy Did.* If strong ideas and action offend you, read no more. Find another companion to share your idle hours. For my part I intend to tell the truth as *I* lived it.

But before I begin relating what happened, you must know something about me as I was in the year 1832—when these events transpired. At the time my name *was* Charlotte Doyle. And though I have kept the name, I am not—for reasons you will soon discover—the *same* Charlotte Doyle.

How shall I describe the person I once was? At the age of thirteen I was very much a girl, having not yet begun to take the shape, much less the heart, of a woman. Still, my family dressed me as a young woman, bonnet covering my beautiful hair, full skirts, high button shoes, and, you may be sure, white gloves. I certainly wanted to be a *lady.* It was not just my ambition; it was my destiny. I embraced it wholly, gladly, with not an untoward thought of anything else. In other words, I think that at the time of these events I was not anything more or less than what I appeared to be: an acceptable, ordinary girl of parents in good standing.

Though American born, I spent the years between my sixth and thirteenth birthdays in England. My father, who engaged in the manufacture of cotton goods, functioned as an agent for an American business there. But in the early spring of 1832, he received an advancement and was summoned home.

My father, an ardent believer in regularity and order, decided it would be better if I finished out my school term rather than break it off midyear. My mother—whom I never knew to disagree with him—accepted my father's decision. I would follow my parents, as well as my younger brother and sister, to our true home, which was in Providence, Rhode Island.

Lest you think that my parents' judgment was rash in allowing me to travel without them, I will show you how reasonable, even logical, their decision was.

First, they felt that by remaining a boarder at the Barrington School for Better Girls (Miss Weed, eminent and most proper headmistress) I would lose no school time.

Second, I would be crossing the Atlantic—a trip that could last anywhere from one to two months—during the summer, when no formal education took place.

Third, I was to make my voyage upon a ship owned and operated by my father's firm.

Fourth, the captain of this ship had acquired a reputation—so my father informed me—for quick and profitable Atlantic crossings.

Then there was this: two families known to my parents had also booked passage on the ship. The adults had promised to function as my guardians. Having been told only that these families included children (three lovely girls and a charming boy) I had looked forward to meeting them more than anything else.

So when you consider that I had but dim memories of making the crossing to England when I was six, you will understand that I saw the forthcoming voyage as all a lark. A large, beautiful boat! Jolly sailors! No school to think about! Companions of my own age!

One more point. I was given a volume of blank pages—how typical of my father!—and instructed to keep a daily journal of my voyage across the ocean so that the writing of it should prove of educational value to me. Indeed, my father warned me that not only would he read the journal and comment upon it, but he would pay particular attention to spelling—not my strongest suit.

Keeping that journal then is what enables me to relate now in perfect detail everything that transpired during that fateful voyage across the Atlantic Ocean in the summer of 1832.

CHAPTER 13

For a second time I stood in the forecastle. The room was as dark and mean as when I'd first seen it. Now, however, I stood as a petitioner in sailor's garb. A glum Fisk was at my side. It hadn't been easy to convince him I was in earnest about becoming one of the crew. Even when he begrudged a willingness to believe in my sincerity he warned that agreement from the rest of the men would be improbable. He insisted I lay the matter before them immediately.

So it was that three men from Mr. Hollybrass's watch, Grimes, Dillingham, and Foley, were the next to hear my plea. As Fisk had foretold, they were contemplating me and my proposal with very little evidence of favor.

"I do mean it," I said, finding boldness with repetition, "I want to be the replacement for Mr. Johnson."

"You're a girl," Dillingham spat out contemptuously.

"A *pretty* girl," Foley put in. It was not meant as a compliment. "Takes more than canvas britches to hide that."

"And a gentlewoman," was Grimes's addition, as though that was the final evidence of my essential uselessness.

"I want to show that I stand with you," I pleaded. "That I made a mistake."

"A mistake?" Foley snapped. "Two able-bodied men have died!"

"Besides," Dillingham agreed, "you'll bring more trouble than good."

"You can teach me," I offered.

"God's fist," Grimes cried. "She thinks this a school!"

"And the captain," Foley asked. "What'll he say?"

"He wants nothing to do with me," I replied.

"That's what he *says*. But you were his darling girl, Miss Doyle. We takes you in and he'll want you back again. Where will that put us?"

So it went, round and round. While the men made objections, while I struggled to answer them, Fisk said nothing.

Though I tried to keep my head up, my eyes steady, it was not easy. They looked at me as if I were some loathsome *thing*. At the same time, the more objections they made, the more determined I was to prove myself.

"See here, Miss Doyle," Dillingham concluded, "it's no simple matter. Understand, you sign on to the articles, so to speak, and you *are* on. No bolting to safe harbors at the first blow or when an ill word is flung your way. You're a hand or you're not a hand, and it won't go easy, that's all that can ever be promised."

"I know," I said.

"Hold out *your* hands," he demanded.

Fisk nudged me. I held them out, palms up.

Foley peered over them. "Like bloody cream," he said with disgust. "Touch mine!" he insisted and extended his. Gingerly, I touched one of them. His skin was like rough leather.

"That's the hands you'd get, miss. Like an animal. Is that what you want?"

"I don't care," I said stoutly.

Finally it was Dillingham who said, "And are you willing to take your place in the rigging too? Fair weather or foul?"

That made me pause.

Fisk caught the hesitation. "Answer," he prompted.

"Yes," I said boldly.

They exchanged glances. Then Foley asked, "What do the others think?"

Fisk shook his head and sighed. "No doubt they'll speak the same."

Suddenly Grimes said, "Here's what I say: let her climb to the royal yard. If she does it and comes down whole, and *still* is willing to serve, then I say let her sign and be bloody damned like the rest of us."

"And do whatever she's called on to do!"

"No less!"

With no more than grunts the men seemed to agree among themselves. They turned toward me.

"*Now* what does Miss Doyle say?" Grimes demanded.

I swallowed hard, but all the same I gave yet another "Yes."

Foley came to his feet. "All right then. I'll go caucus the others." Out he went.

Fisk and I retreated to the galley while I waited for word. During that time he questioned me regarding my determination.

"Miss Doyle," he pressed, "you have agreed to climb to the top of the royal yard. Do you know that's the highest sail on the main mast? One hundred and thirty feet up. You can reach it only two ways. You can shimmy up the mast itself. Or you can climb the shrouds, using the ratlines for your ladder."

I nodded as if I fully grasped what he was saying. The truth was I didn't even wish to listen. I just wanted to get past the test.

"And Miss Doyle," he went on, "if you slip and fall you'll be lucky to drop into the sea and drown quickly. No mortal could pluck you out fast enough to save you. Do you understand that?"

I swallowed hard but nodded. "Yes."

"Because if you're *not* lucky, you'll crash to the deck. Fall that way and you'll either maim or kill yourself by breaking your neck. Still certain?"

"Yes," I repeated, though somewhat more softly.

"I'll give you this," he said with a look that seemed a mix of admiration and contempt, "Zachariah was right. You're as steady a girl as ever I've met."

Foley soon returned. "We're agreed," he announced. "Not a one stands in favor of your signing on, Miss Doyle. Not with what you are. We're all agreed to that. But if you climb as high as the royal yard and make it down whole, and if you still want to sign on, you can come as equal. You'll get no more from us, Miss Doyle, but no less either."

"I understand," I said.

"All right then," Foley said. "The captain's still in his cabin and not likely to come out till five bells. You can do it now."

"Now?" I quailed.

"Now before never."

So it was that the four men escorted me onto the deck. There I found that the rest of the crew had already gathered.

Having fully committed myself, I was overwhelmed by my audacity. The masts had always seemed tall, of course, but never so tall as they did at that moment. When I reached the deck and looked up my courage all but crumbled. My stomach turned. My legs grew weak.

Not that it mattered. Fisk escorted me to the mast as though I were being led to die at the stake. He seemed as grim as I.

To grasp fully what I'd undertaken to do, know again that the height of the mainmast towered one hundred and thirty feet from the deck. This mast was, in fact, three great rounded lengths of wood, trees, in truth, affixed one to the end of the other. Further, it supported four levels of sails, each of which bore a different name. In order, bottom to top, these were called the main yard, topsail, topgallant, and finally royal yard.

My task was to climb to the top of the royal yard. And come down. In one piece. If I succeeded I'd gain the opportunity of making the climb fifty times a day.

As if reading my terrified thoughts Fisk inquired gravely, "How will you go, Miss Doyle? Up the mast or on the ratlines?"

Once again I looked up. I could not possibly climb the mast directly. The stays and shrouds with their ratlines would serve me better.

"Ratlines," I replied softly.

"Then up you go."

I will confess it, at that moment my nerves failed. I found myself unable to move. With thudding heart I looked frantically around. The members of the crew, arranged in a crescent, were standing like death's own jury.

It was Barlow who called out, "A blessing goes with you, Miss Doyle."

To which Ewing added, "And this advice, Miss Doyle. Keep your eyes steady on the ropes. Don't you look down. Or up."

For the first time I sensed that some of them at least wanted me to succeed. The realization gave me courage.

With halting steps and shallow breath, I approached the rail only to pause when I reached it. I could hear a small inner voice crying, "Don't! Don't!"

But it was also then that I heard Dillingham snicker, "She'll not have the stomach."

I reached up, grasped the lowest deadeye, and hauled myself atop the rail. That much I had done before. Now, I maneuvered to the outside so that I would be leaning *into* the rigging and could even rest on it.

Once again I looked at the crew, *down* at them, I should say. They were staring up with blank expressions.

Recollecting Ewing's advice, I shifted my eyes and focused them on the ropes before me. Then, reaching as high as I could into one of the middle shrouds, and grabbing a ratline, I began to climb.

The ratlines were set about sixteen inches one above the other, so that the steps I had to take were wide for me. I needed to pull as much with arms as climb with legs. But line by line I did go up, as if ascending an enormous ladder.

After I had risen some seventeen feet I realized I'd made a great mistake. The rigging stood in sets, each going to a different level of the mast. I could have taken one that stretched directly to the top. Instead, I had chosen a line which went only to the first trestletree, to the top of the lower mast.

For a moment I considered backing down and starting afresh. I stole a glance below. The crew's faces were turned up toward me. I understood that they would take the smallest movement down as retreat. I had to continue.

And so I did.

Now I was climbing inside the lank gray-white sails, ascending, as it were, into a bank of dead clouds.

Beyond the sails lay the sea, slate-gray and ever rolling. Though the water looked calm, I could feel the slow pitch and roll it caused in the ship. I realized suddenly how much harder this climb would be if the wind were blowing and we were well underway. The mere thought made the palms of my hands grow damp.

Up I continued till I reached the main yard. Here I snatched another glance at the sea, and was startled to see how much bigger it had grown. Indeed, the more I saw of it the *more* there was. In contrast, the *Seahawk* struck me as having suddenly grown smaller. The more I saw of *her,* the *less* she was!

I glanced aloft. To climb higher I now had to edge myself out upon the trestletree and then once again move up the next set of ratlines as I'd done before. But at twice the height!

Wrapping one arm around the mast—even up here it was too big to reach around completely—I grasped one of the stays and edged out. At the same moment the ship dipped, the world seemed to twist and tilt down. My stomach lurched. My heart pounded. My head swam. In spite of myself I closed my eyes. I all but slipped, saving myself only by a sudden grasp of a line before the ship yawed the opposite way. I felt sicker yet. With ever-warning strength I clung on for dearest life. Now the full folly of what I was attempting burst upon me with grotesque reality. It had been not only stupid, but suicidal. I would never come down alive!

And yet I had to climb. This was my restitution.

When the ship was steady again, I grasped the furthest rigging, first with one hand, then the other, and dragged myself higher. I was heading for the topsail, fifteen feet further up.

Pressing myself as close as possible into the rigging, I continued to strain upward, squeezing the ropes so tightly my hands cramped. I even tried curling my toes about the ratlines.

At last I reached the topsail spar, but discovered it was impossible to rest there. The only place to pause was three *times* higher than the distance I'd just come, at the trestletree just below the topgallant spar.

By now every muscle in my body ached. My head felt light, my heart an anvil. My hands were on fire, the soles of my feet raw. Time and again I was forced to halt, pressing my face against the rigging with eyes closed. Then, in spite of what I'd been warned not to do, I opened them and peered down. The *Seahawk* was like a wooden toy. The sea looked greater still.

I made myself glance up. Oh, so far to go! How I forced myself to move I am not sure. But the thought of backing down now was just as frightening. Knowing only that I could not stay still, I crept upward, ratline by ratline, taking what seemed to be forever with each rise until I finally reached the level just below the topgallant spar.

A seasoned sailor would have needed two minutes to reach this point. I had needed thirty!

Though I felt the constant roll of the ship, I had to rest there. What seemed like little movement on deck became, up high, wild swings and turns through treacherous air.

I gagged, forced my stomach down, drew breath, and looked out. Though I didn't think it possible, the ocean appeared to have grown greater yet. And when I looked down, the upturned faces of the crew appeared like so many tiny bugs.

There were twenty-five or so more feet to climb. Once again I grasped the rigging and hauled myself up.

This final climb was torture. With every upward pull the swaying of the ship seemed to increase. Even when not moving myself, I was flying through the air in wild, wide gyrations. The horizon kept shifting, tilting, dropping. I was increasingly dizzy, nauseous, terrified, certain that with every next moment I would slip and fall to death. I paused again and again, my eyes on the rigging inches from my face, gasping and praying as I had never prayed before. My one hope was that, nearer to heaven now, I could make my desperation heard!

Inch by inch I continued up. Half an inch! Quarter inches! But then at last with trembling fingers, I touched the spar of the royal yard. I had reached the top.

Once there I endeavored to rest again. But there the metronome motion of the mast was at its most extreme, the *Seahawk* turning, tossing, swaying as if trying to shake me off—like a dog throwing droplets of water from its back. And when I looked beyond I saw a sea that was infinity itself, ready, eager to swallow me whole.

I had to get back down.

As hard as it was to climb up, it was, to my horror, harder returning. On the ascent I could see where I was going. Edging down I had to grope blindly with my feet. Sometimes I tried to look. But when I did the sight of the void below was so sickening, I was forced to close my eyes.

Each groping step downward was a nightmare. Most times my foot found only air. Then, as if to mock my terror, a small breeze at last sprang up. Sails began to fill and snap, puffing in and out, at times smothering me. The tossing of the ship grew—if that were possible—more extreme.

Down I crept, past the topgallant where I paused briefly on the trestletree, then down along the longest stretch, toward the mainyard. It was there I fell.

I was searching with my left foot for the next ratline. When I found a hold and started to put my weight upon it, my foot, slipping on the slick tar surface, shot forward. The suddenness of it made me lose my grip. I tumbled backward, but in such a way that my legs became entangled in the lines. There I hung, *head downward.*

I screamed, tried to grab something. But I couldn't. I clutched madly at nothing, till my hand brushed against a dangling rope. I grabbed for it, missed, and grabbed again. Using all my strength, I levered myself up and, wrapping my arms into the lines, made a veritable knot of myself, mast, and rigging. Oh, how I wept! my entire body shaking and trembling as though it would break apart.

When my breathing became somewhat normal, I managed to untangle first one arm, then my legs. I was free.

I continued down. By the time I reached the mainyard I was numb and whimpering again, tears coursing from my eyes.

I moved to the shrouds I'd climbed, and edged myself past the lowest of the sails.

As I emerged from under it, the crew gave out a great "Huzzah!"

Oh, how my heart swelled with exaltation!

Finally, when I'd reached close to the very end, Barlow stepped forward, beaming, his arms uplifted. "Jump!" he called. "Jump!"

But now, determined to do it all myself, I shook my head. Indeed, in the end I dropped down on my own two India-rubber legs—and tumbled to the deck.

No sooner did I land than the crew gave me another "Huzzah!" With joyous heart I staggered to my feet. Only then did I see Captain Jaggery push through the knot of men and come to stand before me.

The Historical Novel

Historical novels combine facts from history with ideas from an author's imagination. Fictional characters dress, speak, and behave like people who lived at a certain point in history. They have ideas and attitudes that reflect the times. Often the characters are involved in actual events that you can read about in history books. But the fictional characters never lived. The author created them to help you experience a particular moment in history.

In a historical novel, the time, place, and events play an important role in the story. And the conflict often reflects real conflicts that took place in the past. To write an effective historical novel, an author must do a great deal of research about the time period. The novel must given an honest, accurate picture of the time and the true feelings of the people who lived through them.

In *The True Confessions of Charlotte Doyle,* the action takes place on board a ship in 1832. For this book Avi chose a historic time period, although he did not choose a particular historical event. But even though Avi had the freedom to invent many fictional characters and situations, he still had to keep the novel's details historically accurate.

In this lesson we will look at four characteristics of a historical novel, all of which Avi uses in *The True Confessions of Charlotte Doyle*:

1 ◆ The characters look and behave like people who lived in the past.

2 ◆ The details of the time and place show that the novel takes place in the past.

3 ◆ The conflict in the story gives you some insights about a period in history.

4 ◆ You see the events in the novel through the eyes of a character.

1 ♦ People out of the Past

The main character of a historical novel is almost always a fictional character. And even if the character *is* based on a real historical figure, the author creates words, thoughts, actions, and situations that never actually existed. Other characters—townspeople, soldiers, acquaintances—are created by the author as they are needed. As in any other novel or story, the characters in a historical novel help to advance the plot, or action, of the story.

But in a historical novel, the characters also have another job. They remind us that the story is taking place in the past. Everything—their clothes, their speech, and their actions—must reflect the time period of the novel. Otherwise, readers will lose interest because the novel does not seem accurate or believable.

Read the following passage from *The True Confessions of Charlotte Doyle*. What do you learn about Charlotte? How does that knowledge remind you that the novel is set in 1832?

> How shall I describe the person I once was? At the age of thirteen I was very much a girl, having not yet begun to take the shape, much less the heart, of a woman. Still, my family dressed me as a young woman, bonnet covering my beautiful hair, full skirts, high button shoes, and, you may be sure, white gloves. I certainly wanted to be a *lady*. It was not just my ambition; it was my destiny. I embraced it wholly, glady, with not an untoward thought of anything else. In other words, I think that at the time of these events I was not anything more or less than what I appeared to be. . . .

Charlotte's description of herself reminds you that she is not a modern thirteen-year-old girl. Everything about her clothing, from her bonnet to her white gloves, lets you know that she is a character from the distant past.

But what else in the passage reminds you of the past? Think about the way Charlotte speaks. She uses language that seems unfamiliar to us, even though it is obviously English. Phrases like "you may be sure" and "untoward thought" hint that Charlotte lives in a different time, an era when people who belonged to the upper class wrote and spoke in a formal, elegant way.

1♦Exercise A

Read the following passage and answer the questions about it using what you have learned in this part of the lesson. Use your writing notebook or a separate piece of paper for your answers.

> My father, an ardent believer in regularity and order, decided it would be better if I finished out my school term rather than break it off midyear. My mother—whom I never knew to disagree with him—accepted my father's decision. I would follow my parents, as well as my younger brother and sister, to our true home, which was in Providence, Rhode Island.
>
> Lest you think that my parents' judgment was rash in allowing me to travel without them, I will show you how reasonable, even logical, their decision was.

1. How does Charlotte's language show that she is not a modern teenager? List some of the words and phrases that remind you that she is a character from the past.

2. What does this passage teach you about families in the 1830s?

Now check your answers using the suggestions in the Answer Key starting on page 451. Review this part of the lesson if you don't understand why an answer was wrong.

1♦Writing on Your Own

Look at the list you wrote for Writing about a Historical Event on page 404. Now do the following:

1. Think about the details on your list that tell what the character looks like.

2. Write a paragraph that concentrates on the character's appearance. Make sure you include details that remind you of the historical period.

For example, if you are writing about a duchess at Queen Elizabeth I's court, you might mention the stiff high ruff around her neck, the heavy dress studded with jewels, the thick layer of makeup on her face, and so on.

3. You may want to change and rewrite your paragraph several times until you are satisfied with your character's appearance.

2 ◆ Setting out of the Past

Setting is a major part of any story. But in a historical novel the setting is especially important. The authors of historical novels may spend as long learning about a period in history as they do writing the novel. By doing research before they begin writing, they make sure they are creating an accurate picture of the times.

Authors include hundreds of small details that are specific to the period, and they are very careful not to include details that seem out of place. They go through all this work to make sure that the setting gives you the true flavor of a time and place in history.

For example, an author who is writing a novel about a hospital during the Civil War must learn a great deal about the medical equipment available during the 1860s. If a description of an operating room includes an X-ray machine, then the novel is no longer believable.

Even if you don't know very much about a historical period or event, an author's confident use of setting can give you a picture of the time and place. For example, you may not know much about ships in the 1830s. But Avi's careful descriptions, even when they're filled with unfamiliar words, show you the action and give you a flavor of the times.

In *The True Confessions of Charlotte Doyle,* Avi wants to create a realistic picture of a typical merchant ship. So even in a scene with action and suspense, he makes sure that the details are accurate. Read the following passage and notice the description of the ship.

> When the ship was steady again, I grasped the furthest rigging, first with one hand, then the other, and dragged myself higher. I was headed for the topsail, fifteen feet further up.
>
> Pressing myself as close as possible into the rigging, I continued to strain upward, squeezing the rope so tightly my hands cramped. I even tried curling my toes about the ratlines.
>
> At last I reached the topsail spar, but discovered it was impossible to rest there. The only place to pause was three *times* higher than the distance I'd just come, at the trestletree just below the topgallant spar.

In this description you have a clear picture of Charlotte struggling up the mast. You may not be able to define a topsail spar, but Avi makes sure that you understand exactly what's going on in the story.

2 ◆ Exercise B

Read the following passage and answer the questions about it using what you have learned in this part of the lesson. Use your writing notebook or a separate piece of paper for your answers.

> To grasp fully what I'd undertaken to do, know again that the height of the mainmast towered one hundred and thirty feet from the deck. This mast was, in fact, three great rounded lengths of wood, trees, in truth, affixed one to the end of the other. Further, it supported four levels of sails, each of which bore a different name. In order, bottom to top, these were called the main yard, topsail, topgallant, and finally royal yard.
>
> My task was to climb to the top of the royal yard. And come down. In one piece. If I succeeded I'd gain the opportunity of making the climb fifty times a day.

1. In your own words, explain what this passage teaches you about the ship.

2. Why does the author include all these details about the ship? How does the setting contribute to the story?

Now check your answers using the suggestions in the Answer Key starting on page 451. Review this part of the lesson if you don't understand why an answer was wrong.

2 ◆ Writing on Your Own

Look back at the list you wrote for Writing about a Historical Event on page 404. Now do the following:

1. Think about the details on your list that tell you about the setting of the historical event.

2. Write a paragraph about the event that concentrates on time and place. Remember that the details should tell the reader about the historical period.

   For example, if you are writing about a duchess at Queen Elizabeth I's court, you might describe a drafty stone castle, huge tapestries hanging from the walls, and the sounds and smells of the castle dungeon.

3. You may want to change and rewrite your paragraph several times until you are satisfied with your description.

3 ◆ Society in Conflict

Conflict is at the center of every novel. A conflict happens when opposing forces create a struggle or problem. The way the characters react to the conflict produces the action of the story.

In a historical novel, the conflict often centers around a social problem. For example, in a novel set during the Revolutionary War, the conflict will probably tell us about the struggle between British colonial rule and American self-rule. In a novel set during the Civil War, the conflict may give us some insights about the cruelty of slavery. In both cases, the wars themselves are based on deeper social issues. Good historical novels explore those deeper issues while they tell the story of historical events.

The True Confessions of Charlotte Doyle doesn't tell the story of a famous incident in history. Instead, Avi gives you a picture of the times by inventing a story that includes a lot of historical detail. But he still uses the conflict in the novel to explore some important social issues of the times. What do you learn about society from the conflict in this passage?

> "I do mean it," I said, finding boldness with repetition, "I want to be the replacement for Mr. Johnson."
>
> "You're a girl," Dillingham spat out contemptuously.
>
> "A *pretty* girl," Foley put in. It was not meant as a compliment. "Takes more than canvas britches to hide that."
>
> "And a gentlewoman," was Grimes's addition, as though that was the final evidence of my essential uselessness.

The conflict between Charlotte and the crew teaches you several things about the society they live in. First, you learn that it's very unusual for a girl to want to become a sailor. Second, you learn that the crew members agree that girls shouldn't become sailors. Third, you learn that the crew members think that gentlewomen are useless.

The passage gives you a good idea of the roles that girls were expected to play in 1832. It also reminds you that people from different social classes don't necessarily respect each other. Charlotte is struggling against her society's accepted beliefs, and her struggle creates the conflict in the passage.

3 ◆ Exercise C

Read the following passage and answer the questions about it using what you have learned in this part of the lesson. Use your writing notebook or a separate piece of paper for your answers.

Though I tried to keep my head up, my eyes steady, it was not easy. They looked at me as if I were some loathsome *thing*. At the same time, the more objections they made, the more determined I was to prove myself.

"See here, Miss Doyle," Dillingham concluded, "it's no simple matter. Understand, you sign on to the articles, so to speak, and you *are* on. No bolting to safe harbors at the first blow or when an ill word is flung your way. You're a hand or you're not a hand, and it won't go easy, that's all that can ever be promised."

"I know," I said.

"Hold out *your* hands," he demanded.

Fisk nudged me. I held them out, palms up.

Foley peered over them. "Like bloody cream," he said with disgust. "Touch mine!" he insisted and extended his. Gingerly, I touched one of them. His skin was like rough leather.

"That's the hands you'd get, miss. Like an animal. Is that what you want?"

"I don't care," I said stoutly.

1. In your own words, describe the conflict in this passage.

2. What does the passage teach you about social attitudes in 1832? What do you learn from Charlotte's behavior? What do you learn from the crew members?

Now check your answers using the suggestions in the Answer Key starting on page 451. Review this part of the lesson if you don't understand why an answer was wrong.

3 ◆ Writing on Your Own

Look at the list you wrote for Writing about a Historical Event on page 404. Now do the following:

1. Think about the event and the characters you are writing about. What kinds of social problems are related to that event? You might think about age or skin color. You might consider the kinds of jobs that boys did compared to the jobs that girls did. You might think about the way disabled people were treated at that time. You might explore the differences between rich people and poor people.

2. Write a paragraph describing a social problem that your character is struggling against. Remember that it should be related to the historical event.

    For example, if you are writing about a duchess at Queen Elizabeth I's court, you could mention that she was a milkmaid before she married the duke. Then you could talk about some of the social problems that she has to deal with now that she lives at court.

3. You may want to change and rewrite your paragraph several times until you are satisfied with your description.

4 ◆ History on Personal Terms

The lesson about autobiography (see Unit 8, *Anne Frank: The Diary of a Young Girl*) points out that history has more meaning when it is seen through the eyes of real people. This point applies to historical novels too.

If you read all of *The True Confessions of Charlotte Doyle,* you will learn a great deal about oceangoing ships in the early 1800s. Unlike a history book, the novel doesn't tell you how the ship was built or describe the growth of merchant shipping during the century. But it does give you an accurate feeling of what it was like to live and work on a ship. You also learn about the kinds of people who spent their lives at sea during the 1800s.

Historical novels describe historical events. But they also remind you that life in the past wasn't so different than it is today. What details does Avi include in this passage that make Charlotte seem like a modern teenager?

> So when you consider that I had but dim memories of making the crossing to England when I was six, you will understand that I saw the forthcoming voyage as all a lark. A large, beautiful boat! Jolly sailors! No school to think about! Companions of my own age!
>
> One more point. I was given a volume of blank pages— how typical of my father!—and instructed to keep a daily journal of my voyage across the ocean so that the writing of it should prove of educational value to me. Indeed, my father warned me that not only would he read the journal and comment upon it, but he would pay particular attention to spelling—not my strongest suit.

Charlotte uses old-fashioned language, but she still manages to sound like a typical thirteen-year-old girl. She's thrilled to be out of school, and she looks forward to meeting new friends. She even gets annoyed at her father when he tries to improve her spelling.

Avi wants you to think of Charlotte as a girl who lived in 1832. But he also wants you to care about what happens to her. By making her seem like a real girl, he helps you see historical events from a personal point of view.

4 ◆ Exercise D

Read the following passage and answer the questions about it using what you have learned in this part of the lesson. Use your writing notebook or a separate piece of paper for your answers.

I screamed, tried to grab something. But I couldn't. I clutched madly at nothing, till my hand brushed against a dangling rope. I grabbed for it, missed, and grabbed again. Using all my strength, I levered myself up and, wrapping my arms into the lines, made a veritable knot of myself, mast, and rigging. Oh, how I wept! my entire body shaking and trembling as though it would break apart.

When my breathing became somewhat normal, I managed to untangle first one arm, then my legs. I was free.

I continued down. By the time I reached the mainyard I was numb and whimpering again, tears coursing from my eyes.

1. What makes Charlotte seem like a real person in this passage?

2. Imagine that Charlotte climbed the mast quickly, calmly, and easily. How would your feelings about her be different?

Now check your answers using the suggestions in the Answer Key starting on page 451. Review this part of the lesson if you don't understand why an answer was wrong.

4 ◆ Writing on Your Own

Look at the list you wrote for Writing about a Historical Event on page 404. Now do the following:

1. Reread the items on your list. Do any of them remind you that your character is a real person? Do any of them show feelings or behaviors that seem familiar?

2. Write a paragraph about the historical event. Try to include details that make the character seem like a real person.

For example, imagine you are writing about the duchess who meets Queen Elizabeth I. The duchess is worried about tripping on the edge of her dress as she curtseys. Distracted, she stumbles over her words as she speaks. She accidentally calls the queen "Your Majestick." The queen frowns and the duchess thinks, "Forsooth, it's a beheading for me!"

3. You may want to change and rewrite your paragraph several times until you are satisfied with it.

Now go on to Reviewing and Interpreting the Chapter.

Reviewing and Interpreting the Chapter

Answer these questions without looking back at the selection. Choose the best answer to each question and put an *x* in the box beside it, or write your answer on a separate piece of paper.

Remembering
Facts

1. Charlotte's family lives in
   - ☐ a. Liverpool, England.
   - ☐ b. Newport, Rhode Island.
   - ☐ c. London, England.
   - ☐ d. Providence, Rhode Island.

2. Charlotte travels during the
   - ☐ a. summer.
   - ☐ b. fall.
   - ☐ c. winter.
   - ☐ d. spring.

Following the
Order of Events

3. What happens when Charlotte first asks to join the crew?
   - ☐ a. The sailors immediately agree.
   - ☐ b. They ask the captain for his opinion.
   - ☐ c. They say, "You're a girl."
   - ☐ d. They ask, "Are you willing to take your place in the rigging?"

4. What happens after Charlotte reaches the royal yard?

☐ a. She has to come back down again.

☐ b. The sailors cheer.

☐ c. She sights land in the distance.

☐ d. The sailors climb up after her.

5. "Keeping that journal then is what enables me to relate now in perfect detail everything that transpired during that fateful voyage. . . ." *Transpired* means

☐ a. coughed.

☐ b. ran.

☐ c. wobbled.

☐ d. happened.

6. "Even when not moving myself, I was flying through the air in wild, wide gyrations." What does *gyrations* mean?

☐ a. wings

☐ b. footprints

☐ c. spirals

☐ d. tears

7. At the beginning of the novel Charlotte is

☐ a. unhappy with her life.

☐ b. satisfied with herself.

☐ c. anxious to learn about sailing.

☐ d. unfriendly and depressed.

8. The sailors believe that

    ☐ a. gentlewomen are intelligent.

    ☐ b. the captain is always right.

    ☐ c. girls are useless.

    ☐ d. Charlotte is really a boy.

Understanding
Levels of
Meaning

9. The story hints that the sailors

    ☐ a. always believe in Charlotte's abilities.

    ☐ b. think she can't climb to the royal yard.

    ☐ c. hope she'll kill herself.

    ☐ d. plan to notify her father about her decision.

10. You learn from the story that Charlotte

    ☐ a. never doubts her abilities.

    ☐ b. dislikes all the sailors on the *Seahawk*.

    ☐ c. hopes to be a ship's captain in the future.

    ☐ d. sometimes thinks she's made the wrong decision.

Understanding
Character

11. Which adjective best describes Charlotte's attitude about joining the crew?

    ☐ a. stubborn

    ☐ b. shy

    ☐ c. wishy-washy

    ☐ d. boastful

12. Who seems to make most of the important decisions in Charlotte's family?

☐ a. Charlotte

☐ b. her father

☐ c. her mother

☐ d. her brother

Understanding Setting 13. When Charlotte reaches the royal yard, she feels "the *Seahawk* turning, tossing, swaying as if trying to shake me off." The author writes that description to stress

☐ a. the motion of the ship on the sea.

☐ b. the time of day and the season.

☐ c. Charlotte's big mistake.

☐ d. the height of the royal yard.

14. Why does the author include so many sailing terms in the novel?

☐ a. He wants to confuse the reader.

☐ b. He hopes you will take up sailing.

☐ c. He wants to create a picture of the ship.

☐ d. He is showing off his knowledge of boats.

Understanding Feelings 15. How does Charlotte feel before her journey on the *Seahawk* begins?

☐ a. grumpy

☐ b. scared

☐ c. brave

☐ d. excited

16. Which word best describes Charlotte's reaction when she falls backward off the ratlines?

☐ a. calm

☐ b. panic

☐ c. nervousness

☐ d. amusement

Now check your answers using the Answer Key starting on page 451. Make no mark for right answers. Correct any wrong answers you may have by putting a check mark (✓) in the box next to the right answer. Count the number of questions you answered correctly and plot the total on the Comprehension Scores graph on page 462.

Next, look at the questions you answered incorrectly. What types of questions were they? Count the number you got wrong of each type and enter the numbers in the spaces below.

Remembering Facts   _____

Following the Order of Events   _____

Understanding Word Choices   _____

Understanding Important Ideas   _____

Understanding Levels of Meaning   _____

Understanding Character   _____

Understanding Setting   _____

Understanding Feelings   _____

Now use these numbers to fill in the Comprehension Skills Profile on page 463.

Discussion Guides

The questions below will help you think about the selection and the lesson you have just read. If you don't discuss these questions in class, try to think about them or discuss them with your classmates. Perhaps you will want to write a few paragraphs in answer to the questions.

Discussing the Historical Novel

1. There are hundreds of historical novels about sailing ships, pirates, and battles on the high seas. Why do you think so many modern readers are fascinated by sea stories?

2. Imagine that *The True Confessions of Charlotte Doyle* is set on the American frontier in 1890 instead of on a ship in the Atlantic Ocean in 1832. What kinds of details does the author need to include? What subjects does he need to research?

3. Why did Avi choose a girl as the main character of this historical novel? How did that choice affect some of the deeper social issues of the book?

Discussing the Chapter

4. How do you feel about Charlotte when you first meet her? Do your feelings about her change? In what way?

5. In a later chapter of the novel, Charlotte is accused of murder and brought to trial. Do you think she is capable of murdering anyone? Why or why not? Support your answer by using what you have learned about Charlotte's character in this selection.

6. Do you think that Charlotte and the crew members will be friends from now on? Or do you think she will continue to have problems with them? Explain your answer.

Discussing the Author's Work

7. Avi once said that he "is more interested in finding a way to tell a good story and to provide a means of imagining and understanding the past than he is in teaching a historical fact." What does he mean by that statement? Does it describe *The True Confessions of Charlotte Doyle*? Why or why not?

8. For several years, Avi worked as a librarian before he became a full-time writer. How do you think his work in the library helped him write historical novels?

9. *The True Confessions of Charlotte Doyle* is one of Avi's most famous books. Many readers have told stories about bursting into tears of relief when Charlotte breaks out of her traditional ladylike role. Why do you think readers are so affected by Charlotte's struggle?

Writing Exercise

Read all the instructions before you begin writing. If you have any questions about how to begin the writing assignment, review Using the Writing Process, beginning on page 439, or confer with your writing coach.

1. Avi lives in Providence, Rhode Island, a city that is often mentioned in his historical novels. He says "just walking down the street can inspire a story."

   Your town or city has a history too. What kinds of things happened there one hundred years ago? What was the land like before your town was even built? What kinds of people lived in that spot and what did they do?

2. Do a little research about the history of your town. Your librarian can help you find some information.

   Then write a story about an incident in your town's past. Remember to answer the following questions as you write:

   ☐ How do the people look, speak, and behave?

   ☐ What details tell about the time and place?

   ☐ What conflict is at the center of this event?

   ☐ How can I make my characters interesting and believable?

3. As you write, you may want to review the paragraphs you wrote for the four Writing on Your Own exercises.

4. Write, revise, correct, and rewrite your story until you are satisfied with your writing.

Using the
Writing Process

Using the Writing Process

The following reference section will help you with the writing exercises in this book. It explains the major steps in the writing process. Read this section carefully so that you understand the process thoroughly. At the end of this section is a checklist. Whenever you are asked to complete a writing assignment, you can refer to the checklist as a reminder of the things you should think about when you are working on an assignment. This reference is an information source. Use it whenever you feel it would be helpful to review part or all of the process.

Whatever kind of job you do, from carpentry to sewing to cutting the grass, it will be easier if you have a good method for doing the job. People who write—students, authors, reporters, business executives, to list a few—also have to have a method that enables them to write easily and well. Even writing simple notes or memos requires a method.

How to Use a Writing Process

Different writers use different methods, but there are certain techniques that all writers use to make their work easier and their finished product better. These techniques have been put together in a list that is called "the writing process." A "process," of course, is just another name for a method.

Keep in mind that writing is not simply the act of filling a piece of paper with words. It is a form of communication. The purpose of writing is to put *ideas* across to other people. Since ideas come from your mind, not your pen, the writing process begins with the work that takes place in your mind: the creation and organization of ideas. Next, you're ready to actually set the words down on paper. The final stage is polishing your ideas and the words you use to express them.

In this section you will read about the stages and steps that make up a "writing process." These are techniques that writers use to make their job easier and the results better. But this doesn't mean that all writers follow this list exactly as it is written here.

Remember that every writer is different and every writing project is different. You can't always follow the list in one particular way.

Finish step 1 and go on to step 2. Do step 2 and then step 3. Writing doesn't work that way. Some authors write an opening paragraph before they do anything else. Then they make a plan and go after their facts and ideas. Some writers don't find a focus for their writing until they have assembled all of their ideas. Others find their focus first.

To help you understand the process that writers use, we will group the process into three main stages: prewriting, writing, and revising. Remember that the steps in each stage blend into the next, and sometimes a writer moves back and forth through the process. When you write, your goal should be to produce a clear and lively work that expresses interesting ideas. The writing process can help you every time you write and with everything you write.

Stage 1: Prewriting

What will I write about? You will need to think of a subject or an idea. Suppose your teacher says, "Write a story for me. It's due next week." What do you do? Panic, of course.

What is there to write about? How much should I write? Where do I start? With all the things you've done in your life, in spite of all the books you've read and all the movies you've seen, your mind goes blank. Or so many things go through your mind that you become thoroughly confused.

Welcome to the writing club. This is how *all* writing begins.

What should you do? The best thing you can do at this point is to sit back in your chair and think. Let your mind wander. Scribble down ideas as they come to you—even if the ideas seem dumb or farfetched. Good ideas often develop from a crazy thought. You may want to sit around with a few friends and throw ideas at one another as you think of them. This technique is called *brainstorming*. It might go like this:

> "She said we could write about anything we want."
> "How about writing about my vacation at the lake?" (Write down *vacation*.)
> "Nah! Everybody writes about a vacation. We need something different." (Write down *different*.)
> "Different? How about *weird*? How about a weird vacation?" (Write down *weird*.)
> "Yeah! I did see a cave this summer. Maybe I walked into a cave and couldn't find my way out."

"And you walked for miles in the dark."

"And suddenly there was a bright light. And I saw that there was a big underground city!"

By brainstorming you have turned your modest idea about your vacation into a great idea for a science-fiction or fantasy story.

Once you start brainstorming, the ideas can come quickly. So now it's time to get things under control by finding a *focus* for your story.

What will I focus on? Pick your best ideas. Sometimes good writing is ruined because the writer tries to do too much. You might decide that aliens live in the underground city. You want to tell how they captured you. You want to describe how they got there, what they look like, what they did to you, what you did, how you became their ruler, how you escaped and brought an alien friend back with you, and how you took him to school to meet your friends . . . and on and on. Stop! It's too much.

There are many good ideas here. What you want to do is pick out what you think is your best idea and zero in on that. Focus on that one idea just as you focus a camera on a subject. If you concentrate on describing the beauty of the underground city, you will probably have more than enough for your story. If you skip the city and just tell how you brought this wonderful cave person to school, you have a great story by itself.

The point is not to overload your story with too many ideas. Writing is always easier and better if you concentrate on telling about a few things thoroughly and well. When you wander back and forth through too many ideas, you soon become lost and confused. Your reader will also be confused and will soon lose interest in your story.

How will I organize my ideas? Plan your writing. There is very little you can do in life without first making a plan. Even a simple bike ride needs a plan. Where will you go? When? What route? How far? What will you wear? Will it be a leisurely ride, or are you out to set a speed record?

Writing, like any other activity, calls for careful planning. You begin to plan as soon as you decide what to write about and find your facts. Then you do more planning as you decide what facts and ideas you will include in your story? And there are other steps to consider.

Who is my audience? You may write one way for your friends and another way for your teacher. Who will be reading your work? Will the story be serious or funny? What ideas or feelings do you want to emphasize?

As you write, you continue to plan. You may change your mind about your plan just as a coach changes a game plan as the game progresses. Which words will you choose? An idea that seemed good at first may need to be dropped later.

Prewriting is not as hard or as complicated as it may sound. It helps to write down a few notes about your *plan* when you begin: the subject, a few important ideas, where to look for information you need, and who you might interview.

The important part of this stage is to have a plan. Think ahead about what you want your writing to be about, how you want it to sound, who will read it, and how to get it down on paper.

How do I gather facts and ideas? You have already read about brainstorming for ideas when you are searching for a subject to write about. You can also brainstorm to think of facts and ideas you want to include in your writing. Write these ideas down as you think of them. You can pick and choose from your list later.

Freewriting is another way that writers generate ideas. To free-write, quickly jot down anything that pops into your head. Suppose you were asked to write about winter. How to begin? Start writing. Put down the first thought that comes to mind and let ideas begin to flow. You might come up with something like this:

> I don't know what to write. Winter. What can I say that hasn't already been said about winter? It's cold, there's lots of snow . . . well, not in all places I guess. Actually when it's cold here, it's warm on the other side of the world. Do they call that winter then, or summer . . . ?

As you freewrite, you are often able to see the basic ideas of a story or article emerge.

Then there is research. You may think that you can make up everything in a story out of your head. Most times you can't. If you are writing about an adventure in a cave, you will want to describe a cave accurately so that it is believable to your readers. Do some research at the library. Interview people who have seen caves to add realistic touches to your story.

Facts and ideas are gathered in four ways: thinking, reading, listening, and observing.

◆ Thinking means brainstorming and freewriting.

◆ Reading means research in books, magazines, newspapers, encyclopedias, and other sources of information.

◆ Listening means interviewing, listening to tapes and to people with special knowledge.

◆ Observing means carefully looking at a scene, carefully looking at an event, or carefully watching a movie or television show to gather ideas. While you are observing, imagine describing those scenes. What details do you see? What observations can you make?

How do I organize my facts and ideas? There are several ways to organize your information. Some writers make *lists* (informal outlines) of the facts and ideas they have gathered and rearrange the list until they have the information in the correct order that will work well in their writing.

Other writers make formal *outlines,* designating the most important ideas I, II, III, IV, etc., and related details as A, B, C, 1, 2, 3, and so on. An outline is a more formal version of a list, and like a list, the items in an outline can be rearranged until you get the correct order. Outlines help you organize and group your ideas.

Mapping or *clustering* is another helpful technique used by many writers. With this method you write down your main idea in a circle or a rectangle and then show how other facts and ideas are connected to that main idea. Here is an example of how a cluster may evolve from a major idea:

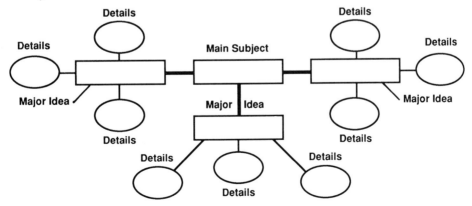

Do you see how a cluster map relates ideas? The farther you branch out, the more detailed you get. When you get to the point where you are ready to write your story or article, you can use the cluster map as a guide to grouping your ideas.

Stage 2: Writing

How do I get my thoughts on paper? What do you do when you step onto the basketball court? You might stretch a bit and then you take the ball and start dribbling, passing, and shooting. You don't stand there and agonize over how you are going to play, or worry that you might lose. You start playing.

Once you have your subject, your plan, and your facts and ideas, the worst thing you can do is worry about the writing—how to start, where to start, how good or bad it might be, what the teacher *really* wants, writer's block, or a hundred other things that only make you panic.

Now is the time to get your thoughts on paper. Like freewriting, quickly writing down your story will make you feel more at ease with writing itself. Once your story is written down, then you can rewrite, revise, and polish.

How will I get started? Start with an opening sentence or paragraph. It can become a guide for the rest of your story or essay.

Here is an opening sentence that was used in a story about a midair collision: "A Boeing 747 collided with a smaller plane over San Diego today and crashed in flames to the ground, killing at least 144 people . . ." With this sentence, you know you will have to tell the details of the crash, why it happened, and how it happened.

You expect something different with this opening sentence: "I ran out in the driveway the other night waving a bag of cold spareribs and shouting to one of my grown kids." Obviously, this story is going to be funny. Humorist Erma Bombeck, who wrote that sentence, knew her story would have to carry on the humorous tone and probably include a few wisecracks about why a mother would want to chase her grown kid with a bag of spareribs.

Now let's look at the opening sentence from a famous short story by Frank O'Connor called "First Confession": "All the trouble began when my grandfather died and my grandmother—my father's mother—came to live with us." The writer has set the tone of the story.

He will have to describe what the trouble is and why it began when his grandmother moved in with his family.

What is a rough draft? You are finally ready to turn all of your prewriting work into a story or essay. This will be your *rough draft*—your sloppy copy. Working from your outline or cluster map, your goal is to turn your loose facts and ideas into sentences and paragraphs that will work together. Write quickly. Refer to your outline and writing plan frequently so that you stay on track and avoid the delays caused by wondering what to write next.

At this stage don't worry too much about choosing exactly the right word or about crafting a sentence perfectly. Cross out, draw arrows showing how you are changing the order of ideas, and make notes to yourself in the margin. In the middle of what might look like a mess, you'll be surprised to find that a story is taking shape.

You're like an artist who is sculpturing your likeness in clay. After the artist's first effort, there is what looks like a muddy pile in the middle of the table. But the general shape is right. It certainly looks like a head. The ears are where the ears should be, and the nose is familiar. With polishing, the rough shape will eventually look like you.

There is nothing that slows a writer down more than thinking that the first draft will be the only draft—that it has to be the neatest and best effort—the one others will read. Your first attempt should be rough and unfinished: a *rough* draft. Plan to revise your draft two or three times. It sounds like a lot of work, but it would be disappointing to come this far and not finish the job of editing, revising, and polishing you story.

Stage 3: Revising

How should I begin my revision? Now you're ready to revise your work. You want to look for ways to polish your writing. Don't be fooled into thinking that revision is a waste of time. Professional writers revise their writing over and over again. They know that careful revision makes a big difference in the final product.

When you are revising, answer these questions:

Is my writing clear and logical? Reread your entire first draft. Make sure the sentences and paragraphs follow one another in logical order. Run-on sentences get confusing: "I entered the cave and it was so dark I couldn't see and all of a sudden a bat flew past me and I was sure it was a vampire because I could see its big teeth and I remembered this movie where a vampire captured this girl and my cousin who was with me said something that made me spill my popcorn." Wait a minute! What's going on in that sentence? You will need to decide what is important and then throw out the rest.

You may need to rewrite sentences or paragraphs, or even add new information. Check your prewriting plan to make sure you have included everything important.

Is my language interesting? Have you chosen strong verbs, nouns, and adjectives? For example, avoid using the verb *to be (is, are, being, become)* more than you have to. Choose precise actions, such as *jumped, ran, grinned, sobbed.* Instead of saying *thing,* choose the exact noun: *bucket, bathrobe, liberty, violence.* The adjectives *beautiful* and *nice* are boring. Replace them with *elegant, tidy, prim, joyous.*

Take out words that repeat the same ideas. For example, don't say "bright and intelligent." The words are synonyms. Choose one word or the other.

What errors do I look for? Check for correct spelling, grammar, and punctuation. If you mention a date or a place, check an encyclopedia to make sure it is correct. Your handwriting must be clear. If your reader can't read your handwriting, he or she is going to lose interest in your ideas.

Be sure to have your editor or writing coach read your work. An editor looks for errors in grammar and spelling. Poor spelling and errors in grammar are confusing to your readers. Your editor or coach can often find problems that you have missed.

Editors should be kind, helpful, and encouraging—not cross, mean, or critical. If you are asked to edit someone else's writing, always start with a compliment or a positive comment. Remember that other writers have the same personal feelings about their work that you have about yours.

A Writing Checklist

☐ What is my topic? Is it focused enough? Should it be broader or narrower?

☐ What is my purpose for writing? What do I want to say about the subject? What are my feelings and ideas about it?

☐ Do I have a prewriting plan? Who is my audience? How do I want my writing to sound?

☐ What do I have to do to gather my facts and ideas? Think? Read? Interview? Research?

☐ How will I organize my ideas? a list? an outline? a cluster map?

☐ How will I develop my ideas? Do I have an opening sentence or paragraph?

☐ Do I need to add more information? Switch the order of paragraphs? Take out unnecessary information?

☐ Do all the sentences in one paragraph relate to one idea? Do I have to rearrange the order of ideas? Eliminate or add information?

☐ Have I used active, precise words? Is my language interesting? Do the words explain what I mean to say?

☐ Is the grammar correct? Have I used correct spelling and punctuation? Have I checked my facts?

☐ Is my final draft clear and legible?

Answer Key

Unit 1: **Summer of My German Soldier**

———————————————— **Character** ————————————————

1 ◆ Exercise A

1. Freddy has spent two years in the fourth grade; he is frightened by crawdads; he gives Patty a half-eaten candy bar as a gift.

2. Answers will vary. Freddy isn't very bright, but he is harmless and somewhat thoughtful.

2 ◆ Exercise B

1. Answers will vary. Patty's only friends are Anton and Ruth. She finds comfort and friendship listening to Anton.

2. Answers will vary. Patty needs someone to confide in since she does not get the love and understanding she needs from her parents.

3 ◆ Exercise C

1. Patty is not allowed to question her father's decisions.

2. Answers will vary.

4 ◆ Exercise D

1. Answers will vary. Anton feels that both men need to inflict cruelty on others.

2. Answers will vary.

——————— **Reviewing and Interpreting the Chapter** ———————

1. a	5. b	9. d	13. c
2. d	6. a	10. b	14. a
3. c	7. b	11. d	15. a
4. b	8. c	12. b	16. b

Unit 2: **I Know Why the Caged Bird Sings**

────────── **How Authors Use Language** ──────────

1 ♦ Exercise A

1. sister, is sho'ly, brother

2. Answers will vary. She is embarrassed because she thinks Momma's dialect makes her sound ignorant.

2 ♦ Exercise B

1. Answers will vary. Most of the paragraph describes the women. The words create a picture of women who live in another time and place.

2. Answers will vary. She wants to make Mrs. Flowers seem rare and unusual.

3 ♦ Exercise C

1. like an old biscuit, simile, uses the word *like*; sweet-milk fresh, metaphor, suggests that an afternoon is the same as fresh, sweet milk; like a thread over an open fire, simile, uses the word *like*

2. Answers will vary.

4 ♦ Exercise D

1. "Children these days would bust out of sheet-metal clothes." "It would be fitting if I got sunstroke and died before they came outside. Just dropped dead on the slanting porch."

2. Answers will vary. You learn that Momma thinks kids today are worse then they used to be. You also learn that she is proud of her sewing. You learn that Maya is very self-conscious.

────────── **Reviewing and Interpreting the Chapter** ──────────

1. a	5. b	9. d	13. c
2. c	6. a	10. c	14. a
3. a	7. d	11. d	15. b
4. b	8. b	12. b	16. c

Unit 3: **Julie of the Wolves**

——————————————— **Setting** ———————————————

1◆ Exercise A

1. the cliffs; a rock
   We are able to see the setting from a different point of view. It is now a setting of happiness.

2. Miyax is happy in this setting because she is with her father. It is not the bleak setting Kapugen sees in his grief. Answers will vary.

2◆ Exercise B

1. the bent woman and Naka
   Answers will vary. They add an eerie sense to the setting.

2. black, blue, purple, red, rose
   Answers will vary.

3◆ Exercise C

1. "He would hail the blue sky and shout out his praise for the grasses and bushes."

2. Answers will vary. Those sentences create an empty and depressing setting.

4◆ Exercise D

1. The scenery changes from the white world to the natural world Miyax knows best.

2. Answers will vary.

——————— **Reviewing and Interpreting the Chapter** ———————

1. c	5. a	9. a	13. c
2. a	6. b	10. d	14. b
3. d	7. c	11. b	15. d
4. c	8. b	12. d	16. b

Unit 4: **To Kill a Mockingbird**

————————————— Tone and Mood —————————————

1 ◆ Exercise A

1. "What is it, Heck?" said Atticus. He seems to concentrate on Sheriff Tate's mood. Atticus knows something serious is about to happen.

2. Sheriff Tate rubs his thigh and his arm. He looks around the room and rubs his neck. Answers will vary.

2 ◆ Exercise B

1. filling with people; scurrying going on; teeming with people; crowded around the one small window; galloped to me; thrust me inside
The mood created is one of confusion and hurrying.

2. Mrs. Merriweather is trying to do too many things at once. The description of the crowd, the band, the children, the stage, the curtain, and even Scout's problem with her costume provide a true-to-life feeling. Answers will vary.

3 ◆ Exercise C

1. Scout and Jem feel the same respect and love for Dr. Reynolds that they feel for Atticus. They trust the doctor.

2. "You all right, Scout?" he added.

4 ◆ Exercise D

1. wind rustling; shuffled and dragged; soft swish of cotton; wheek, wheek; Jem screamed
The phrases create tension and a threatening tone.

2. The tone is threatening. The mood of the children is fear. Answers will vary.

————————— **Reviewing and Interpreting the Chapter** —————————

1. d	5. d	9. b	13. c
2. c	6. a	10. c	14. c
3. c	7. b	11. d	15. b
4. b	8. c	12. a	16. c

Unit 5: **The Westing Game**

──────────── Theme ────────────

1 ◆ Exercise A

1. Answers will vary. Sandy treats Judge Ford like a very important person. Judge Ford doesn't pay too much attention to Sandy.

2. Answers will vary. Sometimes a person's money or job makes other people treat that person as if he or she is very important.

2 ◆ Exercise B

1. Answers will vary. Mr. Hoo is an angry man with stomach problems. He seems to have a grudge against Sam Westing.

2. Answers will vary. She is quieter than Mr. Hoo and seems homesick for China. The difference supports the theme because you get the idea that Mr. and Mrs. Hoo don't understand each other's feelings.

3 ◆ Exercise C

1. Answers will vary. Mrs. Wexler likes Angela and doesn't like Turtle. She worries about Angela's skin but doesn't seem happy to see Turtle.

2. Answers will vary. Mrs. Wexler judges her daughters by the way they look and behave.

4 ◆ Exercise D

1. Answers will vary. The author wants you to dislike Mrs. Wexler. She makes Mrs. Wexler seem silly, whiny, and vain.

2. Answers will vary. Mrs. Wexler is very concerned about the way things look. The author also shows that we, as readers, make judgments about Mrs. Wexler based on looks and behavior.

──────── Reviewing and Interpreting the Chapter ────────

1. c	5. d	9. d	13. b
2. b	6. a	10. c	14. d
3. a	7. b	11. b	15. c
4. c	8. a	12. c	16. b

———————————— Conflict ————————————

1♦ Exercise A

1. George's desires for a simpler life is in conflict with his feelings of responsibility for Lennie.

2. Answers will vary.

2♦ Exercise B

1. Answers will vary. George probably believes that his dream will never come true.

2. Answers will vary. Your dreams can help determine what you will do with your life. The conflicts arise when you try to reach your goal.

3♦ Exercise C

1. Lennie's lip quivered and tears started in his eyes. "Aw Lennie!" Answers will vary.

2. George gets angry with Lennie when he does things that may be harmful. Then he tries to comfort Lennie when he becomes upset.

4♦ Exercise D

1. Lennie pets things so hard that he innocently kills them.

2. Answers will vary. George would probably become upset, but would still try to find some way to get Lennie out of his trouble and take care of him.

——————— **Reviewing and Interpreting the Chapter** ———————

1. b	5. d	9. b	13. b
2. c	6. a	10. d	14. d
3. a	7. d	11. c	15. b
4. d	8. c	12. a	16. a

Unit 7: A Separate Peace

—————————— Symbolism ——————————

1 ♦ Exercise A

1. fear

2. Answers will vary.

2 ♦ Exercise B

1. Finny, who represents confidence, strength, and courage is linked with Gene, who represents fear and uncertainty.

2. They represent common ways that people react to fear: making excuses and doing or saying nothing.

3 ♦ Exercise C

1. Finny trapped me again . . . ; Finny was right; we struggled in some equality for a while

2. Finny made Gene overcome his fears and follow Finny's lead.

4 ♦ Exercise D

1. He feels thankful because he has overcome his fear in the process of growing up.

2. Authority figures—teachers and perhaps parents—were the giants of Gene's childhood. Answers will vary. You may have the same kinds of giants to remember. And you may add things like trains, houses, and school buildings that seemed larger and more frightening when you were younger than they do now.

————— **Reviewing and Interpreting the Chapter** —————

1. c	5. d	9. b	13. b
2. b	6. a	10. d	14. d
3. d	7. a	11. c	15. b
4. d	8. c	12. b	16. a

Unit 8: Anne Frank: The Diary of a Young Girl

———————— Autobiography and Biography ————————

1 ◆ Exercise A

1. Answers will vary. People are watching them; they must wear a big yellow star; the people on the street pity them.

2. Answers will vary. The reader is able to see that the Franks are truly outcasts.

2 ◆ Exercise B

1. jealousy; longing; anger
   Answers will vary.

2. She can tell her diary anything. To complain to the others would make her seem ungrateful.

3 ◆ Exercise C

1. Answers will vary. She learns something about Peter.

2. Peter needs love and affection just as she does.

4 ◆ Exercise D

1. hopefulness and despair

2. returning to school

———————— Reviewing and Interpreting the Chapter ————————

1. c	5. c	9. d	13. c
2. a	6. a	10. c	14. d
3. c	7. d	11. b	15. b
4. a	8. a	12. b	16. a

Unit 9: **The Hobbit**

———————————— **Fantasy** ————————————

1 ◆ Exercise A

1. The far North; this mountain on the map; King under the mountain; mortal men . . . to the South
Thorin's family worked hard and built workshops.

2. The author describes an underground kingdom where treasure was found.

2 ◆ Exercise B

1. The author speaks directly to the reader and asks the reader for his or her opinion. The reader is asked to respond also to the uninvited guests.

2. He is pushy.

3 ◆ Exercise C

1. He hints at what the dragon can do.
he flew into the air; settle . . . in a spout of flame; the woods . . . all went up in fire

2. The dwarves will probably have to battle the dragon.

4 ◆ Exercise D

1. "What am I going to get out of it?" Answers will vary.

2. Bilbo is businesslike. Answers will vary.

——————— **Reviewing and Interpreting the Chapter** ———————

1. c	5. c	9. b	13. c
2. b	6. b	10. d	14. b
3. b	7. d	11. a	15. c
4. a	8. c	12. d	16. a

Unit 10: The True Confessions of Charlotte Doyle

─────────────── Historical Novel ───────────────

1 ◆ Exercise A

1. Answers will vary. Most of the passage reflects Charlotte's old-fashioned use of language.

2. Answers will vary. The father makes decisions, and everyone else goes along with him.

2 ◆ Exercise B

1. Answers will vary. The passage describes the height of the mainmast and tells what it looks like. Then it tells about the different sails supported by the mainmast. We learn that crew members must climb the mainmast many times a day.

2. Answers will vary. Avi wants to show us exactly how dangerous the climb is. The description also adds to our overall picture of the ship.

3 ◆ Exercise C

1. Answers will vary. The sailors don't believe that Charlotte is tough enough or committed enough to join the crew, but Charlotte is determined to succeed.

2. Answers will vary. We learn that upper-class people did not work with their hands. Charlotte is determined to fight that attitude, but the sailors have trouble believing her.

4 ◆ Exercise D

1. Answers will vary. Charlotte is very scared, just as most people would be.

2. Answers will vary.

─────────── Reviewing and Interpreting the Chapter ───────────

1. d	5. d	9. b	13. a
2. a	6. c	10. d	14. c
3. c	7. b	11. a	15. d
4. a	8. c	12. b	16. b

Comprehension
Scores Graph
&
Comprehension
Skills Profile

Comprehension Scores

Use this graph to plot your comprehension scores. At the top of the graph are the names of the chapters in the book. To mark your score for a unit, find the name of the chapter you just read and follow the line beneath it down until it crosses the line for the number of questions you got right. Put an *x* where the lines meet. As you mark your score for each unit, graph your progress by drawing a line to connect the *x*'s. The numbers on the right show your comprehension percentage score.

Number of Questions Answered Correctly	Summer of My German Soldier	I Know Why the Caged Bird Sings	Julie of the Wolves	To Kill a Mockingbird	The Westing Game	Of Mice and Men	A Separate Peace	Anne Frank: The Diary of a Young Girl	The Hobbit	The True Confessions of Charlotte Doyle	Comprehension Percentage Score
16											100
15											94
14											88
13											81
12											75
11											69
10											63
9											56
8											50
7											44
6											38
5											31
4											25
3											19
2											13
1											6
0											0

Comprehension Skills Profile

Use this profile to see which comprehension skills you need to work on. Fill in the number of incorrect answers for each skill every time you complete a unit. For example, if you have two incorrect answers for Remembering Facts, you will blacken two spaces above that skill label. The numbers on the left side show your total number of wrong answers for each comprehension skill. The profile will show you which kinds of questions you consistently get wrong. Your instructor may want to give you extra help with these skills.

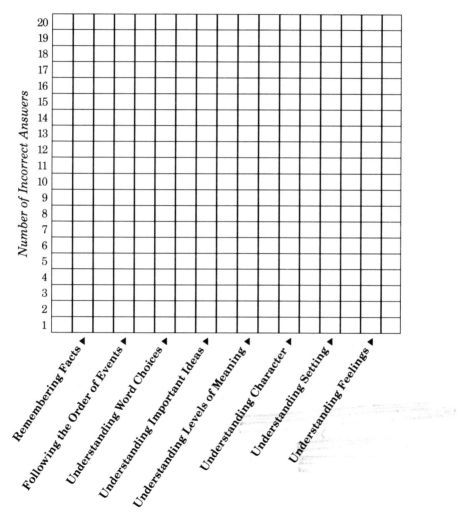

Bibliography

Angelou, Maya. *I Know Why the Caged Bird Sings.* New York: Random House, Inc.

Avi. *The True Confessions of Charlotte Doyle.* New York: Orchard Books.

Frank, Anne. *Anne Frank: The Diary of a Young Girl,* ed. Otto Frank. New York: Doubleday. First published in Amsterdam, Holland.

George, Jean Craighead. *Julie of the Wolves.* New York: HarperCollins Publishers, Inc.

Greene, Bette. *Summer of My German Soldier.* New York: Dial Books for Young Readers.

Knowles, John. *A Separate Peace.* New York: Macmillan, Inc.

Lee, Harper. *To Kill a Mockingbird.* New York: HarperCollins Publishers, Inc.

Raskin, Ellen. *The Westing Game.* New York: Dutton Children's Books.

Steinbeck, John. *Of Mice and Men.* New York: Viking Penguin.

Tolkien, J.R.R. *The Hobbit.* New York: Houghton Mifflin Company.